D0870184

The Intellectual Origins
of Jeffersonian Democracy

The Intellectual Origins of Jeffersonian Democracy

Republicanism, the Class Struggle, and the Virtuous Farmer

Douglass G. Adair

Edited by Mark E. Yellin
With a foreword by Joyce Appleby

LEXINGTON BOOKS
Lanham • Boulder • New York • Oxford

LEXINGTON BOOKS

Published in the United States of America
by Lexington Books
4720 Boston Way, Lanham, Maryland 20706

12 Hid's Copse Road
Cumnor Hill, Oxford OX2 9JJ, England

British Library Cataloguing in Publication Information Available

Library of Congress Cataloging-in-Publication Data

Adair, Douglass.
    The intellectual origins of Jeffersonian democracy : republicanism, the class struggle, and the virtuous farmer / Douglass G. Adair ; edited by Mark E. Yellin ; foreword by Joyce Appleby.
        p.   cm.
    Includes bibliographical references and index.
    ISBN 0-7391-0124-2 (cloth : alk. paper) — ISBN 0-7391-0125-0 (pbk. : alk. paper)
        1. Political science—United States—History—18th century.   2. Political science—History.
    I. Yellin, Mark E.   II. Title.
    JA84.U5 A617   2000
    320'.01—dc21   00-032264

Printed in the United States of America

♾™ The paper used in this publication meets the minimum requirements of American National Standard for Information Sciences—Permanence of Paper for Printed Library Materials, ANSI/NISO Z39.48–1992.

For the students of Douglass Adair

Contents

Foreword *by Joyce Appleby*

I entered graduate studies planning to work on the Progressive Era, met Douglass Adair my first visit to Claremont Graduate School, and became a colonial historian forthwith. What was there about the man to cause such an immediate change of plans? Unprepossessing physically, by no means a spellbinding speaker, Adair drew people to him because he quickened the imagination of all those around him. You left his presence with images and ideas buzzing, feeling yourself more alive just for sharing a few minutes with him. Adair was also a man of successive enthusiasms that captured his own attention completely. When I visited him that summer day in 1961, he had been reading *Ishi: Last of His Tribe*, by Theodora Kroeber, the fascinating story of the last of the Yana Indians who somehow wandered onto the Berkeley campus in 1911. Before that he had been rereading William James' *Varieties of Religious Experience*. I remember the titles to this day, because he strongly recommended that I read both of them as soon as possible and, of course, I did—with great enjoyment to be sure but with some puzzlement as to how they instructed me as an historian. Adair was not as grimly professional as his new student.

Douglass had a very intimate relationship with the past. He confined his attention to a few of the greats in the Revolutionary generation and spent his scholarly life pondering them, their temperaments, preoccupations, and foundational ideas. From these ruminations, he conveyed an ardent love not of the past abstractly —but of the people he had chosen to study, even more precisely, of the people in the past that he had gotten to know quite well. Adair clearly identified with the (mostly) men he studied in his "Age of Jefferson," but his was not a presentist approach in which the concerns of the past were collapsed into contemporary issues. Instead, the hours that he spent reenacting in his mind the choices, decisions, and commitments made by Jefferson, James (always Jemme) Madison, Alexander Hamilton, George Washington, and their friends and associates had created a familiarity that suffused Douglass's conversations about history with an electric immediacy.

When I entered his life he was pondering the implications of Caroline Robbins' work on the Commonwealthmen. He announced during one of my visits to his office that the word *virtue* did not appear in The Federalist Papers. Being something of a natural skeptic, I went through my well-marked Modern Library edition of The Federalist to see if he was correct. He wasn't; I found five or six *virtues* in the eighty-five papers, but he was essentially correct—virtue played no conceptual role in Publius's defense of the new constitution. Years later, of course, when early Americanists decided that virtue was the principal concern of the founding generation, I realized that he had anticipated their interest, perhaps even fostered it.

Adair was something of a daydreamer who got lost in his own cerebrations. I well recall once when he spontaneously invited me to join him for lunch. Having that much of his time was indeed a treat not to be turned down. When we returned to the department, he was greeted by an agitated colleague who told him that he had missed an important and long scheduled meeting. I was on the other side of his dreaminess at the end of my graduate career when an official telephoned me at home to ask if I expected to get my degree that June. Having finished my dissertation two months earlier, I very much did anticipate that longed-for day, but Adair had left town, failing to file the necessary papers, an oversight hastily corrected.

Students always seem to recall the physical appearance of their mentor's office, probably because the moments spent in it are scorched into memory. Adair's was the usual book-lined study, but because the lovely old building in which the graduate school was housed had ten-foot-high ceilings, his bookshelf was outfitted with a handsome, polished wood ladder that I often saw him climb. One particular incident has captured the sensation of being in that office. On an occasion when both Douglass and John Niven were talking to me, something humorous made us all burst out laughing. At that very moment, an awkward young man appeared at the doorway seeking Douglass's signature. He clearly felt embarrassed by arriving at this moment of hilarity. Douglass perceived his discomfiture and found the words, delivered in that lovely, soft Scotch-Irish accent, to put him at his ease and we at ours. His was a kindness bred in the bone and sustained by his acute awareness of the feelings of others.

I spoke earlier of Adair's having gotten to know some people in the past very well. His hallmark as a scholar was the keenly personal approach he took to historical figures. Did Alexander Hamilton die a

Christian? Was Jefferson the father of Sally Hemings's children? Did Meriwether Lewis commit suicide? These were the questions that fascinated him. He talked of Madison and Jefferson as one might speak of relatives or friends. Chatting away, he would allude to the fact that Madison almost had a nervous breakdown when he came back from Princeton to the society of Piedmont planters who idled away their days hunting small game, planning cock fights and drinking too much punch. Adair's second passion was solving historical riddles such as who wrote those Federalist Papers that both Hamilton and Madison had claimed. Having reconstructed the provenance of the various claims by Madison and Hamilton of authorship of a disputed ten essays, Adair determined from internal evidence that they belonged to Madison, not Hamilton. Nothing delighted him more than an analysis done by early computer mavens that confirmed his judgment.

When I entered the profession in 1967 women were neither a novelty nor a conspicuous presence in the corridors of academic departments. Adair's wife, Virginia, who has recently received a flurry of excited praise for her poetry, taught English at California State Polytechnic University and had given him some idea of the second-class citizenship accorded the distaff side of the academy. I would have no trouble in my chosen profession, Adair assured me, if I didn't mind washing up the coffee cups, something I was never asked to do when I joined the history department at San Diego State University. But I do well remember being with Douglass when one of his colleagues—with some incredulity—asked why another graduate student, who like me was a wife and mother, wanted a Ph.D. I replied as prosaically as I could manage that I thought that she was studying in order to write and teach history. Douglass smiled broadly.

The year that I started teaching I drove to Los Angeles to join Adair for a meeting of the old Southern California History Guild, eager to enjoy his company as a fellow working historian. Later that year he committed suicide and I, like countless others, had to nurture carefully the precious memories we had of this remarkable teacher and human being.

Introduction

Douglass Adair's *The Intellectual Origins of Jeffersonian Democracy: Republicanism, the Class Struggle, and the Virtuous Farmer* is one of the most influential dissertations on the history of the American Founding and political thought. Written in 1943 at Yale University, it quickly gained notoriety, with a list of borrowers that resembled "a who's who in early American history."[1] Beyond that, work of Adair's drawn from the dissertation has been highly influential in its own right. While Adair never developed his thesis into the comprehensive monograph he had originally envisioned, it remains an important and substantial study to this day. Its influence can be seen in four areas: in legitimating the study of the role of ideas in historical explanation, in providing a cogent critique of the economic approach of Charles Beard, in drawing connections between the Scottish Enlightenment and the Founding, and in setting the terms of the debate over the relative roles of republicanism and liberalism.

Adair's dissertation is concerned with the intellectual origins of American political thought and practice, as opposed to economic origins. It is clearly a direct response to Beard's earlier volume, *The Economic Origins of Jeffersonian Democracy*.[2] Adair uses the term *intellectual* broadly, including in it notions of ideology, political philosophy, and ways of thinking about history and historical time. Issues of terminology aside, Adair is reconnecting with the scholarship of Carl Becker, who, in his classic *The Declaration of Independence,* explores the philosophical sources of that document, especially emphasizing the role of John Locke as a key influence. In addition, Becker's *The Heavenly City of the Eighteenth Century Philosophers* also advances the importance of the idea of posterity for the eighteenth century.[3] This was a theme to which Adair would return toward the end of his career.

To appreciate *Intellectual Origins of Jeffersonian Democracy,* it helps to place the study in its proper setting. In the decades from 1920 to 1950, the economic approach to historical interpretation of the American Founding, pioneered by Beard, emerged as the prevailing orthodoxy among historians. As Adair's title signifies, he meant to challenge the Beardian paradigm by arguing for the importance of ideas and beliefs in shaping the ways the Founders saw the world and made sense of their experience. In doing so, he explicitly rejected the notion that the Founders' framing of the Constitution was reducible to simple economic interest. Adair did not repudiate the idea entirely, however; in *The Power to Govern* an earlier examination that he coauthored, the mercantilist background of the Constitution is given very serious emphasis.[4] What Adair argues is that economic motives alone are incomplete as a way of explaining the actions and the goals of the Founders: while the Founders may not have been completely disinterested, there were other motivations and designs at work.

Adair's qualified rejection of economic reductionism, or the notion that all moral and political action is ultimately concerned with the pursuit of economic self-interest, was one of his recurring themes. Toward the end of his career, in an essay entitled "Fame and the Founding Fathers," he took up the subject and developed it in a new direction. In that essay he discusses Forrest McDonald's *E Pluribus Unum*, praising it for its thoughtful application of Beardian economic analysis to both state and national politics during the Founding period. Adair criticizes McDonald for sharing with Beard an excessively narrow conception of self-interest and contends that such a limited notion was insufficient to explain fully the motivations and public spiritedness of many of the Founders.[5] Adair posits instead that one of the Founders' unique dimensions was their reflection on experience that "had led them to redefine their notions of interest and had given them, through the concept of fame, a personal stake in creating a national system dedicated to liberty, to justice, and to the general welfare."[6]

Probably the best-known aspect of Adair's criticism of Beard is his analysis of Federalist 10, first in chapter 6 of *Intellectual Origins of Jeffersonian Democracy* and later in two seminal articles, "The Tenth Federalist Revisited" and "'That Politics May Be Reduced to a Science': David Hume, James Madison, and the Tenth Federalist."[7] In these pieces Adair, through his own style of historical detection, elucidates the intellectual connection between Federalist 10 and other earlier works of political philosophy, most notably those of David Hume on the typology of factions and the superiority of a large over a small republic.[8] Adair further demonstrates that Beard's concern with class conflict led him to miss important nuances in Madison's argument.

Beyond this, Adair fundamentally challenges Beard's conception of class struggle, arguing that the notions of class held by the Founding generation owed more to Aristotle and were aimed at a particular political, as opposed to an economic, ideal—how to create a relatively peaceful republican order. For Aristotle, the virtuous farmer was the key ingredient in this process because the combination of discipline and independence fostered in the agricultural class made it the necessary support for republicanism. To this end, Adair emphasizes the importance of historian John Gillies's translation of Aristotle as indicative of the way the eighteenth century interpreted Aristotelian politics. Other significant classical influences, in Adair's view, included Polybius, for the theory of the mixed constitution and the cyclical theory of history, and Tacitus. This classical grounding, Adair contends, not only provided Founders such as John Adams and Alexander Hamilton with theoretical tools that were useful in constructing new institutions, but also led them to interpret events like Shays's Rebellion in an especially ominous light—as anarchic strife that would eventually spiral into despotism.

One aspect of *Intellectual Origins of Jeffersonian Democracy* that may strike readers as puzzling is the lack of explicit discussion about Thomas Jefferson's political thought. There is no chapter on the sources of the Declaration of Independence, which surely is one of the key elements of Jeffersonian democracy. Part of the answer may be that, as far as Adair was concerned, Becker's earlier work on the Declaration was sufficient and did not need challenging or improvement. The other part of the answer is to be found in Adair's concern with confronting Beard's interpretation of Federalist 10, which leads him to concentrate on Madison's political thought rather than Jefferson's. Indeed, some may conclude that a more appropriate title for this work is "The Intellectual Origins of Madisonian Democracy."

Adair's focus on Madison is not misplaced if one bears in mind that he sees no serious distinction between Jefferson and Madison in terms of political thought. For Adair, Madison is the leading Jeffersonian democrat, a view that puts him at odds with those who would drive a sharp wedge between the two. In addition, while Adair's work was of great import for what came to be known as the Republican Synthesis, it does not offer a dichotomy of republicanism (or civic humanism) versus liberalism, or Locke versus Machiavelli. Adair emphasizes the complementary aspects these different thinkers have for the American Founding generation; perhaps he is right not to draw such a sharp distinction between republicanism and liberalism, and perhaps contemporary historiography has exaggerated such distinctions.[9] Those interested in the intellectual history of the American Founding would be well served to return to the work of Adair to find the ways in which these allegedly separate and distinct traditions interpenetrate and complement each other.

In highlighting the importance of the intellectual sources of American political thought from classical, Renaissance, and seventeenth- and eighteenth-century European political thinkers, Adair wanted to get at the frames of reference by which the Founding generation viewed the world and interpreted events. He also sought to identify and trace the evolution of their aspirations. In investigating the sources of the ideas and beliefs of the Founding generation, Adair explored the genealogy of republican thought from classical Greece through Montesquieu and Hume. He believed it was important to know what was in the Founders' libraries in order to apprehend how they looked at the world.

One of Adair's most original contributions is his emphasis on the influence of Scottish Enlightenment thinkers, particularly David Hume, on the American Founders. Adair's initial work opened the door for further scholarship that examined the depth, range, and impact of this connection. Adair's student Trevor Colbourn, in *The Lamp of Experience*, explored many of the libraries of the Founding generation and discovered in them numerous examples of works from the eighteenth-century commonwealth tradition and the Scottish Enlightenment.[10] The connection of Hume to Jeffersonian democracy was complicated, however, by the recovery of evidence that Jefferson harbored great antipathy for Hume's *History of England* because of Hume's partial defense of the Stuart kings, particularly Charles I, and his rejection of the Whig myth of Saxon democracy. Indeed, Jefferson described Hume as "a degenerate son of science" and, as Leonard Levy has documented, tried to thwart University of Virginia students' access to Hume's potentially corrupting work, since many elements in it ran counter to what Jefferson regarded as the proper Whig account of English history.[11]

Other notable attempts to build on Adair's insight into the connection between the Scottish Enlightenment and America include those of Garry Wills and Morton White. Wills connects the Scottish Enlightenment to Jefferson in *Inventing America*, which makes the case for Scottish influence in the Declaration of Independence.[12] *Inventing America* goes beyond Adair to challenge Becker's analysis of the Declaration of Independence. Wills uses Adair's insights about the importance of the Scottish Enlightenment as a springboard to replace an interpretation that emphasizes the influence of John

Locke with one that emphasizes Francis Hutcheson. Wills extended —many thought overextended—Adair's work on Hume's influence in the Federalist Papers in *Inventing America*, treating Hume as a virtual Founding Father.

The work of Morton White in *Philosophy and the American Revolution* and *Philosophy, the Federalist, and the Constitution* has been received with less controversy. In the former, White accentuates Locke's influence on Jefferson and, in the latter, the way in which both Locke and Hume were important for the writers of the Federalist. In *Philosophy, the Federalist, and the Constitution*, White engages in what is arguably the most philosophically acute analysis of the connection between the Federalist Papers and earlier works of political theory.[13] He argues that, while Adair was right to criticize Beard and to find a pronounced Humean influence on the writers of the Federalist, the Founders were content to hold mutually contradictory philosophical viewpoints. White gives the example of Hamilton, who regarded Hume as the most important of political thinkers but who was also insistent on defending a notion of Lockean natural rights.[14] This is significant because Hume's arguments undercut Locke's notion of the social contract and did not give much credence to the notion of abstract natural rights. Although White's work is not as broad in its scope as Adair's or as concerned with historical context, it is probably the most nuanced and sophisticated study of the inner logic of the Federalist.

Forrest McDonald, who criticized Beard while pursuing his own brand of economic analysis, moved more in the direction of intellectual history in *Novus Ordo Seclorum*, a work that explores many of the theoretical sources of the Constitutional debates.[15] McDonald emerges as a champion for the influence of the Scots and the design of a science of politics that taught how to channel self-interest in directions that promote prosperity, stability, and liberty. And he broadened the discussion of the Scottish Enlightenment, bringing in an analysis and comparison of the political economy of Adam Smith and James Steuart. It is also worth noting that McDonald subtitled this book *The Intellectual Origins of the Constitution* in clear homage to Adair, who he hoped would have given this work a "posthumous third cheer."[16]

Adair, along with Zera Fink and Caroline Robbins, was instrumental in setting the terms for what would later become known as the Republican Synthesis, which in turn framed the debate over the relative importance of republicanism and liberalism in the Founding period.[17] Reading *The Intellectual Origins of Jeffersonian Democracy* makes it clear that Adair deserves credit for the initial insights that made the Republican Synthesis possible, even if it eventually moved in directions he might not have fully endorsed. It is possible to read Adair as presenting two different types of republicanism in "Intellectual Origins of Jeffersonian Democracy." The first is a classical republicanism that can be traced back to Aristotle and is concerned with the form of civic virtue that is needed to maintain the small-scale polity or city state. The second version of republicanism is a modern understanding associated with Hume and the Scottish Enlightenment that offers a blueprint for the large-scale commercial republic and places greater emphasis on a psychology of self-interest. Frequently this modern republicanism is identified as liberalism. Adair's analysis seems to suggest that these two kinds of republicanism —one focused on the small scale and primarily concerned with virtue, and the other focused on the large scale and principally concerned with commerce—are reconciled in Jeffersonian democracy. Along with this, Adair introduces the importance of the "country" party opposition led by Bolingbroke to the Whig oligarchy in eighteenth-century Britain and notes the importance of this opposition for the Jeffersonian Republican opposition to the Federalists.

The Republican Synthesis in American historiography emerged most strongly in the 1960s with works by Bernard Bailyn and Gordon Wood.[18] The emphasis on the connection between the British opposition tradition and America was in part a response to interpretations that argued for the dominance of Lockean liberalism in the American Founding that had emerged in the 1950s, most notably in Louis Hartz's *The Liberal Tradition in America.*[19] The argument put forth by Bailyn in *The Ideological Origins of the American Revolution* draws on a thorough survey of pamphlets from the Revolutionary period and emphasizes the importance of self-abnegation for the common good, suspicion of commerce and public debt, fear of corruption through excessive luxury, and a strict opposition to standing armies. It is important to point out that Bailyn does not use the term *republican* and does not explicitly argue that Locke was unimportant. Wood, in *The Creation of the American Republic*, wrote: "Republicanism was essentially anticapitalistic, a final attempt to come to terms with the emergent individualistic society that threatened to destroy once and for all the communion and benevolence that civilized men had always considered to be the ideal of human behavior."[20] Wood qualifies the republican thesis by arguing that the Constitution and its ratification marked a turning point in the direction of liberalism.

If Bailyn and Wood downplay Locke's role in American political thought, it utterly disappears in the work of J.G.A. Pocock. For Pocock, the self-sacrificing, virtuous, property-owning, arms-bearing citizen ideal that constitutes republicanism, or what he calls "civic humanism," was brought to modernity through the teachings of Machiavelli, hence the title of his masterwork, *The Machiavellian Moment*.[21] Machiavellian republicanism was then transmitted to Britain during the seventeenth century through James Harrington, especially in his utopian work *Oceana*. Later neo-Harringtonian writers include Bolingbroke and other Tory opponents to the administration of Robert Walpole. These opposition politicians saw the Robinocracy's use of public debt and patronage as fundamentally corrupt and corrupting, eroding virtue and leading to the loss of liberty. They looked back in time toward a pristine past of true republican virtue. Pocock is the most forceful of all the historians identified with the Republican Synthesis in denying the importance of John Locke for eighteenth-century Anglo-American political thought, a stance that has made his work the target of much criticism.

In *The Jeffersonian Persuasion*, Lance Banning builds on Pocock's insights and takes the republican thesis to its logical conclusion in the American setting. Banning argues that the Jeffersonian Republicans utilized country party opposition language to attack the Federalists, particularly Hamilton, for producing a corrupt, Walpole-like commercial oligarchy that would eventually degenerate into an oppressive monarchy in which hard-won liberties would be lost. Banning even entitles the chapter in which he discusses the election of Jefferson as president "The Country Comes to Power."[22] Adair anticipates Banning's study in explicitly connecting Bolingbroke to Jefferson in chapter 6 of "Intellectual Origins of Jeffersonian Democracy," writing that Bolingbroke "set the pattern for the Jeffersonian opposition to Hamilton."[23]

This is not to suggest that the Republican Synthesis is not without some very substantial detractors, most notably Joyce Appleby, Isaac Kramnick, and John Patrick Diggins.[24] Appleby, another of Adair's former students, argues that the republican interpretation of Jefferson misses Jefferson's commitment to agrarian capitalism and free trade, as well as his determination to look to the future and not to the past. Appleby's analysis undercuts the sharp dichotomy between virtue and commerce posited by Pocock.[25] Kramnick criticizes the absence of Locke in the Republican Synthesis, finding numerous examples of Lockean influence and responses to that influence that had been unacknowledged.[26] Diggins also emphasizes the importance of Locke and Calvinism for what he sees as the dominant liberal tradition in America and further argues that what had been identified as classical republican influence was merely a rhetorical flourish superimposed on liberal politics. Building on Adair's work, Diggins insists that "Hume's presence pervades the Federalist." Diggins connects Hume to John Adams in terms of assessing human motivations.[27]

Two other scholars have produced very different works that owe something to the Republican Synthesis but are best seen as critical responses to it. The Jefferson constructed by Richard Matthews, who has written on both Jefferson and Madison, rejects the aristocratic baggage of classical republicanism. As portrayed by Matthews, Jefferson is a radical egalitarian participatory democrat who advocates a state of permanent revolution and rejects the concentrations of power in both a centralized state and capitalist development.[28] Although Matthews agrees with Appleby that Jefferson is fundamentally future oriented, he argues that Jefferson retains the anticapitalistic emphasis of the Republican Synthesis and deepens it dramatically. Matthews also opposes both Madison and Hamilton to Jefferson as promoters of modern American liberalism. Here he explicitly cites Adair's use of evidence from Hume and the Scottish Enlightenment. This view actually runs counter to Adair's desire to link Madison and Jefferson.

Lastly, Paul Rahe's monumental *Republics Ancient and Modern* covers much of the same ground that Adair was attempting to address in "Intellectual Origins of Jeffersonian Democracy."[29] Indeed, it is not too farfetched to see a work of this scope as being what Adair originally intended (as well as providing a partial explanation for why he never followed through on that intention). Rahe rejects the notion of continuity between ancient and modern republicanism and, in arguing for a sharp discontinuity between them, offers the most thorough repudiation of Pocock's *Machiavellian Moment.* Rahe's study also raises problems for Adair's work. Although Adair implied a difference between ancient and modern republicanism, he does not draw a sharp theoretical distinction between these bodies of thought primarily because he decided to stress the Founders' adaptations of those sources to the challenges of the Constitutional and Federalist eras.

I fully recognize that this brief overview cannot do justice to the work of the many fine scholars writing on the ideology of the American Founding. That said, I hope that it gives some sense of the widespread and continuous impact of Douglass Adair's work. Restoring credibility to the intellectual history of the American Founding, providing a serious refutation to the Beardian school of analysis, highlighting the connection of the Scottish Enlightenment to the American Founding, and helping to set the terms of contemporary debates about republicanism and liberalism are by themselves important contributions to historical scholarship and the study of political thought. That Adair can be credited with all of these accomplishments amply demonstrates his acuity and insight. His scholarship, when added to his many years as a distinguished teacher, shown in part by the work of students such as Trevor Colbourn and Joyce Appleby, and his editorship of the *William and Mary Quarterly* in the period when it became the leading journal of American history, constitutes a very impressive record.

Some may question the appropriateness of the posthumous publication of a work whose author chose not to publish it during his lifetime. While I understand and sympathize with such concerns, the intrinsic value of the dissertation overrides them. In addition, I should mention that this project went forward with the full consent and approval of the Adair family. As far as editorial decisions are concerned, I have endeavored to do as little as possible, changing or removing only the most obvious errors. No significant alterations of either style or substance have been made. The main differences between this volume and the dissertation are that footnotes are now endnotes and that I have added a new bibliography listing all the works cited in the text.

Notes

1. Douglass Greybill Adair, "Introduction," *Fame and the Founding Fathers: Essays by Douglass Adair*, ed. Trevor Colbourn (New York: Published for the Institute of Early American History and Culture, Williamsburg, Virginia, by W.W. Norton, 1974), xv.

2. Charles Beard, *The Economic Origins of Jeffersonian Democracy* (New York: The Free Press, 1915).

3. Carl L. Becker, *The Declaration of Independence: A Study in the History of Political Ideas* (New York: Vintage Books, 1958 [1922]), and *The Heavenly City of the Eighteenth Century Philosophers* (New Haven: Yale University Press, 1932).

4. Walton Hamilton and Douglass Adair, *The Power to Govern: The Constitution Then and Now* (New York: W.W. Norton, 1937).

5. Adair, *Fame and the Founding Fathers*, 32.

6. Ibid., 33. It is worth mentioning that McDonald has, to a certain degree, accepted Adair's insights on this point. In the second edition of *E Pluribus Unum*, he writes: "Most importantly, however, there is a dimension of the Founding Fathers which is neglected here: the ardent desire for Fame, the secular equivalent of Christian immortality. The hope of winning the undying gratitude through noble creative statesmanship was the 'ruling passion' in Hamilton's life. And a similar urge impelled Madison, James Wilson, and other Americans

of their generation." McDonald, *E Pluribus Unum,* 2d ed. (Indianapolis: Liberty Press, 1979; orig. pub. Boston: Houghton Mifflin, 1965), 15.

7. Both articles are reprinted in *Fame and the Founding Fathers*. Usually Adair and Martin Diamond are seen as being key to laying the groundwork of a non-Beardian analysis of Federalist 10. See Charles Kesler, "Federalist 10 and American Republicanism," in Kesler, ed., *Saving the Revolution: The Federalist Papers and The American Founding* (New York: Free Press, 1987), 16-17, on the importance of Adair and Martin Diamond. "Adair sought to restore independence and some of the dignity of political theory, even if only from the historical point of view."

8. One point that Adair does not explore sufficiently is that Madison did not get from Hume his argument for the multiplicity of factions as being the structure for controlling the harmful effects of faction. However much it may seem to be implied in his analysis, Hume deliberately never makes it, seeing the method for restraining the effects of faction in moderating public opinion. Hume's good friend, Adam Smith, does make an argument for a multiplicity of religious sects as the vehicle for dampening religious enthusiasm in *The Wealth of Nations*, as did Voltaire before him.

9. For a work that calls into question the credibility of the Republican Synthesis as a "paradigm," see Daniel T. Rodgers, "Republicanism: The Career of a Concept," *Journal of American History,* 79 (1992), 11-38. For a study that argues that liberalism includes many of the aspects of civic republicanism see Richard C. Sinopoli, *The Foundations of American Citizenship: Liberalism, the Constitution, and Civic Virtue* (New York and Oxford: Oxford University Press, 1992).

10. Trevor Colbourn, *The Lamp of Experience* (Chapel Hill, N.C.: University of North Carolina Press, 1965). See especially chap. 8.

11. Leonard W. Levy, *Jefferson and Civil Liberties: The Darker Side* (Cambridge: Harvard University Press, 1963), chap. 7. Levy's book generated a great deal of controversy for its depiction of Jefferson as an antilibertarian. For a more recent account of Jefferson and Hume's History that aims to exculpate Jefferson from Levy's accusations, see Douglass Wilson, "Hume vs. Jefferson," *William and Mary Quarterly*, 3d Ser., 46 (1989), 49-70.

12. Garry Wills, *Inventing America: Jefferson's Declaration of Independence* (New York: Doubleday, 1978), and *Explaining America* (New York: Doubleday, 1981). Wills's analysis drew critical commentary. For the most important see Ronald Hamowy "Jefferson and the Scottish Enlightenment: A Critique of Garry Wills's *Inventing America: Jefferson's Declaration of Independence*," *WMQ*, 3d Ser., 36 (1979), 503-23; Theodore Draper, "Hume and Madison: The Secrets of Federalist Paper No. 10," *Encounter*, 58 (February 1982); Gordon S. Wood, "Heroics," *New York Review of Books*, 2 April 1981; and Marvin Meyers, "Findings on the Fathers," *New York Times Book Review*, 1 March 1981. Most of these commentators were sympathetic to Adair but thought that Wills had grievously overstated his case. For a writer who thinks Adair is utterly mistaken see James Conniff, "The Enlightenment and American Political Thought," *Political Theory*, 8 (August 1980), 381-402.

13. Morton White, *The Philosophy of the American Revolution* (New York:

Oxford University Press, 1978), and *Philosophy, the Federalist, and the Constitution* (New York: Oxford University Press, 1987).

14. On Hamilton's dependence on Hume, see Forrest McDonald, *Alexander Hamilton: A Biography* (New York: W.W. Norton, 1979), 35-37. For White's discussion of Hamilton's wanting to simultaneously hold contradictory Lockean and Humean viewpoints see *Philosophy, the Federalist, and the Constitution,* 28-31. One of the defects of Adair's work is that he failed to draw the connections between Hume and Hamilton.

15. Forrest McDonald, *Novus Ordo Seclorum: The Intellectual Origins of the Constitution* (Lawrence: University Press of Kansas, 1985).

16. Ibid., ix.

17. Zera Fink, *The Classical Republicans: An Essay in the Recovery of a Pattern of Thought in Seventeenth-Century* (Evanston, Ill.: Northwestern University Press, 1945); Caroline Robbins, *The Eighteenth-Century Commonwealthman: Studies in the Transmission, Development and Circumstance of English Liberal Thought from the Restoration of Charles II until the War with the Thirteen Colonies* (Cambridge, Mass.: Harvard University Press, 1959). For the notion of a Republican Synthesis see Robert E. Shalhope, "Republicanism and Early American Historiography," *WMQ*, 3d Ser., 39 (1982), 334-56, and "Toward a Republican Synthesis: The Emergence of an Understanding of Republicanism in American Historiography," ibid., 29, (1972), 49-80.

18. Bernard Bailyn, *The Ideological Origins of the American Revolution* (Cambridge, Mass.: Harvard University Press, 1967); Gordon S. Wood, *The Creation of the American Republic, 1776-1787* (Chapel Hill, N.C.: University of North Carolina Press, 1969).

19. Louis Hartz, *The Liberal Tradition in America: An Interpretation of American Political Thought since the Revolution* (New York: Harcourt, Brace, 1955).

20. Wood, *Creation of the American Republic,* 418-19.

21. J.G.A. Pocock, *The Machiavellian Moment: Florentine Thought and the Atlantic Republican Tradition* (Princeton, N.J.: Princeton University Press, 1975); also important in this context is *Virtue, Commerce, and History: Essays on Political Thought and History, Chiefly in the Eighteenth Century* (Cambridge: Cambridge University Press, 1985).

22. Lance Banning, *The Jeffersonian Persuasion: Evolution of a Party Ideology* (Ithaca, N.Y.: Cornell University Press, 1978).

23. See page 142, note 19 of this work.

24. In addition to Appleby, Kramnick, and Diggins (whose first chapter in *The Lost Soul of American Politics* is entitled "Who's Afraid of John Locke?"), see Steven M. Dworetz, *The Unvarnished Doctrine: Locke, Liberalism and the American Revolution* (Durham, N.C.: Duke University Press, 1990), and Michael Zuckert, *Natural Rights and the New Republicanism* (Princeton, N.J.: Princeton University Press, 1994).

25. Joyce Appleby's work can be found in *Capitalism and a New Social Order: The Republicanism of the 1790s* (New York: New York University Press, 1984), and a collection of her essays, *Liberalism and Republicanism in*

the Historical Imagination (Cambridge, Mass.: Harvard University Press, 1992).

26. Isaac Kramnick, *Bolingbroke and His Circle: The Politics of Nostalgia in the Age of Walpole* (Cambridge, Mass.: Harvard University Press, 1968), and "Republican Revisionism Revisited," *American Historical Review*, 87 (1982), 629-64, reprinted in *Republicanism and Bourgeois Radicalism: Political Ideology in Late Eighteenth-Century England and America* (Ithaca, N.Y.: Cornell University Press, 1990).

27. John Patrick Diggins, *The Lost Soul of American Politics* (New York: Basic Books, 1984), chap. 3 and 76 (quotation).

28. Richard Matthews, *The Radical Politics of Thomas Jefferson: A Revisionist View* (Lawrence: University Press of Kansas, 1984); *If Men Were Angels: James Madison and the Heartless Empire of Reason* (Lawrence: University Press of Kansas, 1995).

29. Paul Rahe, *Republics Ancient and Modern* (Chapel Hill, N.C.: University of North Carolina Press, 1992).

Editor's Note

In producing this edition of Douglass Adair's *Intellectual Origins of Jeffersonian Democracy*, I worked to stick as closely as possible to the original text. Two editorial interventions, however, deserve some explanation. The first was the addition of translations into English of passages in the original that were simply either in French or Latin. I did this to increase the accessibility of the work. The translations added occur in chapter 4, note 64, and chapter 6, pages 119-120 and note 29. The second had to do with the reconstruction of the bibliography at the end of the work. In the overwhelming majority of cases I was able to determine which edition of a particular text Adair used in his dissertation. In one particular case, a book entitled *Erasmus Darwin and His Circle* by Hesketh Pearson, I was unable to find any information about that work. However, I did locate a book by Hesketh Pearson entitled *Doctor Darwin* that is concerned with Erasmus Darwin, so I substituted that title in the bibliography.

There are many people to thank in getting this classic work of Douglass Adair's into print. First, I would like to thank Carey McWilliams and Gordon Schochet for their encouragement of this project, especially during the inevitable setbacks that accompany such an endeavor.

I am also grateful to the Adair family, Ron Hoffman of the Institute of Early American History and Culture, and Joyce Appleby for their support of this project. This book could not have been produced without their approval. The Institute also provided editorial assistance with the foreword and the introduction. A special thanks is in order to Professor Appleby for agreeing to write a foreword to this work.

Richard Boyd and Jonathan McFall provided timely help with translations. Boyd provided the English translation to passages in French and McFall located the appropriate translation of a Cicero quote through a remarkable display of Latinate sleuthing.

I greatly appreciate the insightful commentary I received on my introduction from Holly Brewer—a Douglass G. Adair Memorial Award winner it should be noted—and Christine Henderson, in addition to that provided by Professors McWilliams and Schochet. Of course, I am responsible for any errors contained in the introduction.

I am most grateful to Stephen Wrinn and Serena Leigh of Lexington Books for recognizing the inherent value of this project and for their enthusiasm and help as the project progressed. In addition, I would like to thank Matt Spaulding and Charles Kesler for suggesting that I propose this project to the Rowman & Littlefield Publishing Group.

Finally, I most acknowledge my greatest debt—which is to my wife Ethel, who has subsidized the time spent on this project with patience, good humor, encouragement, and help with the final corrections.

Summary

The Intellectual Origins of Jeffersonian Democracy

This monograph attempts to uncover certain intellectual assumptions, postulates, and theories which Jefferson and Madison acted upon in organizing the Republican party in 1792, and in formulating the political philosophy of that party.

The ideas that were used in creation of the Jeffersonians' political philosophy were all current in the eighteenth century; they were the ideological commonplace of every literate man. Jefferson and Madison as liberally educated men of their own age could not possibly escape exposure to those ideas. Their receptivity to certain current theories and their rejection of others was undoubtedly conditioned by the fact that they were planters living in the Virginia Piedmont. Nevertheless the most fruitful point of departure in studying their careers as statesmen is acceptance of the fact that all the questions they asked and all the answers they found to them were eighteenth-century questions and answers that their intensive reading had already blocked out into a systematic pattern.

Turning from the general to the specific, the agrarian theory with which the Virginians' names have been so closely identified was one of the most common political doctrines of the Enlightenment. It was also one of the most ancient theories in its origin. It had been cast into fairly definitive form by Aristotle; and all the elements that the Greek included are to be found substantially unchanged in the Virginians' reordering of the dogma. Aristotle's agrarianism was in part an economic theory, in part a theory of human psychology, in part a scheme of ethical values, but above all it was a hypothesis of how to base a stable government on popular suffrage. With a society composed of self-sufficient and economically independent farmers, whose way of life was the golden mean of virtue between riches and poverty, it would be possible, the Greek claimed, to set up a republican government exempt from the class struggle. Variations on this Aristotelian theme of the stable republic had been read by the Virginians in Xenophon, Polybius, Cicero, and Plutarch. A related school of theorists who were well known to Madison and Jefferson, appeared among the Roman authors of the early imperial era; for Augustus laid down and subsidized a propaganda policy that identified his veiled dictatorship with the rustic virtue of ancient Rome, in order to buttress his imperial power by a social myth. How familiar to the Jeffersonian democrats these classical theorists were can be seen by the most cursory examination of their writings.

Jefferson and Madison were also heirs of contemporary English version of this classical agrarianism. The British republicans of the seventeenth-century (notably Harrington, who drew directly from Aristotle's *Politics* for his "agrarian law") were saturated with Greek and Roman political concepts. And though republicanism proved a transitory phase in England's constitutional development, the agrarian theories then evolved proved too useful as ideological weapons for the Tory "landed interest" led by Bolingbroke to drop.

As a result, when Jefferson discussed the virtuous farmer and the vicious city-dwelling artisan in his *Notes on Virginia*, and when Madison wrote the tenth *Federalist* paper, they were not simply voicing novel theories serviceable to an American farm bloc, nor were they enunciating dogma spontaneously generated upon the frontier. The leaders of "Jeffersonian democracy" were summing up in American terms a traditional theory whose origins date back to the Fourth Century before Christ; that an agrarian base is necessary for a free republican state.

Chapter 1

A Polemical Prologue

It takes "considerable courage," as a reviewer in the *American Historical Review* noted in a recent issue, for anyone today to write anything about Thomas Jefferson that pretends to be original. "The story of [his] life, of his political doctrine, and of his influence in American history, has been told so often and in such detail that it has become a difficult task to add anything to knowledge of the man, or to give any fresh interpretation of his work."[1] This is almost equally true for his friend and political associate, James Madison. Yet if one examines the oft told story of their two careers as they have been presented by their historians and biographers one wonders if there is not a need for reinterpretation of their thought. Certain aspects of their political activities and their influence on American history have never been clearly elucidated.

A reanalysis of old history is well justified when it can fit into the pattern of cause and effect certain primary data, which, failing to conform to some scholar's research, have heretofore been left out. Historians who have written during the last century on the origins of Jeffersonian democracy have had a tendency to shun discussion of certain charges its founders used to combat the Federalist opposition. One charge, it seemed, became increasingly hard to explain as time flowed more deeply over the period. That is, the Jeffersonians' obsession that the result most greatly to be feared from the Federalist fiscal policy was not the obvious—to us—plutocracy, but an American monarchy. There are many letters in their own handwriting, too many of their spoken statements vouched for by competent witnesses, for us to dismiss the accusation out of hand.[2] And indeed, with all the scholarly debate over Jefferson's ideas, motives, private character and public policy, no satisfactory commentary has yet been written on his organization and leadership with James Madison of the republican opposition that drove the Federalists from office. This

opposition culminated in one of the great climaxes of Jefferson's life
—his election as President of the United States in 1800. The meaning
of that climax to the historian, its importance for American history
still remains controversial.

To Thomas Jefferson and his political lieutenant, James Madison,
the significance this victory of the republicans in 1800 was by no
means ambiguous. It is clear beyond question that they thought the
election of Jefferson to the Presidency marked a decisive event in
American history. To both of them the election was "the revolution
of 1800"—a "revolution as real in the principles of government," to
quote Jefferson's own words, "as that of 1776 was in its form."[3] This
was Jefferson's considered opinion written eleven years after he had
retired from the Presidency. His convictions were not different on
this score from those he held in 1801 when he took office. Writing to
John Dickinson two days after the inauguration he stated, "the tough
sides of our Argosie have been thoroughly tried. Her strength has
stood the waves into which she was steered with a view to sink her.
We shall put her on her republican tack, and she will show by the
beauty of her motion the skill of her builders."[4] Jefferson apparently
believed that the defeat of the Federalists was an event comparable in
the history of the United States to the Declaration of Independence;
the electoral revolution had restored to the Constitution republican
principles commensurate with its republican form.

Madison is as explicit as Jefferson in treating the election of 1800
as a revolution that preserved free government in America. In 1798
when drafting the Virginia resolutions he declared that the "obvious
tendency and inevitable consequence" of Federalist policy "would be
to transform the present republican system the United States into an
absolute, or, at best, a mixed monarchy."[5] This was not merely a case
of public exaggeration for propaganda effect. For reasons we shall
examine later, Madison sincerely feared that the Federalists had
repudiated government by consent. In private letters to Jefferson just
before the latter's inauguration he was thankfully noting that lack of
a standing army had blocked a Federalist attempt at a military *coup
d'etat*, designed to retrieve the loss at the Polls. It was only this lack,
he believed, that allowed the Jeffersonian "revolution" to be a
peaceful one. If the monocrats controlled a professional army
Madison did not doubt that they would have used it.[6]

The chief actors in "revolution of 1800" were convinced that
there was a radical difference between their system and that of their
predecessors. They appear to have believed that somehow the issue
turned on the issue of monarchy, and that the name of their party—
Republican—was concretely related to the program that they carried

out. But later commentators, for all their familiarity with Jefferson's career, political doctrines and personal character, have had great difficulty in marking the exact cleavage and definite bounds to the policies the Jeffersonian Democrats were so sure that they had inaugurated. American historians during the last century have violently differed as to the nature of Jefferson's and Madison's "revolution." Few of them have accepted the monarchy issue as valid; although if Madison's and Jefferson's words are to be trusted that issue was the essence of their opposition.

Among these historians neglectful of the monarchy issue or unimpressed by it, there have been two exceptions. Henry S. Randall, whose life of Jefferson published in 1858 still remains in mnay ways the best biography of the man, considered the monarchy issue so important that he devoted a chapter to it.[7] The evidence he presents is designed to show that every one of the early presidents of the United States from Washington to John Quincy Adams took the threat of monarchical usurpation in the United States more or less seriously. He argues further, that on the basis in part of personal conversations with Madison and other friends and associates of Jefferson who survived in the 1830's and 1840's, that Alexander Hamilton's monarchism was the leading cause of Jefferson's joining Madison in opposition to the Federalist program.

Louise B. Dunbar, a recent historian, fortifies Randall's thesis in a work unfortunately ignored in the twentieth century as Randall's was in the nineteenth.[8] While not attempting to relate her study to actual politics and parties, she maintains most persuasively that a great many sane and well-informed men considered the revival of kingly government in the United States quite possible up until 1800. Miss Dunbar moreover demonstrates how seriously the Republican paladins, Jefferson, Madison, and Monroe, took this threat of monarchical usurpation by cataloguing their reiterated statements to competent witnesses and reprinting the numerous private letters that they wrote on the subject. The opposition to Hamilton's fiscal program by these men visualized not merely some phase of plutocratic government, but ultimately the subversion of free government with the emergence of a king over the American people.

In spite of all the discussion of Jeffersonian democracy in the last hundred years we still lack a comprehensive study that analyzes the formation of the Republican party by Jefferson and Madison, in terms which comprehend these factors that they themselves stressed. A survey of the explanations advanced by American historians as to the nature of the Republican party, and its achievement in bringing about the "revolution of 1800" reveals wide discrepancies. Even though

Madison believed the election of that year signalized the end of one epoch in the course of American history and the commencement of another, some historians have gone so far as to deny that the "revolution" Jefferson talked of so confidently ever took place.

The most magisterial representative of the "no-revolution" school is John Bach McMaster in his *History of the People of the United States*. Ignoring Madison, and training his guns on Jefferson, he is willing to concede to Washington's Secretary of State a species of sincerity, however marred by economic ignorance, in opposing a sound fiscal policy.[9] "But by far the larger part [of this opposition] sprang from intense hatred of Hamilton. He could not bear to see the greatest place in the Cabinet filled by any but himself." While Hamilton "was perfecting a financial policy that drew upon him the eyes of a whole continent," Jefferson was condemned to the tedious tasks of notewriting to foreign ministers, chiding our envoys abroad, and umpiring the petty disputes of rival inventors.

> The Revenue Bill, the Assumption Act, the Funding System were fast bringing the country to a state of prosperity which seemed marvelous... All over the land mills and factories were going up, and such a demand was made for money that the price of it was already one percent a month. Yet the sight of this business activity excited in the breast of Jefferson, the stern patriot, only malignant hatred for the man whose fertile brain and untiring labour it was due.[10]

Thus McMaster attributes to personal jealousy the rise of the opposition. Since the organization of the Republican party resulted from one man's malice, there could be no real issue and no revolution.

Edward Channing believed that the center of republican opposition is to be found in a differing interpretation of the constitution; but that the election of 1800 marked no sharp split even in constitutional interpretation. For in winning the election the Republicans were in a position to bring in only new men, not measures—owing to the narrowness of the electoral vote that raised Jefferson to the post of Chief Executive. The "revolution," if any was really contemplated, was frustrated by the new party's insecurity; for no matter how many exulting letters Jefferson wrote, he "realized that his victory, such as it was, had been merely accidental."[11]

Following such a meager triumph, there could be no all-out attack upon the legislative fabric of the Federalist System; and Channing depicts Jefferson as a politician who cannily realized that the supreme problem of his administration was to consolidate his party's power by converting the New England masses into loyal Republicans, and thus undercutting the Strength of the Federalist leaders. If there was anything new in the actual performance of the new Administration, Channing conceded it might lie in its stress on economy.[12]

"Economy," in the eighteenth century, was a political term as well as an economic one. Jefferson, Madison, and their cohorts were to consider such measures as the payment of the national debt, the abrogation of excise taxes and the consequent dismissal of tax collectors, as among their great political contributions in preserving constitutional government. In their eyes, accordingly, such "economies" were valued for their political consequences alone. But it is obvious that Channing considers these measures simply in the light of common sense frugalities, rather than as the basis or programme of a new departure in government.

A stand somewhat removed from Channing is taken by Henry Adams on the question of the republican policies. In his study of the United States during the administrations of Jefferson and Madison, he is intensely preoccupied with the question of "the revolution." As the great-grandson of John Adams, who was swept from office by the republican broom, Henry Adams' extremely subtle and delicately balanced mind was emotionally involved in finding a reasonable pattern of cause and effect in the events leading up to the defeat of his renowned ancestor. Fully aware of the "self-deception inherent in every struggle for personal power" Adams summarily read out of court the Federalist attack on the Virginians as envious demagogues.[13] He granted that Jefferson at least meditated a programme "new in a system of government."[14]

According to Henry Adams, Jefferson's domestic policy envisioned the American republic, founded or secured in 1801, "as an enlarged Virginia"; a "society to be kept pure and free by the absence of complicated interests, by the encouragement of agriculture and of commerce as its handmaid, but not of industry in a larger sense."[15] But the revolution contemplated seemed to Adams no more than a dreamer's design to strip the Federal Government of most those powers which the Federalists had been at such pains to give it. The "radical distinction," then, between Jefferson and his worthy predecessors, lay in "opposite concepts of the National Government."[16] Only, and on this point Henry Adams is inflexibly certain, the revolution always remained in the stage of an elaborate theory; Jefferson never prepared, consciously or unconsciously, to put those Utopian concepts into practice.

In all the early dissections of the first great party battle in American history, historians followed the lead developed by Adams and laid their emphasis on the Constitutional doctrines of the contestants; the struggle was analyzed almost entirely as it focused on the "strict" or "liberal" construction of the United States Constitution. With the start of the nineteenth century, however, a new note was heard. Charles A. Beard published his two volumes on the Constitution and Jeffersonian Democracy, and in so doing established his position as one of the great American historians.[17] When Beard commenced his career Americans were becoming increasingly conscious of the pervasive effect of economic conflict upon the theory and practice of government. Applying the knowledge learned from contemporary events to the politics of the early national period, Beard presented proof that just as in 1896 and 1912, so also in 1787 and 1800 the basis of politics could be shown in economic terms. It became impossible, after Beard had presented his solidly documented case, for any serious writer on the subject to treat the early story of the American republic from a non-economic point of view. And with Beard's studies, new support was given to Jefferson's and Madison's belief that 1800 was a crucial date in United States History.

This view was in sharp contradistinction to that of earlier historians who had scarcely looked beyond the Constitutional aspect of the struggle between the two parties. The Jeffersonians having come into office used their political power as the Federalists before them. The Federalists now being out of office began to repeat the same old Jeffersonian pleas for strict constitutional interpretation. The election of 1800 then resulted in the appearance merely of new men in office, with no new departures in Constitutional practice; and on this fact the nineteenth-century historians had based their arguments that no revolution had taken place. This sort of juristic analysis Beard contends did no more than "skim the surface of politics."[18] But assuming, as Beard does, that both Madison and Jefferson looked consciously at political power as a device for furthering the interest of specific economic groups, then the election of 1800 was assuredly a "revolution." To Beard the party battle was a real one centering on the political desires of two economic groups as distinct in their outlooks as were the attackers and defenders of "big business" at the time Beard published his book.

The distinction of outlook between the embattled parties was that of two groups owning different types of property. As Beard sees it, the Federalists under Hamilton had turned the energies of the state they had created for that very purpose to the fostering of certain economic interests; their record by 1792 showed a deliberate and carefully wrought system designed to benefit definite economic classes.[19] "Wanting above all to gain certain economic ends, the Federalist party naturally came to the conclusion that the Constitution was to be construed freely enough to permit a straight march to the goal."[20] Since their program was based on exploitation of the masses, "it was equally natural that its sponsors should fear the triumph of the populace at the polls."[21]

Behind the frenzied attacks of the Anti-Federalists, Beard contends the motive for opposition is, in turn, purely economic. Madison, Jefferson, and other leaders of this group, while favorable to the strengthening of American credit and to improving the standing of the country abroad, "dissented, with varying emphasis, from propositions contained in the Federalist economic programme." Above all, as Southern planters, they were "tender of the people engaged in agriculture," (thus Beard over-simplifies the very complex bases of their agrarianism)—and every fiscal and commercial measure drawn up in the temporary capital at New York had imposed a burden on agriculture and labor for the benefit of the dominant interests.[22] "In a word the Anti-Federalist leaders saw in Hamilton's policies schemes for exploiting farmers, planters, and laborers for the benefit of capitalists, shipowners, and manufacturers." Beard claims this is the key to the opposition, and that "far from being the mere froth of excited politicians, this view represented the matured convictions of leaders given to deliberation and analysis."[23] Beard's evaluation is undoubtedly illuminating as far as it goes. It does ignore, as a whole century of historians before him, certain of their purely political grounds for opposition, which the Republican leaders stressed time and time again.

Accepting Beard's party split on this single basic issue of economic exploitation, the ambiguities of the Jeffersonian programme during the period of opposition and Jeffersonian practice after coming to power cease to be a problem. The "revolution of 1800" is an economic revolution; and Beard stresses Jefferson's statement "that he wanted 'the agricultural interest' to govern the country, and presumably to pursue policies advantageous to that social group." The constitutional doctrines and political theories that sprang from this underlying urge were, to Beard, merely verbal shadows signifying little in themselves, but standing in "precise relationship" to the economic appetites of the interest groups involved. The actual assumption of power by Jefferson as Chief Magistrate does not demonstrate "the mutability of human affairs and the hollowness of political profession."[24] Jefferson out of power was a strict constructionist for fear that the power of the national government held by commercial and financial men would hurt agriculture. Whereas,

Jefferson in power was for liberal interpretation—for the farmer could not but benefit from power wielded by the farmer's friend. Beard uses Jefferson's reversal to underline the essential dominance of the economic drive in politics.[25] The period of Jefferson's presidency does not inaugurate a frustrated political revolution; in truth an economic revolution had been consummated and the furling of the State's Rights banner meant simply that the Republicans controlled both the Federal Congress and Executive. Political victory, "in economic terms," permitted "a reversal of means not ends."[26]

Beard's arguments are impressive, even irrefutable as far as they go; but they do exhibit a scheme of motivation in the history of the period that seems unnecessarily meager. Reduced to its simplest statement, his claim is that the driving impulse behind both parties is pecuniary, without qualification. The Federalists exerted themselves in the interest of certain well-defined economic blocs, while their opponents shuddered as representatives of economic interests about to be sacrificed. They accordingly turned on their exploiters, to use Beard's Marxian term, and exploited them as they were able. Thus Beard succeeds in reducing the war-cries and the slogans which covered the attack on the bastions of Federalism to "rhetorical defense mechanisms;"[27] thus, too, in one short sentence he can dismiss to the realm of the irrelevant the charge of "monarchy."[28]

Charles Beard's support of Jefferson's claim that the election of 1800 was a "revolution" thus appears equivocal from the Virginians' viewpoint. If Beard is correct, Jefferson's contention that his party was putting the Constitution back on the "republican tack" which its "builders" in the Convention of 1787 had intended, becomes the most arrant sort of self-deception. In the Beardian view, 1776, the date of the Declaration, and 1800, the year of Jefferson's election are set in sharp contrast to 1787, the year in which the Constitution was framed.[29] The fact remains that Madison and Jefferson regarded all three dates as admirably progressive stages in the development of American republicanism. Jefferson and Madison never looked on the Constitution as the source of the trouble, nor did they repudiate the ideas which it embodied. Jefferson believed the *Federalist Papers* one of the best commentaries on free government ever written, and insisted that it be used as a text in his fledgling university's politics course.

It is true that Jefferson and Madison were "tender" of the agricultural interest; but if their words are to be believed it was far less for economic reasons, than for political reasons. If part of the gravamen of their charges against the Federalists was that of economic exploitation, included also and with equal emphasis, was the indictment of monarchism. Assuming, then, the sincerity of Jeffersonian opposition, its roots must be uncovered somewhere beyond the field of economic strife of real and personal property. If one recalls the remark of James Madison that a man can have "property in his opinions,"[30] some of the obscurity about the organization and leadership of the Republican party by Jefferson and Madison vanishes. To put it differently; opinions and ideas can own men. Political theory alone, it is true, is incapable of bringing about a social movement, but it cannot be pretended that ideas and the literature of ideas are not dynamic factors in history. The political leader who expects to attain any measure of success must mobilize most of his followers behind some clearly formulated idea. A Declaration of Independence possibly would have been written in 1776, even if John Locke had never sent pen to parchment; but the Declaration of Independence that was actually proclaimed on that hot day in Philadelphia, studied without reference to Locke's *Second Essay on Government* written a century before, would always contain something unfathomable.[31]

All history is, of course, partial truth at best; and each generation learns something different about the past from its own present. Charles Beard and the men who participated in Wilson's "New Freedom" knew by their own experience how important and all pervading the fact of economics was in American life. To carry back that knowledge as Beard did to 1787 resulted in a great flood of light being directed toward much that was obscure and confused in our early history; he can pride himself for having at one blow, emancipated large sections of the historical profession form a slavish and sterile repetition of cant about the background of the Constitution and the origins of our first political parties. Now, however, the hurrying course of events has made us aware of things that were less obvious when Beard wrote; we suspect that some of the data of the past which he dismissed as irrelevant may be important after all. It is not that many of us can hope to equal the wisdom of Charles Beard as historian, but only that we come after him in period of time.

And it may well be that the time has come to ask, whether the economic base is in truth the best point of departure from which to explain some of the puzzling facts about Jeffersonian democracy that no historian has quite succeeded in weaving into a believable pattern. We know that Hamilton at least in 1782 considered Madison's economic ideas as practically identical with his own; and yet Mr. Madison, the great antiparty philosopher of the Constitutional Convention, went into opposition and helped organize a highly effective party with Jefferson—supposedly Hamilton's direct antithesis in economic doctrine.

A real revolution "in the principles of government," Jefferson called the results of this opposition. Whether as philosophers of the frontier, or as gentlemen farmers (both tags have been abused to explain and identify their policies), Madison and Jefferson may well have been modified by their nonurban origins. And it may indeed be normal enough for gentlemen farmers to dislike a plutocracy; but why, not simply for the purposes of the "revolution" of 1800, but throughout their lives, did they insist what they really feared was a monarchy? This transmutation of an economic grievance into a political accusation puts the burden of proof on admirers of the Virginians. Assuming they were neither consistent hypocrites with a sharp eye for propaganda appeal, nor partisans blinded by a narrow regional belief, can some change of scholarly approach to the problems show then a new validity in their protestations?

Against this fear of monarchy, which history has passed over almost incredulously, the Jeffersonians opposed as a firm bulwark their ideal of an agricultural commonwealth. The Jeffersonian agrarian state is a concept on which historians can almost unanimously agree: its organization, and virtuous implications. What historians have perhaps failed to consider fully is the negative force of this concept to combat those principles of government which Madison and Jefferson feared as a direct path to monarchy.

To comprehend the Virginians' agricultural state as they envisioned it, that is, as the only sure safeguard of republicanism, it will be necessary to examine a strangely neglected bulk of evidence on the formation and growth of their political theories. The easy judgments, that Madison and Jefferson were "tender of farmers," or above all, formed by the frontier, have long enough served as the base from which to view their agricultural state as "a revolution...in the principles of government." What observers from this viewpoint have almost incredibly turned their backs upon is a source of influence on both Madison and Jefferson, confessed and discussed and emphasized in the letters, speeches, and miscellaneous writings of their two lifetimes. This source is the vast impact of classical traditions of political theory on two of the most widely read and scholarly statesmen America has ever known. Not only the authorities of Greece and of Rome did they cite for presage and resolution of events in their political world, but the more recent European writers whose political wisdom was already a tradition among seasoned statesmen of England, the Continent, and America.

The presentation here will be first, to establish that as men of the Enlightenment, Madison and Jefferson could not escape the cultural flood of ideas of their time, in which every men's concept of government must be swept along, diverted by this current or that, stopping against this or that opposing rock of query or refutation. Second, to show how in the great stream of ideas, classical and recent, the Virginians took perhaps the most traditional course in formulating their theories of government. Third, to illustrate that their "revolution of 1800" strove to establish values—however dubious they may now seem—which to them were proven by the long record of man's struggle toward a more perfect state. And since the long historic record was the groundwork for their belief, this paper must go far afield, from fourth-century Greece up through the rebellious patterns of seventeenth and eighteenth-century England, in an effort to review those intellectual terrains in which Madison and Jefferson moved as citizens and contemporaries.

Notes

1. *American Historical Review*, vol. XLVIII, 2, Jan., 1943, 356-357

2. Louise B. Dunbar, *A Study of "Monarchical" Tendencies in the United States, from 1776 to 1801* (Chicago: 1920).

3. To Judge Roane, Sept. 6, 1819, H.A. Washington, ed. *The Writings of Thomas Jefferson* (Washington, 1854), VII:133 (hereafter cited as *Writings*, Washington, ed.).

4. *Writings*, Washington, ed., IV:365, to John Dickinson, March 6, 1801.

5. Virginia Resolutions, Dec. 24, 1798, Included in *Documents of American History* (New York: 1940), edited by H.S. Commager, 182.

6. To Jefferson, Feb. 28, 1801. "The result of the contest [Jefferson's election] in the House of Representatives was generally looked for in this quarter. It was thought not probable that the phalanx would hold out against the general revolt of its partizans out of doors, and without any military force to abet usurpation. How fortunate that the latter has withheld! And what a lesson to America and the world is given by the efficacy of the public will, when there is no army to be turned against it." *Letters and other Writings of James Madison* (Philadelphia: 1865), II:171 (hereafter cited as *Letters*).

7. H.S. Randall, *The Life of Thomas Jefferson* (New York: 1858), I:589ff

8. Louise B. Dunbar, *A Study of "Monarchical" Tendencies.*

9. Most of the biographers of Hamilton, while agreeing with McMaster that the opposition to Washington's great Secretary of the Treasury was essentially pure demagogy, are aware that chronologically Madison went into opposition before Jefferson arrived in Philadelphia to become Secretary of State; see for example Henry Cabot Lodge's *Alexander Hamilton* (Boston and New York: 1898), 137-138; Frederick Scott Oliver, *Alexander Hamilton: An Essay on American Union* (New York: 1932), 176, 180, 187. This was probably due to

the fact that Hamilton's son and first biographer (whose work served as a basis for later authors) felt that Madison, not Jefferson, was the diabolical master mind who plotted and finally brought about the downfall of his illustrious father.

10. John Bach McMaster, *A History of the People of the United States* (New York: 1895-1920), II:36-37.

11. Edward Channing, *The Jeffersonian System* (New York and London: 1906), 22.

12. Cf. Allen Johnson, *Jefferson and His Colleagues* (New Haven, CT: 1921), who finds no revolution meditated (except perhaps a secret attack on the Supreme Court, 31), and not clear-cut policy except "a programme of humdrum economy." 28.

13. Henry Adams, *History of the United States during the Administration of Jefferson and Madison* (New York: 1889), I:195. It should be noted that by heredity and conscious preference, Henry Adams was completely indisposed to view Alexander Hamilton as alpha and omega of all wisdom, as McMaster, for example, was inclined to do.

14. Henry Adams, *History of the United States,* 215.

15. Henry Adams, *History of the United States*, 210.

16. Henry Adams, *History of the United States*, 215.

17. Charles A. Beard, *An Economic Interpretation of the Constitution* (New York: Free Press, 1913). *The Economic Origins of Jeffersonian Democracy* (New York: Free Press, 1915).

18. Charles A. and Mary Beard, *The Rise of American Civilization* (New York: 1927), I:350. (Hereafter referred to as *American Civilization).*

19. Beard, *American Civilization*, I:351.

20. Beard, *American Civilization*, I:355.

21. Beard, *American Civilization,* I:356.

22. Beard, *American Civilization,* I:352.

23. Beard, *American Civilization,* I:353. Cf. 354, "Of course, Jefferson expressed his alarm in letters to Washington over the liberal way in which the Constitution had been construed by men who formulated and enacted Federalist policies into law, but the gravamen of his complaint was that Hamilton's economic measures exploited one section of society for the benefit of another."

24. Beard, *American Civilization*, I: 355.

25. Which, it should be noted, drove the Federalists fighting the acquisition of Louisiana into "a narrow and crabbed provincialism that made Jefferson's juristic argument against the United States Bank seem broad and generous in comparison."

26. Beard, *American Civilization*, I:392.

27. Beard, *American Civilization*, I:349.

28. "With a show of defiance, Anti-Federalists had branded the Hamiltonians as monarchists and assumed for themselves the name Republican." Beard, *American Civilization*, I:372.

29. A disciple of Beard's, Vernon Louis Parrington, actually organized his intellectual history of the period around which considered to be the antithetic poles of the Declaration and Constitution. To each of these famous documents, he attached an intellectual pedigree from abroad, the former expressing "liberal"

French thought, and the latter embodying "conservative" English doctrine.

30. Gaillard Hunt, *The Writings of James Madison* (New York and London: 1906), IV:101 (hereafter referred to as *Writings*).

The distinction between "property holding" and "property attitudes" is made by Max Lerner in his *Ideas are Weapons* (New York: 1939). To set up the dynamic of history in terms entirely of the stark struggle of the concrete economic interests imputes to the participants in that struggle a singleness of purpose and an awareness of interest that experience seems to belie. Any economic interpretation stands in precise relationship to that great nineteenth century abstraction, "the economic man," who, long after the enlightenment, was drowned out in the blood of the guillotine and the Napoleonic wars, theoretically was still making his decision by the light of pure reason.

31. Albert Mathiez, article on the French Revolution, *Encyclopedia of the Social Sciences*. "The influence of abstract thinkers on the great social crises has sometimes been denied. 'The most eloquent dissertations on the revolution' writes George Sorel, metaphysician of revolutionary syndicalism. 'Have no practical issue, and the course of history is not altered by literature.' If this statement implies that literature alone is incapable bringing about a social movement it is on firm ground; but if it pretends that literature is an utterly negligible factor it lays itself open to serious question. The great majority of men are unaware of this injustice until it is pointed out to them. The denunciation of abuse is an essential preliminary to a demand for reform; a clearly formulated ideal, the prerequisite of a loyal following. It is extremely doubtful whether without the writing of the *Philosopher* the bourgeoisie would have risen in 1789 with the same unanimity, the same resoluteness; whether without the writing of Karl Marx, the Russian Revolution would have been the same. Robespierre without Rousseau remains an enigma; so does Lenin without Marx."

Chapter 2

The Constant and Universal Principles of Human Nature

Its [history's] chief use is only to discover the constant and universal principles of human nature—David Hume

Thomas Jefferson's statement that "those who labor in the earth are the chosen people of God...whose breasts He has made His peculiar deposit for substantial and genuine virtue" sets up a doctrine that is neither astonishing on its face nor uniquely American in its origin.

Agriculture of all the occupations seems most clearly to manifest the divine finger of Deity; God and the farmer stood in a primary relationship long before Jefferson proclaimed it, as is testified by the worship of Osiris in Egypt, Ceres in Greece, Saturn in Italy, and fertility rites of innumerable other peoples. The farmer, of all men, most directly participates in the yearly cycle of growth and decay— the birth, death, and rebirth that is life. For thousands of years all the associations of the "customary"—what is normal and hence right —have clustered about the word agriculture, giving it a highly ethical connotation.

Stated in more secular terms, the belief in the primacy of agriculture has always received support from the fact that most men on this earth have lived by it; the minimum of security without which human life remains "poor, nasty, brutish, and short" has historically depended on the invention and diffusion of techniques of husbandry. A textbook studied by Madison at Princeton, eschewing in enlightened eighteenth century style any religious interpretation of history, takes exactly this view. This volume, seeking to discover *The Origins of Laws, Arts and Sciences and their Progress among the Most Ancient Nations* conscientiously "treated of the origin of agriculture before that of all other arts, as it has been the occasion in great measure of their invention, multiplicity, and progress."[1] Not only is farming the most "natural" of occupations it is also the most technically important for the rise of civilizations.

Jefferson's and Madison's preoccupation with agriculture, however, does not spring from nor stress the religious, anthropological, or common sense aspects of the word. No doubt all of these elements unconsciously entered into their valuation of farming as a way of life, as no doubt too did the fact that they were successful planters who loved the soil. The doctrine that Jefferson enunciated and Madison subscribed to stresses the relation of agriculture and politics—the connections between a sturdy yeomanry and a free state. The virtue which Jefferson designated as "substantial and genuine" was political virtue. The two Virginians were not primarily interested in agriculture as the producer of abundant crops and as the source of wealth; they were interested in the agrarian way of life as the producer of the ideal type of citizen for a republic.

The agrarianism of Madison and Jefferson is political agrarianism. The "virtuous farmer" as he figures in their writings is not necessarily the product of the frontier, although certain of their over-civilized eighteenth century contemporaries tended to endow frontiersmen, including trappers and hunters, all dwellers beyond the limits of civilization, and even the red Indian, with the farmer's quota of virtue. Neither did they consider the "honest farmer" mainly as an economic man, although there are undoubted economic aspects to his character. Jefferson and Madison were concerned with him, moreover, not because they themselves were planters from Piedmont, Virginia, but because they were eighteenth century inheritors of an agrarian tradition that runs directly back to the fourth century before Christ when Plato and Aristotle, Xenophon and Thucydides, attempted with varying degrees of scientific precision to delineate man as a political animal.

A motley mixture of soldiers, geographers, social scientists and propagandists, have recently spawned what purports to be a brand new science, tracing the relation of the military potential of a state to such factors as climate, geography, type of political organization, ethnic make-up, population density, and technological development. This hodge-podge of social research and imperial appetite goes under the name of Geopolitics and apparently arose from a consideration of the question: what will make my nation utterly invincible in war? Greek thinkers some twenty-four hundred years ago—starting with the ethical question of how to produce the good life—worked out a comparable series of propositions on the relation of the individual to his natural and social milieu.[2]

This store of social information, without benefit of faddish label, was the common intellectual pabulum of any educated man in the eighteenth century. For by definition education *was* classical education when Jefferson and Madison were growing up; willy-nilly the students who attended Princeton of William and Mary, Edinburgh or Amsterdam, Oxford or Konigsberg, had drilled into their heads these specific concepts of the geographic, social, and political prerequisites best fitted to enable a commonwealth to expand in power or survive in freedom. It would have been as hard for our Virginians to have shed their physical skin as to have escaped this Greek intellectual cast of thought.

Their later political lives were to put no strain on this classical intellectual conditioning which Madison and Jefferson received as students. In the eighteenth century there was no contradiction between an interest in the most current events and in Greek and Roman antiquities. The most momentous problem that Madison ever faced as a practical statesmen, was the actual organization of some sort of political union for the American states. The policy memorandum he produced on this occasion for the presentation to an assembly of matter-of-fact lawyers, businessmen, planters, and politicians, drew as heavily on ancient historians like Thucydides and Xenophon as it did on moderns like Stanyan. A copy of this memo was made and preserved by as indifferent a scholar as George Washington, without the slightest suspicion that the citations from Strabo, Polybius, or Potter's *Grecian Antiquities* were in any way pedantic or esoteric information.[3] Jefferson, the most modern of men, whose mind was sensitized to the vanguard of thought for his own day, in considering the up to the minute problem of the impact of Bonaparte's career on European affairs casually seeks for a comparison in Roman history and the character of Octavius Caesar.[4] Eighteenth century practitioners of politics sometimes seem as naively anachronistic about classical civilization as were the medieval artists toward the ancient Hebrews when they arrayed Kind David or Joshua in the costumes and armour of the high middle ages.[5] The eighteenth century intellectual canon that all but obliged every statesman to become an amateur classical historian was supported with the strongest possible reasoning by professional historians themselves. David Hume, in whose approach to history there is nothing amateur or dilettante, never doubted that the antique past must be used as a guidebook to the present.

> It is universally acknowledged, that there is a great uniformity among the actions of men, in all nations and ages, and that human nature remains still the same, in its principles and

operations... Would you know the sentiments, inclinations
and course of life of the GREEKS and ROMANS? Study well
the temper and actions of the FRENCH and ENGLISH: You
cannot be much mistaken in transferring to the former *most* of
the observations, which you have made with regard to the
latter. Mankind are so much the same, in all times and
places, that history informs us of nothing new nor strange in
this particular. Its chief use is only to discover the constant
and universal principles of human nature, by showing men in
all varieties of circumstances and situations, and furnishing us
with materials, from which we may form our observations, and
become acquainted with the regular springs of human action
and behavior. These records of wars, intrigues, factions, and
revolutions, are so many collections of experiments, by which
the politician or moral philosopher fixes the principles of his
science; in the same manner as the physician or natural
philosopher becomes acquainted with the nature of plants,
minerals, and other external objects... Nor are the earth, water,
and other elements, examined by ARISTOTLE, and
HIPPOCRATES, more like to those, which at present lie
under our observation, than the men, described by
POLYBIUS and TACITUS, are to those, who now govern
the world.[6]

Madison was thus doing the normal and appropriate thing by
eighteenth century political standards, when in the Federal Convention, he "ran through the whole Scheme of Government—pointed out
the beauties and defects of the ancient Republics; compared their
situation with ours wherever it appeared to bear any analogy."[7] His
listeners, too, judging the speech "very able and ingenious," were
typically men of the Enlightenment in accepting his classical research
and finely drawn historical analogies as sound and relevant material
for the matter at hand—the institution of a government for
eighteenth-century American citizens who were presumed to be
moved in all important matters by the "same springs of action and
behavior" as the long dead Greeks and Romans.

Even the most obtuse nineteenth-century writers could not entirely ignore the eighteenth century's outlandish habit of treating
ancient history as though it were significant and contemporary. The
glib, so often repeated accusation that all eighteenth-century social
thought is *a priori*—that it deals with the false abstraction "Man"
instead of the actuality of Englishman, Frenchman, or American—is
in large part a reflection upon the Enlightenment's tendency to
equate in its own day Washington and Cincinnatus, Marart and
Cataline, Burke and Demosthenes. This charge, however, the most

crushing that the practical Victorian could lay, also mirrors the difficulty that the nineteenth century, preoccupied with national uniqueness, had in assessing eighteenth-century intellectual achievements in eighteenth- century terms. At any rate, the substitution of national systems of education for the traditional classical discipline that Jefferson and Madison had been exposed to, so successfully drove the Greeks and the Romans from modern political life that it was hard to believe that they were ever there.[8] It became possible, then, to talk of the supreme originality of Madison's political philosophy without checking the classical authors from whom he had admittedly gained ideas. And it became the usual thing to assay the quality of Jefferson's thought as though it was as purely American in origin as corn bread.[9]

The men of the eighteenth century viewed the past no more—and no less—anachronistically than we do; each generation merely favors its own type of anachronism. When the political theorists of the eighteenth century looked at classical civilization through the historical telescope they generally saw progress as cyclical; and in revolting against the values of the ages that they called "dark," they hoped to rival the achievements of the golden eras of antiquity before the time when corrupt kings, barbarous nobles, and an infamous church had combined to stamp out reason. So the Enlightenment was a revolutionary period that prided itself on looking backward; it gloried in returning to primitive virtue, in rediscovering original compacts, and in reestablishing Nature's simple plan in fields as various as trade, religion, and landscape gardening.

During the nineteenth century, on the other hand, progress came to be conceived of as automatic and vertical. All the past became but a curtain-raising prologue to what was latest and therefore inevitably the best. The Greeks who had lived and written so many centuries ago were necessarily less important than those eighteenth century individuals who in some instances had foreshadowed that climax of civilization, the Victorian Age. The orientation of this preferred anachronism thus tended to reduce Madison to an embryonic Karl Marx, to exhibit Jefferson, the most cosmopolitan of native heroes, as the "John the Baptist" of nineteenth-century populism and to laud Alexander Hamilton, neo-mercantilist worshiper of the Leviathan state, as the genius who envisioned an America run by the National Association of Manufacturers.

To understand the Agrarian doctrines of Thomas Jefferson and James Madison we must concede that the prodigious span of time and social development separating revolutionary America from Periclean Athens seemed far less formidable to them than it does to us. It will be worth our while to see how this peculiar historical perspective first

took root in the minds of the young Virginians; how in an environment not far removed from the pioneering settlements they could
enter so enthusiastically, through books, into a classical world, and
find it not unlike their own.

*   *   *

Since Frederick Jackson Turner advanced his frontier theory of
American democracy in the 1890's it has been almost impossible for
any writer on Jefferson not to insert a glowing paragraph or two
describing his youth in a frontier environment and the positive effect
that living in Albermarle County had on his mature thought.[10]
Strangely enough, none of the recent biographers of James Madison
have felt that it was necessary to stress the frontier as a factor in his
development, in spite of the fact that his background and Jefferson's
were practically identical.[11] Yet by the yardstick Turner himself
proposes, James Madison is as much the "John the Baptist" of
American democracy as was his great friend.

For James Madison, Sr. had the same doubtful right as Peter
Jefferson to be called "pioneer"—the greatest landowner in his
county, and one of its leading local magistrates, prominent as
vestryman of his church, and exercising an influence that almost
automatically came to the owner of broad acres in colonial Virginia.
And James Madison, Jr. stands as plainly as Jefferson for "the
conception that democracy should have a broad agricultural basis, and
that manufacturing and city life were dangerous to the purity of the
body politic." He emphatically agreed that "simplicity and economy
in government, the right of revolution, the freedom of the individual,
the belief that those who win the vacant lands are entitled to shape
their government" were worthy and true ideals for America. He lent
his aid and support to the reform program in revolutionary Virginia
that repealed entails and primogeniture, and thus helped destroy the
"coastwise aristocrats basis of power"; and it was Madison who finally
forced the complete separation of Church and State along lines
planned by Jefferson, while the latter was abroad in 1795. Undoubtedly all of these ideals and policies "are eminently characteristic of the
Western democracy"; undoubtedly they "tended to throw the power
of Virginia into the hands of the settlers in the interior."[12] Yet one
hesitates to concede that the frontier theory really throws as much
light on either Madison's or Jefferson's political ideas as Turner would
have us believe.

"I cannot live without books," Jefferson told his friend, John
Adams, in 1815;[13] and this remark, as self-revealing as any he

made during his long life, applies as well to his friend James Madison, Jr. Chinard has pointed out with prodigious understatement that Jefferson's early reading and schooling "was not exactly a frontier education with the usual connotation of that word."[14] Strict truth requires a stronger statement. Actually it is doubtful if any practicing statesmen ever entered upon high office with a more consciously thorough intellectual preparation in the field of what we call the social sciences. The two Virginians, both of whom served as President of the United States during the opening years of the last century, had read widely and pondered deeply on a great body of the literature available in their own day dealing with history, public law, sociology, economics, and government.

James Madison and Thomas Jefferson were men of the Enlightenment, and shared with their fellow philosophers across the Atlantic all the great hopes and expectations that the word implied. It was still possible, though barely, in the eighteenth century, for sensible men to hold as valid the Greek ideal (the rediscovery of which so excited Renaissance thinkers) of "the universal man," encompassing in one mind all knowledge.[15] It was an age that found most satisfaction in the broad sweeping attack that reached to the outmost limits of knowledge. Montesquieu sought for the spirit of laws "in their most general signification" which he considered to comprehend "the necessary relation" resulting from the very "nature of things." Gibbon would magnificently erect the history of an Empire that covered centuries, not years, in order to reveal the canker of decay and dissolution that had brought it down. And Adam Smith, intent on increasing the wealth of England, could casually set up in one section of his great book an essay on "the different Progress of Opulence in different Nations" from the earliest times.

It is ironic that these enlightened students of man and society, who hoped to discover and present in a clear and popular manner the simple fundamental laws which they believed governed the whole social world, should be treated by later generations simply as the "fathers" of this or that academic specialty. The present day adherents of Adam Smith and the Physiocrats bicker pedantically as to who is the real originator of "economics" as a sovereign and self-sufficient field of study. Voltaire is credited, not with just writing the first self-consciously "new" history, but rather with creating a novel "social" history; a specific subhead type within a separate general category. A student of sociology goes back to Adam Ferguson, and discovers not a plain professor of Moral Philosophy, who luckily was able to find a publisher for his lectures at the University of Edinburgh, but the great founder of "modern" sociology.

It is impossible, of course, to keep the taint of our own age out of our judgment of the past; nevertheless we should always try to remember that these men of the eighteenth century were not primarily writing "classics" for posterity. Social knowledge has made tremendous advances through specialization and division of labor, but in the 1760's when Jefferson attended William and Mary, and young James Madison sat at the feet of John Witherspoon at Princeton, academic training did not imply the preparation of scholars for scholarship. In a way that seems childishly naive to us they really believed that the books they studied in class furnished and absolutely essential and complete preparation for an active political career.

Madison and Jefferson, however, deserve to be called "intellectuals," in the best sense of that word, by both nature and nurture. In college both were exceptional students, marked by an unusual seriousness. Few undergraduates, then or now, would be disgusted that the scholastic standards of their school were too low, yet Jefferson expressed himself clearly on this point;[16] and as soon as he came to power as the governor of Virginia he instituted a thorough reorganization of his alma mater.[17] He seems to have taken full advantage of all that William and Mary could offer, sometimes reading sixteen hours a day to work through its library. The tradition that young Tom Jefferson squandered large sums in dissipation during his stay at Williamsburg appears now to be founded actually on the fact that he badly overspent his allowance in the bookstore of Dixon and Hunter.[18]

Probably of equal importance in Jefferson's collegiate career with his fully developed taste for reading was contact with three men all older than himself. To Doctor William Small of Scotland, acting professor of Moral Philosophy, Jefferson traced his "first views of the expansion of science, and the system of things in which we are placed."[19] Through Small he probably met Francis Fauquier, friend of Bolingbroke and Pope, disciple of Shaftesbury, Fellow of the Royal Society, and cultured man of the world serving in 1760 as his majesty's Governor of Virginia.[20] The last of the group was George Wythe, philosophic lawyer, too young yet to be called the Cato of America, but already exhibiting wisdom, inflexible integrity, and that mixture of religious and political liberalism that was to make him Virginia's most distinguished signer of the Declaration of Independence.[21] That the seventeen year old undergraduate from Albermarle was accepted by this group and admitted as a fourth in their "*parties carrees*" speaks volumes for his maturity and high intellectual purpose.

Americans of a later day have not shown any decided preference for the scholar in politics, but it cannot be too strongly stressed that this title will describe both Madison and Jefferson. Henry Randall, the latter's mid-nineteenth century biographer, makes it very plain after graduation "the systematic industry of this college life continued." Marvel of marvels, Jefferson somehow managed to combine a decided taste for conviviality with double the average number of hours of study. He kept a clock in his bedroom—presumably this was unusual —and during the summer "as soon as he could distinguish its hands, he rose and commenced his labors." In the winter he slept later; not rising before five. And winter or summer, a schedule of early to bed (at nine or ten depending on the season) allowed him to put by "fourteen or fifteen hours for study and reading."[22] Public duty interrupted but never disrupted his carefully planned life.

Madison's college career seems to have been every bit as exemplary and studious as Jefferson's.[23] At least President Witherspoon reported afterwards to Jefferson that during the whole time he was an undergraduate he had never known him to say or do an indiscreet thing. John Witherspoon took up his post as President of Princeton practically cotemporaneously with Madison's entrance as a freshman; and this remarkable man stands in relation to Madison's thought somewhat as Jefferson's triumvirate of friends in Williamsburg do to his. For President Witherspoon seems to have been the prime awakener and inspirer of James Madison. And his sojourn at Nassau Hall, as an undergraduate, proved so stimulating and satisfying that after getting his degree as Bachelor of Arts he returned to study for an extra year directly under Witherspoon's direction. As Professor Smith points out, James Madison was probably America's first graduate student.[24]

John Witherspoon, just imported from Scotland by the Presbyterian Church to head up their college in New Jersey, was a remarkable man.[25] All his life he moved through the fire of controversy. A fundamentalist in religion, his career in Scotland had been one long tumultuous brawl in which his undoubted talents as a debater, both in pulpit and pamphlet, had been directed against what he considered lapses from orthodoxy. The Scottish hierarchy, however, was too firmly entrenched in the seats of power, and too deeply tainted with the new secular thought to be routed even by the vehement Doctor; so in 1769 he accepted the call to come to the small college in New Jersey. There his political liberalism found at once a congenial environment; and in the period leading up to the overt break with England, Princeton became red-hot Whig, in tone and temper.[26]

Witherspoon undoubtedly was a great educator; and Princeton must have been an exciting place to study during his years as

President. He introduced graduate courses; instituted the study of
modern languages—students had learned no French at Princeton
before his day—and was probably the first lecturer on history and
philosophy in America.[27] The most important feature of his
educational theory, however, lay in his strongly held conviction that
the College should prepare its students for leadership in Church and
State.[28]

Witherspoon's somewhat rigid theological views interfered not at
all with his search for truth. In the first lecture of his course on Moral
Philosophy, covering Ethics, Politics, and Jurisprudence, he cites an
unnamed "author of New England" who held that "moral philosophy
is just reducing infidelity to a system," and at once dismisses him as
"specious" since his objections "will be found at bottom not solid."
For "if the scripture is true, the discoveries of reason cannot be
contrary to it; and therefore it has nothing to fear from that quarter.
And as we are certain it can do no evil, so there is a probability that I
may do much good." Indeed, "reason and observation" may illustrate
and confirm inspired writings; and thus "greatly add to their beauty
and force."[29]

At any rate, the authors whom he quotes and the volumes which
he mentions in the two series of his lectures that have been preserved
show an amazing range and variety.[30] Montesquieu is there, of course,
and Collins states that for some years *The Spirit of the Laws* was used
as a text.[31] The Anglican divines are prominent; Warburton, Swift,
Tillotson, Clark, and Evans, being mentioned repeatedly. Shaftesbury,
Adam Smith, Hutcheson, Hume, Mandeville, and Locke are referred
to; Lord Kames and John Brown, the author of *Estimates of the
Manners and Principles of the Times*, are cited; and even Hogarth is
called to bear witness on a question of innate beauty. There is some
evidence that the learned Doctor was not a brilliant mathematician or
scientist, but this limitation did not prevent his lecturing on Leibniz,
Newton, and Descartes. He appears to have been solidly grounded in
Shakespeare, Milton, and the English poets of the seventeenth
century—he quotes Marvell and Donne—but although he mentions
Pope, Young, Swift, and Butler, in passing, he obviously found modern
poetry not to his taste. For our purposes, however, his list of the
"chief writers" upon government and politics is the most important.
The older classics lead off the catalogue: they are: Grotius, Pufendorf,
Barberac, Cumberland, Selden, Burlamaqui, Hobbes, Machiavel,
Harrington, Locke, Sydney. Crowding close behind them come "some
late books." Montesquieu's *Spirit of the Laws*; Ferguson's *History of
Civil Society*; Lord Kames' *Political Essays*; Montesquieu's *Grandeur
and Decay of the Roman Empire*; Montague's *Rise and Fall of*

Ancient Republics; Goguet's *Rise and Progress of Laws, Arts, and Sciences.*"[32]

In these few treatises are summed up much of the brave new learning of the Enlightenment about men in society; and in their short titles is indicated the source of many of the "facts" on which they based their new and startling generalizations. For the eighteenth century is the second stage in the rediscovery of antiquity. The Renaissance delving in the records of Greece and Rome had been primarily a matter of specialists; now two centuries later this ancient wisdom was democratized and popularized to an amazing degree.[33] The political, economic, and social data on which the self-evident truths of the age of reason were grounded, in large part were drawn from antiquity; the footnotes in inumerable tracts of the period present a curious grafting of quotations from the classics onto the most recent and up-to-date statistical information. Madison's courses at Princeton and Jefferson's at William and Mary revolved around the study of the writings of Greece and Rome. Here were to be found the "standard" authors; the classic presentations of man in relation to his social world; and here was the great quarry from which the most modern minds drew the facts that gave meaning to human history.[34]

It was still possible for a great statesman of England, who read the *Aeneid* on his death bed, to question the advantages of studying Adam Smith; what had happened in Pericles' Athens and Caesar's Rome seemed to him a more valid basis for deciding the policy of His Majesty's government than figures on the trade of Liverpool.[35] The history of the ancients was not dead history in the eighteenth century, but completely "contemporary" in Croce's sense of the word. And this explains why Madison, seeking a pseudonym to cover discreetly, but not entirely conceal, his authorship of pamphlets which damned the Federalist proclamation of neutrality in 1793, almost automatically turned to Tacitus for the name "Helvidius."[36] It makes clear that inevitable choice of names—"appellations for certain official characters"—in the cypher used by Alexander Hamilton and Gouverneur Morris to discuss the political maneuvers at Philadelphia in 1792.[37] And it explains why is was so completely natural for Jefferson, his eye cocked at the fiscal policy of his own government, to seek exact information from Ezra Stiles on the public debt situation under the later Caesars.[38] It was this cross-fertilization of the "old and curious" and the "new and useful" that in large part explains the amazing breadth and suggestiveness of eighteenth-century thought.[39]

There can be no doubt that these men took their books most seriously; if ever individuals read with a purpose they did. Madison, one year out of college, uses terms of solemn conviction in advising his fellow graduate William Bradford to make a "judicious choice" of "History" and the "science of morals" for his winter's study. They are of "the most universal benefit of men of sense and taste in every post," and are of inestimable benefit especially "to youth" in "settling the principles and refining the judgment, as well as in enlarging knowledge and correcting the imagination."[40] And two years later upon learning that his friend had taken up law he consoles him with reflection that in spite of the dullness it was really putting first things first.[41] Study of jurisprudence in the long run truly bears important "fruit"; and thought perhaps "sour" in the beginning, once "gathered and pressed and distilled" it really brings "pleasure or profit." And then Madison confesses that he himself used have "too great a hankering after...amusing studies. Poetry, wit, and criticism, romances, plays captivated me much." Finally, however, he had discovered that "they deserve but a small portion of mortals time, and that something more substantial more durable and more profitable, befits a riper age."[42] Madison at this time had reached the ripe old age of twenty-two.

It is no wonder then that Fisher Ames, a political opponent, would characterize Madison as "a thorough master of almost every public question that can arise, or he will spare no pains to become so. He is well versed in public life, was bred to it, and has no other profession... It is rather a science than a business with him."[43] It is not surprising that an intelligent and able foreign observer of the American scene would feel that he had the "meditative" aspect of a "profound politician"; that while his "look announces a censor, his conversation discovers the man of learning, and his reserve was that of man conscious of his talents and duties."[44] Some at least of the practicing politicians of the eighteenth century were well equipped to govern without benefit of a brain-trust.

We have proof, then, of Madison's and Jefferson's conscientious efforts to study all the phases of government treated by writers from ancient times to their own day. The breadth of their research refutes the suggestion of economic ignorance implicit in the discussion of the great Virginians by McMaster, and also by so many of the biographers of Alexander Hamilton. They were far from being economic morons; indeed, there is every indication that they had read as deeply in economic theory and pondered as wisely the facts of economic life as Hamilton.

So, too, a *caveat* must be set before Chinard's deferential nod in the direction of Turner's frontier thesis. After brilliantly breaking new ground in the discussion of Jefferson's early reading in a chapter significantly entitled "An American Disciple of Greece and Old England," he betrays his thesis in his concluding paragraphs. "No man," he states, "can become genuinely interested in things he has never seen and cannot imagine"; and goes on to conclude that from all his reading Jefferson merely "had culled facts and definitions rather than principles and theories."[45] But surely the craving to extend the narrow horizons of one's single lifetime is a mortal and universal experience; and books offered the surest passage men have discovered into other times, other places, other philosophies than their own. Perhaps the historian, of all men, is least to blame if he argues that the extension of the individual's personality in time and space by means of books is no impossibility.

With Jefferson and Madison, it seems to me fairly obvious that the Piedmont area—the geographic section in which they lived—exerted little positive influence in stimulating their thought to take the turn it did. Cicero and Montesquieu, Dr. Small and Dr. Witherspoon, Aristotle and Locke, were far more important in shaping the way their minds worked than any of the settlements on the hither side of free land. On the other hand, it should be noted that the actual situation of the average American farmer in the settled area back of the squatters' moving frontier offered evidence to corroborate the theory that men with piece of ground to work would be industrious and reasonably law-abiding; inclined to live in harmony with each other. But that the mere observation of this harmony of their neighbors could generate and elaborate the rather complex political theory of James Madison and Thomas Jefferson, is a hypothesis too startling to accept.[46]

An "impending crisis" almost always is the proximate cause of the proclamation of a political faith. It is impossible to understand Hobbes without some knowledge of the English Civil wars; Locke is mystery without the hurried departure of James II for France; and an account of "Shays' Rebellion" explains the wording of many an article and clause of our own Constitution. But once a political theory is proclaimed by a great speculative thinker, it acquires a vitality of its own. It becomes after its enunciation an independent force on its own; and, however interpreted, its text carves channels into which future history will flow. We cannot understand the development of English political institutions in the eighteenth and nineteenth centuries until we read the *Leviathan* and the *Essay on Civil Government* written in the seventeenth; in twentieth century America, Shays' forgotten band of "desperate debtors" is far less important than the paper charter of 1787.

So it is usually wise not to treat political ideas as dead bric-a-brac, automatically becoming museum specimens after the passage of a given number of years. These old theories in which speculative men sought to answer the questions and solve the problems of their own times are still, in their crystallized forms, dynamic today. And if we would know the thought of James Madison and Thomas Jefferson that produced these forms we must deliberately set their ideas in the frame of the great and conscious intellectual tradition in which they were born and educated. We dare start no later than the fourth century B.C. if we would understand the Agrarian Republic that Jefferson and Madison idealized in 1800.

Notes

1. *The Origins of Laws, Arts and Sciences and their Progress among the Most Ancient Nations.* Translated from the French of President de Goguet (Edinburgh: 1761), Vol. I:xii. Witherspoon's copy of this book, which was a recommended text in his course in Moral Philosophy, is still preserved in the Princeton Library. It is an erudite study in the field of what would today be labeled "comparative sociology" of the institutions of the Jews, Babylonians, Assyrians, Egyptians, and the Greeks of the Homeric Age. De Goguet's research led him to argue that all the early civil codes of these civilizations were the results of their agricultural organization and that their greatest gods and mythological sovereigns—Osiris, Ceres, Saturn in the Mediterranean area, like Manco Oapac in Peru, and Yao in China—were agrarian discoverers or innovators (I:34-35).

2. In a volume owned by Jefferson there occurs this general statement: "The manners of a people receive their tone from a great variety of circumstances; climate; soil; extent of territory; population; religion; government, monarchical or republican, vigorous and permanent, or weak and changeable; system of jurisprudence; administration of justice, ready and certain, or feeble and irregular; science; arts; commerce; communication with strangers" (William Mitford, *The History of Greece*, Boston, 1823, Vol. I:153).

Substitute the words "military power" for Mitford's word "manners" and you get in fairly exact detail the prospectus of the studies that Hausfhofer and his Geopolitical Institute concern themselves with. For the purposes of this paper the significant thing to note is that this highly touted "new science" utilizes a comprehensive approach to the study of man, his institutions and his natural environment, that was commonplace in the eighteenth century.

3. Sparks, the earliest editor of Washington's writings, published as an appendix to his 9th volume a copy in the General's own handwriting of Madison's "Notes on Ancient and Modern Confederacies." There could be no question of Madison's authorship after the publication of the original memorandum in his *Letters*, I:293, footnote.

4. Jefferson, *Writings* (Washington ed.), VII:3.

5.The artistic anachronisms of the eighteenth century carried on into the nineteenth century, keep pace with the political ones. The most notorious example in American history is Greenough's heroic statue of Washington as Capitoline Jupiter, which sits today, inadequately clad in marble toga, perpetually hurling imaginary thunderbolts, in the National Museum's most out of the way cellar. Greenough's work executed in the second quarter of the nineteenth century when the frontier was presumably exerting its maximum influence is aesthetically atrocious. It reveals, however, a psychological urge that should neither be ignored nor derided. The fierce symbolical insistence that America's coonskin politics corresponded to the great humanist political tradition of western civilization, was incredibly audacious, incredibly Utopian, but probably the only way to partially square the tobacco-chewing, whiskey-drinking, pioneer actuality with an ideal dream. Heaven only knows what the life would have been in the backwoods log-shacked, muddy-streeted villages, where the frontier did strip off so much of the veneer of civilization, if some of the inhabitants had not insisted that potentially they could live up to their incongruous names of Rome, Georgia; Syracuse, New York; or Athens, Kentucky.

6. David Hume, *An Enquiry Concerning Human Understanding*," CH. VIII:1, "Of Liberty and Necessity." Compare Bolingbroke's conviction that: "The course of things has always been the same... National virtue and national vice have always produced national happiness and national misery in a due proportion, and are, by consequence the great sanctions of the law of nature... He, who made, preserves the world, and governs it on the same principles, and according to the same invariable laws, which he imposed at first." Bolingbroke, *Works* (London: 1754), V:472.

7. "Notes of William Pierce of Georgia in the Federalist Convention of 1787," *Documents Illustrative of the Formation of the Union of the American States*, edited by Charles C. Tonsill (Washington: 1927). Hereafter referred to as *Documents*.

8. There is plentiful evidence to show that the ancients retreated from the American forum only after the middle of the century. Von Holst, writing his *Constitutional and Political History of the U.S.* In the 1870's (he had arrived in the U.S. in the 'fifties), comments then on the American's "disposition to overload their political reasoning with analogies, for the most part not pertinent, for Greek and Roman history. This tendency...has already perceptibly decreased. This is to be attributed in part to a clarification of political thought; but in part to the fact that the majority of members of legislators and members of Congress know too little of Greek and Roman history" (I:31, footnote). Von Holst's last clause seems to indicate that the stream of classical quotations which had continued interminably since pre-Revolutionary days was being cut off at the source, with classics' loss of their dominant position in the school curricula.

9. The researches of Professor Chinard are a landmark in the study of Jefferson's intellectual habits (see especially *Jefferson's Literary Bible* and *Jefferson's Commonplace Book*). Strangely enough, the implications of Jefferson's classical reading for his political doctrines are not worked out to any logical result in Chinard's very good biography entitled: *Thomas Jefferson:*

Apostle of Americanism.

One can only hazard a guess as to the reason. Chinard, a potent admirer of his subject, found the greatest problem in writing on Jefferson in the twentieth century is to clear away the 100-year-old libels of Federalist clergymen and historians as to his theories, character, and motives. Now the gravamen of the Federalist indictment of Jefferson was that he had drunk at the fountain of French atheistic writers; that he was un-American. Chinard at the beginning of his research accepted as true this charge of French influence; to his surprise he discovered it was negligible. Jefferson had not been corrupted by Rousseau. Most of his ideas were fixed before he went to France, and his reading throughout his life was mainly classical literature, English history, and the newspapers. It is probably that Chinard's delight in being able to incontrovertibly refute the hoary lies about Jefferson's un-Americanism tipped the focus of his book toward high-lighting the American frontier background where he did his reading. As a result Chinard does not follow the leads that he himself had developed that would show the place of Jefferson's agrarianism, for instance, in its true perspective as an American variation of a long European tradition originating in ancient Greece.

10. See, for example, Claude G. Bowers, *Jefferson and Hamilton* (Boston and New York: 1925), 95. It was from his father "and his early environment that he received his earliest and most lasting political impressions... His thousand acres at Shadwell were in the wilderness and the frontier, and his son was as much a Westerner in his boyhood as is the boy of Idaho today, for the West is a relative term. This Western boy at the most impressionable age was sent to school in Louisa County, which was then the hot-bed of radical democracy and Presbyterian dissent. The natives...buckskin breeches...coonskin caps... The small proprietor farmers lived in crude cabins, and theirs was the hard lot of the pioneer."

11. Madison, though born in Tidewater, Virginia, was moved to Orange, the County exactly contiguous to Albermarle, at the age of three months. The Piedmont region of the State remained his home for the rest of his life.

12. The quotations are all from Frederick Jackson Turner's essay entitled "Contributions of the West to American Democracy," first published in 1903, and included in *The Frontier in American History* (New York: 1920), 250. Turner believed that the "wilderness masters the colonist and strips off the garments of civilization." The environment is "too strong for the man. He must accept the conditions which are furnished or perish...little by little he transforms the wilderness, but the outcome...is a new product that is American." Turner, *The Frontier*, 4.

13. Paul Leicester Ford, ed. *The Writings of Thomas Jefferson* (New York: 1892-99), VI:460 (hereafter referred to as *Works* [Ford, ed.]).

14. Gilbert Chinard, *Thomas Jefferson: Apostle of Americanism* (Boston: 1929), 6. This is the best single volume biography of Jefferson, and broke new ground in considering his intellectual antecedents.

15. Consider Jefferson the lawyer and legal philosopher, political theorist, writer, architect, scientific agriculturalist. In a more amateur way he dabbled in zoology, comparative philology, geology, comparative theology, and music. He

made crude beginnings in a study of the scientific management of slaves, in order to get maximum efficiency of labor by standardizing the movements required for a given task. He contemplated writing a history of Virginia and a biography of George Wythe, and did the preliminary research required for each. He worked out a comprehensive system of primary education, and almost single-handed designed and set up a University. And all this was during a life in which forty years were actively devoted to the public service.

16. "Admission of learners of Greek and Latin had filled the college with children. This rendering it disagreeable and degrading to young gentlemen, already prepared for entering on the sciences, they were discouraged from resorting to it, and thus the schools for mathematics and moral philosophy, which might have of some service, became of very little." *Notes on Virginia*, Query XV, Jefferson, *Works* (Ford ed.), IV.

17. Jefferson, *Works*, (Ford ed.), I:69; "Autobiography."

18. Chinard, *Jefferson*, 11.

The catalogue of books offered for sale by Dixon and Hunter in an advertisement in the Virginia Gazetter of Nov. 25, 1775, is published in *The William and Mary Quarterly*, 1st series, VIII, 108 (Oct., 1906). It includes over three hundred separate titles. The standard Greek and Roman classics are there; also a sprinkling of novelists, represented by Fielding, Richardson, Smollet, Goldsmith; and a fairly catholic selection of English poetry. The French section includes Essays from the Encyclopedia, Pascal, Montesquieu's *Persian Letters*, and some of Voltaire's miscellaneous writings. The modern history division includes Robertson's *Scotland*, Swift's *History of the Last Four Years of Queen Anne*, Hume, *Temple's Works*, and Rapin in 21 vols. The philosophical volumes number among others Locke (naturally), Hume, Bolingbroke in four volumes, Bacon, and both Hutcheson's *Introduction to Moral Philosophy*, and his *Inquiry into...Beauty and Virtue*. A large number of dictionaries is listed; and, as in almost all colonial catalogues, there is an imposing section devoted to every-man-his-own-doctor, lawyer, or veterinary, treatises.

It is hoped that Louis Wright will match his seventeenth-century study of the *First gentlemen of Virginia* with a companion piece on eighteenth-century gentlemen which will throw as much light on libraries and literary tastes of that period.

19. Dr. Small was nominally professor of Mathematics, but he appears to have been practically omnicompetent. He gave the first regular lectures at William and Mary "in Ethics, Rhetoric, and Belles-letters." *Works* (Ford ed.), Autobiography, I. Dr. Small is an important factor in the intellectual development of Jefferson, and it is unfortunate that we know so little about him. He has no biography in the D.N.B. and the bare mention of his death in *Gentlemen's Magazine* furnishes no details of his life and thought. He was one of the group of "enlarged and liberal" minds that congregated around the famous Erasmus Darwin. It included Wedgewood, the potter and philanthropist, James Watt, Priestley, and John Day, the English disciple of Rousseau who wrote *Sanford and Merton*, and attempted to educate several orphan girls on the principles of *Emile*, in order to have a perfect wife; see Hesketh Pearson, *Erasmus Darwin and His Circle* (London: 1940).

Dr. Swem's *Index* of the *William and Mary Quarterly*, etc. leads one to expect some material there. As a matter of fact, the various citations, aside from setting the dates of Small's relatively short stay at Williamsburg, refer to the statement of Jefferson quoted above; and one or two others made at separate times. They become an impressive series of references (that turns out to be woefully disappointing) by the device of having a second article on colonial teachers quote the first article; a third quotes the first and second; and a fourth quotes the first, second, and third and so on *ad nauseam*.

20. See D.A.B. and D.N.B.

21. "No man left behind him a character more venerable than George Wythe. His virtue was of the purest tint; his integrity inflexible and his justice exact; of warm patriotism, and devoted...to the liberty and the...equal rights of man, he might truly be called the CATO of his country." Jefferson, *Writings* (Washington ed.), I:114.

Jefferson contemplated but failed to write a biography of Wythe; none exists to this day. He was the first great teacher of law in America, numbering both Jefferson and Marshall among his students. He also has the curious distinction of being the only signer of the Declaration of Independence to be murdered. His nephew poisoned him (perhaps accidentally) with arsenic-dosed coffee; see D.A.B.

22. Henry S. Randall, *The Life of Thomas Jefferson* (New York: 1857), I: 32. This biography reveals a hero worship kept well in bounds by stringent standards of research. Since Randall seems to have questioned Jefferson's immediate family and every surviving friend for information, his work should be treated as source material.

23. Madison was a sickly youth and the year after his graduation he remarked with resignation. "I am too dull and infirm now to look out for any extraordinary things in this world, for I think my sensations for many months past have intimated to me not to expect a long or healthy life." Madison, *Letters*, I: 5; to William Bradford, November, 1772. Madison was twenty-one at that time; he outlived all his contemporaries, dying in 1836 at the ripe age of 85.

24. Abbot E. Smith, *James Madison: Builder* (New York: 1937), 9.

25. There is a fairly good biography by Varnum L. Collins, *President Witherspoon* (Princeton: 1925).

26. See Madison's description of the student demonstration in 1770, when the New York merchants broke their non-importation pledge. Madison, *Letters*, I:4. It is interesting to note that even at this early date Madison, the economic nationalist, rejoices that graduates at commencement are to wear "American cloth."

27. Witherspoon was the most important early popularizer of the Scottish "common-sense" philosophy of Reid in the United States; Woodbridge Riley, *American Philosophy; The Early Schools* (New York: 1907). For evidence of Jefferson's adherence to this school see Charles M. Wiltse's brilliant *The Jeffersonian Tradition in American Democracy* (Chapel Hill, N.C.: 1935), 67-68.

Witherspoon's ideas were spread far and wide by a zealous group of preacher-teachers who were graduated by him. A phenomonal number became college presidents in their turn, especially in the South and in the new states of Tennessee and Kentucky; see Collins, *op. cit.*, II:222-229.

28. An indication of how well he succeeded on the secular side can be gathered from the fact that of the 478 graduates during his regime, one became President of the United States; one, Vice President; ten, Cabinet officers; thirty-nine, U.S. Representatives; twenty-one, U.S. Senators; twelve, State Governors; and fifty-six, members of the State Legislatures. Of the thirty-three judges who studied under him, three were eventually raised to the Supreme Court. Nine of the twenty-five college graduates serving in the Constitutional Convention in 1787 held Princeton degrees; Collins, *op. cit.*, II:229.

29. *The Works of John Witherspoon*, D.D. (Edinburgh: 1805), VII:1.

30. Besides those on Moral Philosophy we have his lectures on public speaking—a well-digested analysis of the eloquence suitable for the pulpit, the bar, and for "promiscuous deliberative assemblies"; both series are included in Witherspoon, *Works*, VII.

31. Collins, *op. cit.*, II:207.

32. This list to be found in Witherspoon, *Works*, VII:152; the other titles mentioned are scattered throughout the same volume.

33. James Randall, *The Making of the Modern Mind* (New York: 1935) discusses the most persuasively, Tom Paine is an example of the self-educated type which could not have conceivably appeared before this period.

34. For an indication of how all-pervading the influence of the classics was in college work during this period see the appendix to Ashbel Green's *History of Princeton*.

35. Elie Halévy, *History of the English People in 1815,* I:244 (Diary of Lord Colchester, June 19, 1806, II:71). "In talking of books upon political economy, [Charles Fox] said (as I often heard him say in debates) that he had but little faith in Adam Smith or any of them, their reasons were so plausible but so inconclusive. That...in Greece, arts and arms engrossed the whole efforts of the human mind, and their progress and eminence in those pursuits had probably been the greater for their abandonment of all other pursuits, such as engaged modern nations in commerce, manufactures, etc."

36. Helvidius Priscus was a Stoic philosopher and statesman, who anachronistically still held strongly held republican views in the time of Nero and Vespacian. As praetor (A.D. 70), he maintained in opposition to the latter that the management of finances ought to be left to the discretion of the Senate. Up until his death (he was eventually executed) he insisted on saluting Vespacian by his private name and refused to recognize him as Emperor. Tacitus, *History*, IV:5ff.

37. Henry Cabot Lodge, ed., *The Works of Alexander Hamilton* (New York and London: 1886), VII:266-267. "I will call, the President, Scaevola; Secretary of State, Scipio; Sec'y of the Treasury, Paulus; The Vice-President, Brutus; Sec'y of War, Sempronius; The Attorney-General, Lysander." Then follows a list of eight leading Senators who will be masked behind the names of Cato, Leonidas, Saevius, Sydney, Virginius, Portius, Marcus, Themistocles. The House leaders are to be referred to as Tacitus, Cicero, Chronus, Hampden,

Titus, Valerius, Solon, Livy, Cromwell, Quintus. James Madison leads the list as "Tarquin." (Hamilton quite unnecessarily notes that he has "avoided characteristic names.") The interesting thing from our viewpoint is that of a list of twenty-six name applied to "official characters" only three—Cromwell, Hampden, and Sydney—are not ransacked from the classics.

38. W.C. Ford, ed., *Thomas Jefferson Correspondence* (Boston: 1916), 43-44. Letter from Ezra Stiles to Jefferson, August 27, 1790. This collection, which seems to have been little used by most writers on Jefferson, is intensely interesting in that it gives letters to and from the master of Monticello, and thus shows an intimate view of his mind in action. It will be referred to hereafter as *Correspondence.*

39. The expression is one of Jefferson's made while in France, offering to help Madison fill out his library. It is quoted by Madison in his note of thanks (*Letters,* I:146): "I cannot...abridge the commission you were so kind to take on yourself... Of procuring me...such books as may be either 'old and curious, or new and useful.' Under this description will fall these particularized in my former letters, to wit: Treatises on ancient or modern Federal Republics, on the Law of Nations, and the History, natural and political, of the new World; to which I will add such of the Greek and Roman authors...[that] are not on the common list of school classics." Then listed specifically for purchase are, among others, "Pascal's provincial letters; Don Ulloa in the original; Linnaeus, Ordonnances Marines; Collection of Tracts in French...referred to by Smith on the Wealth of Nations." He would also like Jefferson to check Amelot's "Travels into China," which if well done "must be very entertaining"; and to remember that he wants to add to his fifty-seven volumes of Buffon as new supplements appear.

40. Madison, *Letters,* I:6. To William Bradford, Nov. 9, 1772.

41. It is "hard to give up such refined and exquisite enjoyments [of belles lettres] for the coarse and dry study of Law. It is like leaving a pleasant flourishing field for a barren desert. Madison, *Letters,* I:11.

42. Madison, *Letters.* President Witherspoon was wont to dismiss modern novels as "a class of writing to which the world is very little indebted"; Collins, *op. cit.,* II:185.

Jefferson's judgment seems to have been quite familiar. Chinard notes in the preface to *The Literary Bible of Thomas Jefferson* (Baltimore: 1928), that after 1780 poetry in general became of decidedly minor interest to him. Randall makes it clear that "for fiction he had so little taste, that nearly every work he *ever* read of this could here be stated." [italics his] Randall, *op. cit.,* I:28. The list includes the works of Smollet, Sterne, and Fielding; *Gil Blas* and *Don Quixote.* The last named seems to be the only novel Jefferson really relished or bothered to re-read.

43. Quoted in Charles Warren, *The Making of the Constitution* (Boston: 1937), 57.

44. Ibid., 60. Quoting T.B. Brissot de Warvilles's, *New Travels in the United States of America.*

45. Chinard, *Thomas Jefferson: Apostle of Americanism,* 32-33.

46. It is interesting to remember that John Marshall was second cousin once

removed of Thomas Jefferson. He was born and raised in the identical Piedmont region. He attended, somewhat abortively, William and Mary and sat under Wythe (his untidy and completely disorganized law notes are still in existence). He seems to have had neither taste nor aptitude for study. His great decisions as Chief Justice lean almost entirely for precedent quoted and the backing up of theory with citation, upon the briefs and arguments of the pleaders who appeared before his court. Marshall is never called a great Democrat even by his most adoring biographer, the late Senator Beveridge.

Chapter 3

According to Aristotle

> Tribunal of 100...at Sparta, according to Aristotle...instituted to balance the Generals and the Senate.—James Madison

Before Jefferson published his *Notes on Virginia* the most forceful and persuasive presentation of the thesis that an agricultural base was best suited for popular government was to be found in Aristotle's *Politics*. In the sixth book of this treatise, among those chapters in which Aristotle attempts to describe empirically the functioning of the Greek city-states of his own day, he sets down a classification of democratic governments that had achieved or failed to achieve stability.

> Every democracy is a government of the majority; but this government may be more or less tempered in proportion as wealth, birth, morals, and other circumstances, besides mere strength of numbers, are respected in the fundamental laws of the constitution, and preferred in the distribution of offices and honors. The principal differences of democracies result, however, from the different qualities of the people that enter into their composition; and communities are thus marked with characteristic distinctions by their various modes of procuring the necessaries of life; or according to the various occupations of agriculture, pasturage, manufactures, and commerce. Agreeably to this division, the best kind of democracy and likewise the most ancient on record, is that in which the people subsist by agriculture; because the best class of working people are those employed in the rural labors of agriculture and pasturage, especially the former; and the manners and habits of husbandmen are also the best adapted to counteract the evil tendency of democratic institutions.[1]

In this fashion, Aristotle in his *Politics* (as englished by John Gillies, a distinguished classical scholar of the eighteenth century)[2] anticipates some two thousand years before Madison and Jefferson were born, their emphasis on the free state which would reconcile popular control with constitutional authority. And the Virginians were to hope, even as Aristotle, that the farming interests would be kept pre-eminent as a safeguard to the stability of the state.

Aristotle's praise for the farmers as "the best sort of working people" is unqualified, but his remarks on democracy reveal less than complete esteem. Nor is this merely the bias of a congenital aristocrat. He wrote after the conspicuous failure of the democratic city state to provide security for its citizens. Athens, the great example of popular sovereignty, had fallen before the disciplined power of Sparta, the exponent of aristocracy, as Jefferson observed, was organized as "the rule of military monks over the laboring class of the people."[3]

The great war that left Athenian liberty a broken and defaced column had been punctuated throughout by bloody intestine broils, that threw into ironic relief the proclaimed purpose of the democratic ideal as an inclusive and harmonious partnership of all free men in the life of the city. Nor were voices lacking to cry out that weakness abroad and disorder at home would inevitably result from a continuance of democratic rule. It is against the background of what was to him contemporary history that Aristotle's joining of pastoral virtue and the vices of democracy must be viewed. The connection was not accidental but implies a single pattern of ideas. The indestructible farmer whose occupation was to recommend him to Madison and Jefferson as it had to Aristotle, appears from the beginning with a definite role to play in a specific political drama. To understand that role requires some attention to the theories worked out in the Athenian schools on the ideal city, the good citizen, and the potentialities of the common man for self-government.

A theoretical argument for hedging off the promiscuous mass of working people from political power had been cogently argued before Aristotle's time by his teacher Plato. The formula commenced with the impeccable premise that political intelligence was rare and political virtue rarer.[4] It continued, with logic that the best state could not by definition be the best unless the most wise and virtuous ruled. And this thesis marching from superlative to syllogistic superlative, ended with a plea for the philosopher king. Plato's theory was premised upon the belief that virtue, including political virtue, was disciplined knowledge. His disillusionment with democratically se-lected magistrates had been magnified by the outcome of the Peloponnesian War and the trial of Socrates. As he saw it, the only

wisdom required of leaders in a democratic polity was that of
pandering to the unwise; ignorance was the prime characteristic of
those Athenian statesmen who, too feeble and inefficient to defeat
Sparta, were yet strongly enough infused with malice and envy to
martyr the great Socrates. Therefore, Plato, in violent reaction to the
existing structure of government in Athens, proposed in his *Republic*
a government by a benevolent despot.[5]

Aristotle, although he was as convinced as Plato of the need to
vest power in the hands of the more virtuous members of society,
entered a caveat against all kings who were above the law. Personal
ambition cannot be separated from absolute rule. There is strong
feeling in his assertion

> that it is impossible to modify kingly power into any thing
> like reason and justice...that placing a prince on the throne is
> nothing else than raising passion and a wild beast to the seat
> of sovereignty. That no man is a fair judge in his own cause;
> and that a king, therefore, can never judge fairly between
> himself and his people[6]... That the only just sovereigns,
> therefore, are God and the laws, especially those unwritten,
> moral, and universal laws, founded in nature, reared and
> perfected by education and custom... That the laws must be
> administered, and their general language adapted to particular
> cases, by the discernment of upright judges, affords not any
> argument in favor of the judges as superior to the law. For it is
> acknowledged that in every case to which laws are applicable,
> they only ought to judge and govern; and from law itself men
> derive those principles that enlighten their reason and direct
> their decision.[7]

Plato's tendency to gloss over the inevitable personal ambitions
of even the most benevolent despot—which was enough in itself to
prejudice Aristotle as well as eighteenth century liberals against his
totalitarian solution of the political problem[8]—was not the only
weakness of the *Republic*. An even greater objection, according to
Aristotle, was Plato's failure to treat politics as the art of the
practicable. "In all matters of practice," Aristotle pointed out,
"possibility is to be considered as well as perfection; and things easily
accomplished are preferable to those barely possible." Plato's
government is manifestly impossible. Political philosophy is
irresponsible if it merely produces dream-world formulations. "Above
all, [it] ought most diligently to investigate that form of government
adapted to mankind in general; circumstanced as they are most
commonly found to be."[9] Otherwise political theory will deserve the

sarcasm that Madison poured upon "that artificial structure and
regular symmetry which an abstract view of the subject might lead an
ingenious theorist to bestow on a Constitution planned in his closet or
in his imagination."[10]

In these terms Aristotle shifted the discussion of democracy from
the plane of the perfect republic to that of the best State possible for
actual men who were all more or less imperfect. If the legislator would
make citizens what they ought to be, Aristotle believed he must take
them as he finds them. "Government is nothing else but the arrangement of individuals in a state, and the propriety of every
arrangement or composition must depend on the number and nature
of its materials."[11]

Aristotle's study of one hundred and fifty constitutions of the
Greek States of his day, further convinced him that

> the cause of the wide variety in governments must be sought
> in the wonderful diversity of their constituent parts; for a state
> is a very complex object, composed of individuals and
> families; some rich, others poor; some subsisting by ag-
> riculture and pasturage, others by manufactures and commerce;
> and some are provided with arms, while others are altogether
> defenceless. The higher classes of men are also variously
> distinguished by their abilities, their virtues, their birth, or
> merely by their wealth; which last enable them to train horses,
> a circumstance which alone has been sufficient to decide the
> nature of the government. For in ancient times, whenever the
> national force consisted of cavalry, oligarchy was prevalent.

If one would see how formal constitutions were "preserved, subverted,
or amended" in functioning commonwealths it was necessary, the
Stagirite argued, to consider well the conditions which upon occasion
make individuals, who were neither angels nor devils normally, become politically devilish or angelic. The circumstances in which men
live governs to a large extent their potentialities for citizenship.[12]

The problem of democracy, therefore, has other aspects besides
the arrangement of magistracies in the state. The constitutional
distribution of offices among the few or the many, Aristotle had
discovered, explained only partially the recent developments of
Hellenic history,[13] for the city-state as well as being a legal structure
was an arrangement of social classes, skill groups (such as soldiers),
and economic interests. The search for virtue and wisdom in political
institutions raises a practical question of where among these social
groups power should be lodged to achieve the best approximation of
intelligence and fidelity to the general good. For "it is plain...that

governments vary according to the differences of those constituent parts of the State which either share or engross the sovereignty." Then, in words that Madison was later to echo, Aristotle pointed to a paramount factor influencing the political organization of every state in Greece during his lifetime: "The most palpable, and also the most specific difference (as will appear hereafter) is the distinction of riches and poverty; wherefore, all governments have been divided into oligarchies and democracies, as the winds are divided into north and south...and as melodies into the Dorian and Phrygian" (scales).[14] In the Grecian politics which Aristotle investigated political power was never purely political.

In three books of the *Politics* Aristotle then proceeds to analyze and compare the effect that political constitutions, economic factors, and various combinations of political and economic institutions have on the actual functioning of the governments he had studied. From this point of departure he presents, not one type of popular state characterized by incompetence, as Plato had earlier, but several types of historic democracies that range from the absolutely evil to the relatively good.

It was the Hellenic city-dwelling artisan whose misuse of popular sovereignty had cast a dark shadow over the term democracy down through the ages. Alexander Hamilton, twenty centuries after Aristotle's death, found it impossible "to read the history of the petty republics of Greece and Italy without feeling sensations of horror and disgust at the distractions with which they were continually agitated, and at the rapid successions of revolutions by which they were kept in a perpetual vibration between the extremes of tyranny and anarchy."[15] Hamilton's "disgust" at the class hatreds spawned in the commercial cities of Greece was not to delay in the least his attempt to create an urban and industrialized America. The New Yorker's special bias allowed him to blame the "distractions" on the democratic form rather than on the capitalistic conditions that produced them.

The fourth and worst type of democracy, according to Aristotle, which is the opposite of "the simple and frugal kind...naturally establishes itself in consequence of wealth acquired by conquest or commerce." Historically considered, it was the latest to appear in Greece

> because it cannot take place till cities have acquired a certain measure of population and wealth. A great population, and that condensed in cities, makes the multitude feel, and enables them to exert their strength. All men indiscriminately claim a share in government; and as most people cannot, without

> reducing themselves to beggary, afford time for exercising the
> functions of the citizen or the statesmen, their public services
> must be paid by the commonwealth, and the revenues of the
> state must supply the deficiencies of their private fortunes. By
> such an expedient the poorer citizens obtain greater command
> of leisure than even the rich themselves...[who] on every
> occasion [are] so much outvoted, that they often cease to
> attend any assemblies whatever... thus abandoning their
> country to the licentious and lawless multitude.[16]

   This resultant anarchy, which Aristotle refuses to dignify by the
name of the state

> is governed not by permanent laws, but by occasional
> decrees... But where law is set aside, the authority of wise and
> good men is overturned, and that of demagogues established
> on its ruins; the people in the assemblies assuming the power
> of one complex monarch; tyrants not individually but
> collectively... Of the real individual tyrant, and this tyrannical
> corporation, the manners are precisely the same. The decrees of
> one are as despotical as the edicts and ordinances of the other.
> Both prove the bane of human society, the oppressors of
> virtue, the munificent rewarders of vice...[17]

   On and on Aristotle continues his indictment of the evils incident
to the unchecked urban democracy. Where a city proletariat gains
political power there can be no cure for its viciousness until sheer
excess produces the inevitable tyrant. The despot's rigid absolutism
will be a welcome relief from the spasmodic reign of democratic
terror. And down through the years, from Machiavelli to Burke, from
Florence to Philadelphia, quotations and paraphrases and quotations
of paraphrases of Aristotle's original indictment were to be repeated
interminably every time that hydra-headed monster, the mob, stirred
restively and shook the ladder of degree.[18]
   Set against this dark picture of the turbulent and lawless *demos*
that dwelt in great cities corrupted by commerce, was the portrait of
one type of common man to whom the legislator could safely trust
the vote. Under certain circumstances Aristotle believed a government could be based on the broadest sort of suffrage. If a state was
composed of farmers or herdsman its people could be trusted with
political power to form a just commonwealth. The political principles
of this sort of democracy "requires that all men should be treated
alike; that the rich and poor should indifferently share the
government." Yet its administration is strictly constitutional; "it is

governed by general and fixed laws, which it is the duty of the magistrates and assemblies to administer and apply, without ever interposing their own authority."[19]

The people qualified to enjoy this "best and cheapest" form[20] are those

> subsisting chiefly by agriculture, and possessed, as is usual with such a people, of every moderate fortunes, [who] naturally arrange themselves into a legal and well-constituted democracy. They may subsist comfortably by labour, they would soon be ruined by idleness; they contrive a government, therefore, which requires as little expence of time as possible; and employ on all occasions, when it is practicable, the great machine of law to save the labour of man... A certain census [property qualification] is requisite for enjoying a share in government; but this census is so moderate that it may be acquired by every industrious citizen, without greater exertions of labour than are necessary to make provision for his family. Among such a people, government is carried on without salaries, without revenues, and without taxes. The affairs of the community, therefore, are left to assume this natural order; since men have no undue motive to engage them to abandon their own profitable concerns, in order to employ themselves in matters which will be much better managed without their unseasonable interference.[21]

The farmer, of all common men, is fittest to be trusted with political power; because by the very nature of his daily life he is inclined to use it moderately.

Twenty-two hundred years after Aristotle's death a similar contrast of the politically untrustworthy urban commoner and the politically sound yeoman was to be the center of a debate on the form of government most suitable for a new nation on a new continent that the Greeks did not know existed.

*   *   *

John Adams in 1787 used a memorable illustration in this *Defence of the Constitutions of the United States* to admonish Americans in the necessity of studying Greek history if they would renovate their government according to sound principles. "The history of Greece," he said "should be to our countrymen what is called in many families on the continent a boudoir, an octagonal apartment in a house, with a full length mirror on every side, and another in the ceiling. The use of it is, when any of the young ladies, or young gentlemen if you will, are at any time a little out of humor, they may retire to a place where, in whatever direction they turn their eyes, they see their own faces and figures multiplied without end. By thus beholding their own beautiful persons, and seeing, at the same time the deformity brought upon them by their anger, they may recover their tempers and charms together.[22] Adams' advice was unnecessary as far as the Constitutional Convention was concerned.[23] Madison, Hamilton, and others were already holding up the historic mirror for the delegates to see in Greek experience under democracy a preview of things to come in America if certain drastic steps were not taken. But neither Adams, nor Madison, nor the other classically conditioned citizens of the United States who were so quick to draw parallels out of the past ever stopped to consider carefully just how far it was safe to apply them as guides to contemporary problems. In many instances, as a consequence, the reflecting *boudoir* glass of Greek history threw back an image that was distorted in certain specific particulars. Among these misproportioned shadows must be included the linked figures of the over-virtuous farmer and the overdebauched city artisan.

The shape ideas take is relative to the culture and the age in which they develop; and certainly every element in Aristotle's theory of the hierarchical pattern of democratic government bears marks of the social stresses that had appeared in the Greek world of the fourth century. Mixed in, therefore, with Aristotle's enduringly valuable formulations of scientific truth about the nature and potentialities of the common man in politics, were bound to appear some conclusions that were relevant only to the unique historical character of the Greek city-states. Nor were certain other hypotheses advanced by the head of the Lyceum altogether lacking in personal and class bias. As a result the classical agrarian theory which Jefferson, Madison and their fellow Americans knew was a composite thing: made up in part of sound social science and in part of social science applicable only to a long vanished Hellenic society; the whole flavored to some degree by the prejudices of the Greek philosophical aristocrats.

The fact that some of the materials that Madison, Jefferson, and their contemporaries quarried out of the classics were of dubious value for the state they were building, was hidden from them by the obvious utility of the rest. For the social and economic forces which were operating in Europe in the eighteenth century had combined to pose questions that the leaders of the great philosophical schools of Greece, under roughly similar circumstances, had been forced to face in Alexander's time. The record of Greek experience in handling them, however compromised in detail, was the only considerable body of fact and theory applicable to the problems raised by a commercial revolution that had altered every aspect of European society after the fifteenth century.

The change in the organization of economic life that occurred in Greece from the sixth to the fourth century before Christ was every bit as violent as that which transformed the European economy between the end of the Middle Ages and beginning of the nineteenth century.

> During the period extending from the beginning of Greek history properly so-called to the departure of Alexander for Asia, the economic development of the Greeks altered the conditions of life over the greater part of the Mediterranean basin... The agricultural and pastoral land at the disposal of man was greatly increased and much better worked. Industry developed in a manner hitherto unknown: there was constant increase in the number of raw materials, both those obtained in Greece, and those imported from abroad; often from distant regions; the crafts were specialized and improved... Trade relations became more numerous and more extensive; the invention of money gave them an easiness and elasticity which had never been afforded by the old practice of barter... The producer did not work only for local needs, but for many different markets, some at a great distance. The consumer looked abroad for the satisfaction of his normal appetites and desire for comforts and superfluities... This economic development had a decisive influence on the character of property, the organization of labour, and the nature of commercial operations. Movable wealth assumed an important position by the side of landed wealth. Then what is known as capitalism made its appearance... A series of essential stages had been passed in from the evolution of economic activity as a whole. From being domestic, it had become urban, then interurban, and even international. The geographical area which it would henceforward cover might be increased...but its characteristic features were now fixed, and til the birth of machinery they would not alter in their fundamental nature.[24]

Substitute for the word "Greeks" the term "Europeans" and Toutain's summary would describe the background of what to eighteenth-century Anglo-Americans was modern history. Therefore it is not surprising that Madison, Jefferson and contemporaries, searching through the ancient writers for hints on the solution of their pressing social problems, would find themselves in familiar territory. Their world, after the medieval period of material retrogression, had reached, and was just surpassing, a comparable stage of economic organization. During their lifetime the European economy was to pass over the threshold into a world ruled by the machine. And although many of the questions raised by this new departure were insoluble by any classical formulas, Jefferson, Madison, and men of the their generation continued to look backward for help in puzzling out an answer.

In Greece, as in Europe of the seventeenth and eighteenth centuries, economic and social development was accompanied by political change. Aristotle summarized it in a series of stages that was to appear in practically every text book on government used during the Enlightenment. "Kings were originally established by the gratitude of small communities in which there were but few persons of considerable weight or distinguished merit. But as the number of men deserving the name of peers, or equals increased, the kingly government was changed for an aristocratical republic." This resulted, Aristotle believed—characteristically putting the political cart before the economic horse—in an increase of wealth: "under this government nations flourished, and riches were accumulated. Riches were followed by luxury, and luxury by rapacity. The wealth of the state became the plunder of individuals. Oligarchies, and then tyrannies, successively prevailed...till this power...was easily overturned by the just resentment of the multitude. Democracy then arose, and prevailed in its turn; and it is a matter, perhaps of some difficulty to establish any other form of government in large cities and populous communities."[25] Remembering the sage's sour estimate of urban democracy one might add, it was a matter, also perhaps, of some regret for Aristotle.

For although the marvelous flowering of the Greek spirit in arts, philosophy and letters was bound up with the commercial development of the mercantile cities and was nourished by the new surplus wealth channeled into them by traders and skilled artisans, Aristotle always considered the increasing opulence and its creators as somehow "unnatural." Long before Quesnay and Jefferson's friend Dupont stumbled on the great secret, Aristotle was preaching the doctrines of the physiocrats.[26]

The ideal city would "cultivate commerce...for accommodation only, not for gain; our citizens are not to degrade themselves into brokers and carriers, nor to squander away in the arts of luxury that labour which may far more profitably as well as more honourably be employed, in the cultivation of the soil and in the production of necessaries;[27] the occupation which is of all others the best adapted to the bulk of mankind, the most favourable to the health of their minds and bodies, and therefore the best fitted to promote national prosperity.[28] Our commerce must be limited to the purpose of supplying our domestic wants;[29] and in order to obtain this purpose without endangering the purity of our domestic manners, we may...have... docks and harbours enclosed by walls and fortifications, and separated at a due distance from the capital."[30] In 1784 a curious echo of Aristotle's desire to separate his capital city from the degrading influences of commerce was to appear in a memorandum of Jefferson's entitled, "Temporary Seat of Congress—" Jefferson was at that time a member of this august body which was meeting at Princeton under all the discomforts and inconveniences incident to the overcrowding of that village of eighty-odd dwellings.[31] None of the members were happy about the living arrangements; but in spite of Princeton's admitted "deficiency of accommodation" Jefferson felt that several counter-balancing arguments could be marshalled in favor of staying. Among them was "the risque in case of removal from Princeton of returning under the commercial & corrupt influence of Philadelphia."[32]

If commerce was bad the mechanical arts and their practitioners were worse. Aristotle can find no epithet harsh enough to describe artisans. "A life of mechanical drudgery, or a life of haggling commerce is totally incompatible with that dignified life which it is our wish that our citizens should lead... Men, habitually addicted to the lowly pursuits of providing necessaries and accumulating gain, are unfit members of our republic... They are to be classed with things necessary to the commonwealth, but not to be ranked with its citizens... Such men, therefore...are not parts of a common wealth, any more than food though necessary to an animal, is part of an animal; or than the instruments employed in producing any work, are themselves part of that work."[33] It is only after considerable hesitation that Aristotle is willing to rate them as one step of humanity above slaves.[34]

The quality of the city-dwelling handicraftsmen to transform humane and normally balanced individuals into dogmatic extremists is astonishing. One of the very few unpleasant statements of Jefferson's was evoked by mechanics and their urban habitat. Writing to Dr. Benjamin Rush in 1800 he comments on the prevalence of yellow fever in Baltimore, Providence, and Norfolk, "when great evils happen I am in the habit of looking out for what good may arise from them as consolations to us, and Providence has in fact so established the order of things, as that most evils are the means of producing some good. The yellow fever will discourage the growth of great cities in our nation, and I view great cities as pestilential to the morals, the health, and the liberties of men."[35] Even the ardent admirer of Thomas Jefferson must regret this ferocious Pollyannaism coolly discounting a plague with a sociopolitical moral on the defects of the artificers. As with Aristotle before him, the mere mention of urban workers sufficed to prick some exposed intellectual nerve of the Virginian and set it irrationally to throbbing.

For Aristotle the melioristic providence of the Deity did not go quite so far. However, divine wisdom did fortify all right thinking men's haughty contempt for wage earners generally, by indicating their spiritual degradation with obvious outward signs. Just as Jefferson was to fasten on the phrase, "rickety paupers and dwarfs" to describe English manufacturers, so Aristotle emphasizes the artisans' physical defects. "Wretched laborers and mean mechanics" tend to exhibit deformed and twisted bodies, resulting from the "unwholesome air and distorting postures" to which their occupations condemn them.

Xenophon, using the great Socrates as his "collocutor"—the term is Jefferson's—testified like Aristotle to the same effect.

> The illiberal arts, as they are called, are spoken against, and are, naturally enough held in utter disdain in our states. For they spoil the bodies of the workmen and the foremen, forcing them to sit still and live indoors, and in some cases they spend the day at the fire. The softening of the body involves a serious weakening of the mind. Moreover, these so-called illiberal arts leave no spare time for attention to one's friends, and city, so that those who follow them are reputed bad at dealing with friends and bad defenders of their country.[36]

Meanness of spirit and physical malformation go together. Plato's discussion of social classes by an analogy of gold, silver, and lead, was to his aristocratic contemporaries more than a poetic figure: the common manufacturer actually was conceived of as differing in significant physical and spiritual details from his agrarian counterpart.

This disdain for the manual worker was characteristic of those Grecian cities and states in which the commercial revolution had least development. It was typical of areas in which the old feudal nobility held most tightly to its political power. Gustave Glotz lists a number of these: Thebes, Thespiae (where even the farmer was despised), Epidauros, and most of all, Sparta. To what extremes this hereditary pride is to be seen in Plutarch's argument, as a Boeotion aristocrat, that no high-minded man could wish to be an artist like Praxiteles or Polycleitos—mere craftsmen—who, since they worked for wages were in the same caste as perfumers and dyers.[37]

In the mercantile cities won over to democratic ideas these primitive notions of the oligarchs were obstinately held by minorities. But these minorities, though often numerically infinitesimal, as in Athens, included the greatest portion of the theorists and philosophers whose writings were to interpret Greece's great achievements for later ages.

> Most of the philosophers were led to defend [these anti-artizan prejudices] by their mania for things Spartan and their tenderness for the manners and constitution of their forefathers. They had a personal reason for attaching themselves to them still more in the repugnance with which intellectual labour regards manual labour, as keen as that which landed property feels of trade and industry. The belief in the superior dignity of science dug a trench between the elect and the mass, between those who had leisure for meditation and those who had not.[38]

It is easy enough today to dismiss these philosophical diatribes of Aristotle, Plato, and Xenophon against the democratic and politically powerful artisan of fourth century Greece as merely "the joy of little circles in which they consoled vanities weary of waiting and ambitions run to seed."[39] It is true that at the time they were written their political and social effect was nil, and that they carried little authority in democratic cities strongly attached to the idea of equality. But in a later age susceptible to the "authority" of antiquity, this stylized contrast of "good" farmer with "bad" laborer carried weight far out of proportion to anything history could indicate as to their capacities for orderly participation in the government.

It was not merely as accepted dogma, however, that Greek attacks on the urban artisan carried conviction in post-Renaissance Europe; for common sense views which were apparently supported by observations made it easy for eighteenth-century Englishmen or Americans to accepts theories like Aristotle's as precious truths. For the dramatic contrast between farmer and mechanic did indeed focus upon an enduring phenomenon of social life—the difference that membership in an urban or rural society produce in the habits and psychology of all men.

What is the common denominator of these changes which the cities of all ages have made in artisan, landowner, legislator, soldier, or scholar?

> In the city the relationship of man to man becomes vastly more determinative of character than that of man to nature.

> Livelihood and success depends on the matching of mind with
> mind, on agility, on quick-wittedness, detachment...
> Convention rules [the city-dweller] as well as custom. He
> grows at once more critical and more competitive.[40]

The commercial towns of fourth century Greece, like the cities of
eighteenth century Europe, concentrating within their walls all the
new economic forces, were both symptom and instrument of a
transformed society. The most obvious aspect of this urban centered
transformation was the extreme inequality of wealth produced
wherever commerce flourished. And for Jefferson, Madison, and
Aristotle, the conflicts en⸗ ˏdered by the division of society into the
corrupted rich and degraded poor was the greatest obstacle for
legislators to surmount if they would establish a free government
dedicated to justice.

Notes

1. *Aristotle's Ethics and Politics, Comprising his Practical Philosophy*,
translated from the Greek by John Gillies (London: 1787), II: 407-409 (hereafter
cited as Gillies' *Aristotle*).

Throughout this paper I have deliberately used (wherever possible)
eighteenth-century translations of the Greek and Roman classics. In many
instances these translations are "inferior" by modern scholarly standards and fail
to accurately report the authors' intentions; but for our purposes what Aristotle
or Tacitus intended to say is less important than what eighteenth century men
thought they said.

The desires, hopes, and fears of every age make its reading of the literature
of the past highly selective. Each generation inevitably overaccentuates certain
aspects of historical reality to the detriment of other aspects which seem less
relevant to its own problems. This unconscious overemphasis results in subtle
but significant shifts in idiom from translation to translation. No matter how
literal the rendering, the act of translating the thought of the past into modern
words with modern undertones, transposes the original image into terms which
are always too contemporary.

Warner Fite's *The Platonic Legend* cites as an example the modern usage of
the word "Guardian" to translate the *phylakes* in Plato's *Republic*. Fite insists
that the addition of the ending "ian" to the root word reflects the late eighteenth
century and nineteenth centuries' belief in a natural harmony of social interests,
and by so doing softens and distorts Plato's thought into a gentle
liberalism. The clean monosyllabic "guard," uncompromisingly stressing the
function of force in human affairs, not only represents more clearly Plato's
original idea, but certainly carries a more pregnant meaning for us today.

2. Gillies' translation went through three editions before 1813. Jefferson
knew it by report; "In answer to your inquiry as to the merits of Gillies'

translation of the Politics of Aristotle I can only say that it has the reputation of being preferable to Ellis's, the only rival translation into English." Jefferson's *Works* (Memorial ed.), XV:65; to I.H. Tiffany, Aug. 26, 1816.

Madison used Gillies' once famous *History of Ancient Greece* (London: 1786) in preparing his "Notes on Confederations" (see citation on the Amphictyonic League and references to Gillies in Madison's *Writings*, I:296).

John Adams also used Gillies' *History* extensively in preparing his *Defence of the Constitutions of the United States*. He characterized it as a "valuable and excellent" production, and thought it deserved "to be carefully studied by all America." *The Works of John Adams...with a life...by his grandson, Charles Francis Adams* (Boston: 1850-56), 10 vols., IV:559 note.

3. To Monsieur A. Coray, Oct. 31, 1823, *The Writings of Thomas Jefferson*, ed. Albert Ellery Bergh (Washington, D.C.: 1905) (hereafter referred to as Jefferson, *Writings*, [Mem. ed.]).

4. Aristotle's statement of this: "That one man or a few may be adorned by an accumulation of virtues, is what experience will justify; but that the multitude in any country should be so illustriously distinguished is inconsistent with experience." Gillies' *Aristotle*, II:178.

5. The theory that virtue was Knowledge, and the prime indictment against democracy as incompetence, appears to have been appropriated by Plato from Socrates. At least it is implicit in Xenophon's quotation of the heresy charge against Socrates for "calling it Madness to leave to Chance the election of magistrates; while no one would be willing to take a Pilot, an Architect, or even a Teacher of Music, on the same Terms; though mistakes in such Things would be far less fatal than Errors in Administration." Xenophon's *Memoirs of Socrates*, translated by Sarah Fielding (Bath: 1762). Jefferson, who owned a copy of this translation, felt that Xenophon and not Plato was the only reliable source for Socrates' ideas. "Of Socrates we have nothing genuine but the Memorabilia of Xenophon; for Plato makes him into one of his collocutors merely to cover his own whimsies." To William Short, Oct. 31, 1819. Jefferson, *Writings* (Mem. ed.), XV:220.

6. Madison, in connection with the argument that absolute and centralized power was the best cure for the special interest legislation which compromises to some extent all free government, was to advance a like argument: "In absolute Monarchies the prince is sufficiently neutral towards his subjects, but frequently sacrifices their happiness to his ambition and avarice." Madison, *Letters*, I:327.

7. Gillies' *Aristotle*, II:198-200.

8. See Madison's remark that "a nation of philosophers is as little to be expected as the philosophical race of Kings wished for by Plato." *Federalist*, XLIV.

9. Gillies' *Aristotle*, II:280.

10. *Federalist*, XXXVII.

11. Gillies' *Aristotle*, II:200.

12. Gillies' *Aristotle*, II:282.

13. Aristotle never sharply differentiated the state from society. The contract theory bases on this division, which dominates Anglo-American political

thought after Locke's time, emerged first in Roman law. Citizenship implied for the Greeks membership as in a family, not the possession of private rights. The city-state was a way of life. All the Athenian interests and activities were interconnected and they all centered in the city. "His art was civic art. His religion, in so far as it was not a family affair, was the religion of the city, and his religious festivals were civic celebrations. Even his mean of livelihood were dependent upon the state far more frequently than is the case in modern life." George Sabine, *A History of Political Theory* (New York: 1937), 13.

14. Gillies' *Aristotle*, II:282. Compare Madison's catalogue of the social forces that influence politics with its climactic sentence, "the most common and durable source of faction has been the various and unequal distribution of property," in *Federalist* X.

15. *Federalist* IX.

16. Gillies' *Aristotle*, II:290-291.

17. Gillies' *Aristotle*, II:286-287.

18. One of the curious aspects of Edmund Burke's nineteenth century reputation is the attribution to him of almost mystical insight for prophesying that a revolution in France would lead to a dictatorship—that the deposing of the Bourbon monarch would start an inevitable cycle, progressing through anarchy, to armed despotism.

It was, of course, the most obvious argument to make in the eighteenth century if one opposed the Revolution. And though no one in England could trumpet the warning as eloquently as Burke, its instantaneous and overwhelming appeal can be explained only by its dramatic manipulation of fairly common ideas. Before Burke uttered a word, before the Revolution had passed beyond its honeymoon stage, his classically educated contemporaries who distrusted experiments in leveling, were already half convinced that the restive French populace would end by enthroning the equivalent of Bonaparte. (See, for example, Gouverneur Morris, *A Diary of the French Revolution* [Boston: 1939] under date March 16, 1789, for his prophecy of "tyranny as a *Consequence* of Anarchy.") To what extent the external hostility to the new régime, in part, generated by Burke and other conservatives should be credited with provoking the anarchy and preparing the way for Napoleon is still a moot question.

19. Gillies' *Aristotle*, II:286.

20. Thus Gillies' marginal annotation.

21. Gillies' *Aristotle*, II:289-290.

22. John Adams, *Works*, IV:469.

23. See Madison's slighting remark on Adams' book in his letter to Jefferson, of June 6, 1787, reporting that "men of learning find nothing new in it; men of taste many things to criticize." John Adams, *Works*, I:332.

24. Jules Toutain, *The Economic Life of the Ancient World* (London: 1930), 78-79.

25. Gillies' *Aristotle*, II:197-198.

26. See Gustave Glotz, *Ancient Greece at Work* (New York: 1926). "Thus there grows up a system which is already capitalist, in opposition to the primitive company, and is called *Chrematistike*. Of the two systems Aristotle has made an analysis which is as penetrating as it is biased. 'Economy' had for

its object the satisfaction of natural wants by the acquisition of such natural goods as were strictly necessary for life in common, and it legalized the use of natural means, agriculture, stock breeding, fishing, hunting, war, and piracy. The 'chrematistic' system set out to satisfy artificial wants and to accumulate wealth in the form of money, which is useless in itself by means of trade, which creates no value and has no other object than gain. After making the reservation that Aristotle is the first of the Physiocrats, we may accept this as a true picture of the order of things which begins in Greece in the VIIth century," 69-70.

27. "A prosperity built on...agriculture is that which is most desirable to us, because to the effects of labor it adds the effects of a greater portion of the soil." Jefferson to C.W.F. Dumas, 1792 (Ford ed.), VI:70; "to the labor of the husbandman a vast addition is made to the spontaneous energies of the earth... For one grain of wheat committed to the earth, she renders twenty, thirty, and even fifty fold, whereas to the labor of the manufacturer nothing is added. Pounds of flax in his hands, yield...but penny weights of lace." Jefferson to Benj. Austen, 1816 (Ford ed., X:8ff).

28. "The pursuits of agriculture are the road to affluence and the preservative of morals." Jefferson to George Washington, 1787 (Wash. ed.), II:252. "Agriculture may abandon contentedly to others the fruits of commerce and corruption." Jefferson to H. Middleton, 1813 (Wash. ed.), VI:91.

29. "The exercise...of so much commerce as may suffice to exchange our superfluities for our wants may be advantageous..." Jefferson to William Crawford, 1816 (Ford ed.), X:34.

30. Gillies' *Aristotle*, II:226.

31. Madison in September, 1783, had written from Princeton to warn Jefferson, who was on this way there, that it would be almost impossible to secure decent quarters. Even the warning was composed under difficulty. "I am obliged to write in a position that scarcely admits the use of any of my limbs, Mr. Jones and myself being lodged in a room not 10 feet square." Madison, *Writings*, I:22.

32. Jefferson, *Works* (Ford ed.), IV:314.

33. Gillies' *Aristotle*, II:230. Aristotle includes in this category of unfit citizens, peasants bound to the land and farm labour, living on a wage. The "modes of productive industry" were rated by Aristotle in a descending scale: "those of them are vile and sordid, which hurt the health or deform the body; those are truly servile, which may be exercised by the corporeal powers alone; and those are the...most contemptible, which require not any vigorous exertion of either mind or body," II:45.

34. Gillies, though no admirer of the working man, indicates in a footnote that this decision appears "harsh in the extreme."

35. To Dr. Benjamin Rush, Sept. 23, 1800, Jefferson, *Works* (Mem. ed.), X:173.

36. "Oeconomicus," *Xenophon with An English Translation* in the Loeb Classical Library (New York: 1921-1930), IV:2-4. Xenophon's Socrates, when asked, "what arts, pray, do you advise us to follow," gave the expected question-in-answer. "Need we be ashamed of imitating the King of the Persians? For they say that he pays close attention to husbandry and the art of war,

holding that these are two of the noblest and most necessary pursuits." Jefferson believed that while Plato used Socrates as a "collocutor" to cover his own "whimsies," Xenophon was a faithful transcriber of Socratic ideas, Jefferson, *Works* (Mem. ed.), XV:220. It is probable that Xenophon in putting antimechanic propaganda in his mouth was being "whimsical" in truth; for among all the philosophers Socrates appears to have been in this regard the exception. See Glotz, *Ancient Greece at Work*, 161-162.

37. "Polygnotus [the painter] was not an ordinary mechanic, nor was he paid for this work, but out of his desire to please the Athenians painted the portico for nothing." Plutarch's *Life of Cimon* (Drydon translation). Glotz, *Ancient Greece at Work*, part II, ch. II, has an admirable discussion of the Greek ideas on labor during the Athenian period.

38. Glotz, *Ancient Greece at Work*, 161.

39. Glotz, *Ancient Greece at Work*, 163.

40. R.M. MacIver, *The Modern State* (London: 1926), 73. Compare Franz Oppenheimer, *The State* (London: 1923). "The psychology of townsman...is radically different from that of the country man. His point of view is freer and more inclusive, even though it be more superficial; he is livelier because more impressions strike him in a day than a peasant in a year. He becomes used to constant changes and views, and thus is always *novarum rerum cupidus*," 167.

Chapter 4

The Desperate Debtor and
the Hall of Mirrors

> If Shays had not been a *desperate debtor,* it is much to be doubted
> whether Massachusetts would have been plunged into a civil war.
> —Alexander Hamilton

In 1786 after Dr. John Gillies finished his *History of Greece*, he
penned a respectful dedication to George III:

> Sir, the History of Greece exposes that dangerous turbulence of
> Democracy, and arraigns the despotism of Tyrants. By
> describing the Incurable evils inherent in every form of
> Republican policy, it evinces the inestimable benefits,
> resulting to Liberty itself, from the lawful dominion of
> hereditary Kings.

Madison used Gillies' history to clarify his ideas on the best organization of a republican Constitution. A year and a half later, in a appeal
for ratification of this constitution, Madison echoes Gillies on the
dangers of democracy while denying that these are irremediable.
Admitting that vices were inherent in the Republican form, Madison
claimed that the Constitutional Convention had found a cure for
them:

> Among the numerous advantages promised by a well
> constructed Union, none deserves to be more accurately
> developed than its tendency to break and control the violence
> of faction. The friend of popular governments never finds him-
> self so much alarmed for their character and fate, as when he
> contemplates their propensity to this dangerous vice. He will
> not fail, therefore, to set a due value on any plan which,
> without violating the principles to which he is attached,
> provides a proper cure for it. The instability, injustice, and

> confusion introduced into the public councils, have, in truth,
> been the mortal diseases under which popular governments
> have everywhere perished; as they continue to be the favorite
> and fruitful topics from which the adversaries to liberty derive
> their most specious declamation.[1]

Whether Gillies' "declaration" had stuck in Madison's mind is hard to say. He had leafed through the learned Doctor's *History* almost as soon as it was issued, but in 1787 there were so many "adversaries" to Republicanism vocally drawing parallels from Greek history to explain the vices of America the Gillies' slur may well have been overlooked in the mass.

The observed phenomenon masked Madison's term "faction" and Gillies' word "turbulence"—both deriving from Aristotle's phrase, "the evil tendencies of democracy,"—is the struggle of groups and classes to engross political power, leading to the ultimate appearance of a dictator.

Aristotle believed that the class conflicts in Greece could be traced to the shift from the natural economy of agriculture and pasturage cultivated in the Homeric period to the capitalism, or *chrematistike*, that followed after the discovery of the uses of coined money, "...the invention of money necessarily precedes that artificial traffic, of which the main object is not comfort, but gain." To the merchant, "wealth and money are synonymous; and to heap up money is in his mind to acquire all worldly advantages."[2] As one who considered "the productive arts...far more deserving of attention than exchange or traffic" Aristotle could dismiss the merchants' ideas as beneath contempt. Human industry is praiseworthy when "it selects and arranges the gifts of Nature, suitably to the exigencies and demands of human life."[3]

If the merchant's confusion of pecuniary value with use value was an example of shallow economic reasoning, nevertheless, the effect on society was profound. For this fallacious theory of merchants leads to the growth of a species of traffic "in which money is the end and object as well as the element and principle; a traffic ultimately centering in the augmentation of factitious riches, applicable to no other use than that of indefinitely multiplying themselves."

Dr. Samuel Johnson, the oracular contemporary of Jefferson and Madison, demolishing an eighteenth-century restatement of Aristotle's thesis of false mercantile wealth, maintained that making money was an admirable outlet for the energies of the average man; in no other activity could his faculties be so innocently employed.[4] Aristotle, however, conceived the search for pecuniary values not only as debasing the individual dedicated to it, but as dangerous to the society of which he was a member.

> Of such factitious riches, the desire, as Solon said, must necessarily be boundless; the blindness of avarice mistaking for an object agreeable in itself, and as such indefinitely desirable, that which is barely an instrument, and of which the desire ought to be strictly limited by the purposes which it is fitted to serve. There is a limit, therefore, to accumulation for provision, but none to accumulation for gain.[5]

The result for society is not "innocent." The individuals living in a state where the standard of emulation is measured in pecuniary terms dishonor their skills, weaken their bodies, and deteriorate their characters.

> At the name of money, they recall all those deceitful enjoyments of pride and voluptuousness which it is fitted to procure, and in which wishing forever immoderately to indulge, they cannot fail to desire that which promises to gratify their inordinate passions. If money is not to be obtained by traffic, the purpose for which it was first instituted, men thus minded will have recourse for obtaining it, to other arts and other contrivances; prostituting even skill and courage in this mean and mercenary service. Victory over the enemies of his country forms the proper ambition of a general; the health of this patients ought to be the main pursuit of a physician; yet how many military and how many medical men have no other end in view but gratifying their senseless, because unbounded, rapacity.[6]

More ominous still than the rotting away of moral integrity was the political result of this "artificial traffic which adds nothing to the common stock, but only enriches one man or one nation at the expence of another."[7] And on this point Aristotle was on surer ground than when he argued the productive sterility of commerce.

The possibility of increasing wealth and luxury without end, the insatiable greed incident to such increase led throughout Greece to the extension of pauperism over a great part of the population. The strategic political position of the agrarian aristocracy guaranteed that they would be beneficiaries of much of the new wealth. Other classes, however, amassing property by the new techniques, and using gold as the key, entered the ranks of the oligarchs, to the great disgust of such proud nobles as Theognis of Megara. His fulminations on the subject were to serve John Adams and Thomas Jefferson as the starting point for a discussion of "natural aristocracy" in 1813.[8]

As some individuals rose in the economic and social scale others were depressed. Commercial agriculture and business enterprise required plentiful and cheap workers; in the countryside peasants were reduced to serfdom, in the maritime cities the commoners became a depressed proletariat.

> Thus the individuals who were once united in the same group and dedicated to the same task were separated from each other by an increasing divergence of interests, and on the other hand they felt they were at one with individuals who once belonged to other groups and had left them for the same reasons. Everything was ready for a class struggle. The landed nobility defended its privileges and its revenues either against the newly enriched merchants, who demanded a better distribution of justice and fairer distribution of political rights, or against its tenants, who were crushed down by rent and wished to shake off their burden. Everywhere there were dissentions, disorders, revolutions. Finally the conflicts of interests, which set the citizens of one town against each another, let loose the great wars of rival cities, and in the VI century we see all of Greece crashing together in a furious confusion of struggles.[9]

Only the threat of Persian imperialism could force the Greeks to form up in a united front against the barbarians. When that threat was removed, the savage revolutions and counter-revolution of the rich few and many poor within the city commenced again. Foreign relations between the Greek states degenerated into a search for ideological allies in the never ending wars. Only when Macedonia imposed upon all of Hellas a monarchical system did the Greeks achieve lasting peace and order.[10] Well might Alexander Hamilton, considering some centuries later the "perpetual vibrations of between the extremes of anarchy and tyranny" exhibited in Greece, believe that the "disorders that disfigure the annals of those republics" allow "the advocates of despotism" to array "arguments not only against the forms of republican government, but against the very principles of civil liberty."[11]

In the fifth book of Aristotle's *Politics* nearly a hundred revolutions are mentioned. The quality characterizing almost all of them was their bloodiness. As David Hume noted, "In ancient history, we may always observe, where one party prevailed, whether the nobles or people (for I can observe no difference in this respect) that they immediately butchered all of the opposite party that fell into their hands, and banished such as had been so fortunate as to escape their fury."[12] Hume's scholarly footnote on "a few massacres, which passed in the course of sixty years, during the most shining age of Greece," as reported by Diodus Siculus, was extracted by John Adams and printed verbatim in his *Defence of the Constitutions of the United States*.[13] The fifty-six thousand citizens killed, and the eighteen thousand banished during the revolutions in such republics as Thebes, Sybaris, Corinth, Ephesus, would serve, Adams hoped, to warn his fellow Americans against the "unbalanced parties" of the rich and the poor. "Human nature is as incapable now of going through revolutions with temper and sobriety, with patience or prudence, or without fury and madness, as it was among the Greeks so long ago... Without three orders, and an effectual balance between them, in every American constitution, it must be destined to frequent unavoidable revolutions; though they are delayed a few years they must come in time."[14]

The "rebellion" led by that "desperate debtor" Daniel Shays a year earlier in Adams' own state of Massachusetts was enough to make all thoughtful property owners of the United States pause to consider the problem of faction in its relation to political liberty. This "ominous" event, as Madison termed "Shays' Rebellion," was the precipitating cause of his rereading his Thucydides, Xenophon, and Aristotle.

The most cursory examination of Greek history was sufficient to show that the organization of property, the maldistribution of wealth, the perpetual revolutions of the poor against the economically powerful rich, and of the rich against the politically powerful poor was the major problem of internal policy for the Greek legislator. Aristotle was speaking but the truth when he laid down the proposition that "the most palpable, and also the most specific difference... [in governments] is the distinction of riches and poverty: wherefore, all governments have been divided into oligarchies and demo-cracies..."[15]

Moreover, this "palpable and specific difference of riches and poverty" existing in every state in Hellas had produced a condition resembling a permanent revolution. The interplay of economics and politics was of crucial importance. When Madison in 1787 wrote that "the most common and durable source of factions has been the various and unequal distribution of property" his generalization was based on a view of history that related the turbulence of Shays' followers to ancient Greece. His belief that "those who hold and those who are without property have ever formed distinct interests in society" was a truth that both reading and experience had combined to reveal. The most pressing problem facing the Greek lawgiver and the American politician appeared to be the same. "The regulation of various and interfering interests forms the principle task of modern legislation, and involves the spirit of party and faction in the necessary and ordinary operations of the government.[16]

While the rich and poor struggle for power, Aristotle observed that, "In the contentions which take place, both parties pretend to have justice on their side; but there is a democratical justice and an oligarchical justice, which strongly savours of iniquity. Most men are wretched judges in their own cause. Passion narrows their understanding; and in every complicated case they see those circumstances only which are favourable to themselves, and obstinately shut their eyes to whatever favours their adversaries."[17] Madison also was to comment on the ambivalence of such words as "justice" and "right" in republican America when the emission of paper money in the summer of 1786 threatened to destroy the property rights of creditors, in many of the states. "There is no maxim," he wrote to Monroe, "in my opinion, which is more liable to be misapplied, and which, therefore, more needs elucidation, than the current one, that the interest of the majority is the political standard of right and wrong. Taking the word 'interest' as synonymous with 'ultimate happiness,' in which sense it is qualified with every necessary moral ingredient, the proposition is no doubt true. But taking it in the popular sense, as referring to immediate augmentation of property and wealth, nothing can be more false. In the latter sense, it would be the interest of the majority in every community to despoil and enslave the minority of individuals... In fact, it is only re-establishing, under another name and a more specious form, force as the measure of right..."[18]

Aristotle was as certain as Madison that seizure of political control in any state by a greedy economic group transformed the very nature of the government. Since "every commonwealth...forms a sort of partnership or community; and in this community or partnership each individual has his share,"[19] any state in which either the poor or the rich gained control ceases to be a true commonwealth and becomes a perverted caricature of itself.

> Aristocracy degenerates into oligarchy, when the few, who are rich, govern the state as best suits the interests of their avarice and ambition; and a republic degenerates into a democracy, when the mass who are poor, make the gratification of their own passions the only rule of their administration. Whenever wealth alone opens the road to preferment, oligarchy prevails; poverty, on the other hand, is the constant attendant of democracy; and the distinctive character of those governments consists not in this, that the many or the few bear sway, but in

the one case, that rapacious poverty be armed with power, and in the other that contemptuous opulence be vested with authority. But as eminence in wealth can only fall to the share of the few, and as *all*[20] may participate in the advantages of equal freedom, the partisans of the rich and of the multitude agitate republican states, each faction striving to engross the government.[21]

Aristotle's last sentence, restricting the class struggle to "republican states," rings strangely in the ears of the twentieth century student familiar with the writings of Marx. From the point of view of the Greeks, however, and of those eighteenth century theorists who were intent on underscoring the interplay of economics and politics, it did not appear illogical to restrict economic analysis to those states where political power was widely diffused.[22] They felt no need to elaborate a general theory of economic determinism applicable to all forms of government since a species of political determinism seemed to explain more adequately the historical development of the autocratic state. It was almost impossible to conceive of anything being mightier than the sceptre and sword as long as absolute monarchies were characteristic features of the political landscape.

$$* \qquad * \qquad *$$

Economics—significantly labeled political economy—was to remain a subhead of politics during the whole of the eighteenth century. Man, the *homo-politicus*, was most likely to become economic man only under the special political circumstances to be found in a relatively free State. Thus Madison, whose death antedated the publication of the *Communist Manifesto* by less than two decades, never seems to have doubted that the conflict of classes could be sterilized by decisive application of political power. A sure way "of curing the mischief of faction" was to destroy the "liberty which is essential to is existence." For "liberty is to faction what air is to fire, an aliment [i.e., nourishment] without which it instantly expires."[23]

The belief that political arrangements could control economic forces explains the great enthusiasm of so many Americans from 1785 on, for a stronger central government. In the minds of some at least a new Constitution with strong powers was conceived of as the only way to forestall a class conflict on the Grecian pattern. "The rage for paper money, for an abolition of debts, for an equal division of property," which the commercial depression had generated to a greater or lesser extent in all sections of the Confederation was interpreted by great numbers of the rich, well-born and educated Americans as the first signs of imminent social revolution.[24] And while it is true that much of the demand for a "higher toned government" issued from the distinct economic interests of this group, it falsifies the picture of the so-called "critical period" to overlook certain strong and purely political convictions which entered into the conflict. Hundreds of intelligent men were gripped by the fear that the disunited states were verging on a series of class struggles; and that the anarchy incident to them would result either in the rise of domestic dictators or the reconquest of the petty republics by a strong European power, as had befallen Greece at the hands of Macedon and Rome.

The bromide that "history repeats itself" can be taken too literally by a classic conscious age; and surely the classical literature with which some of the Fathers saturated their brains of 1787 sometimes served less to clarify than confuse their view of the American social situation in the last years of the Confederation. One can understand John Adams' "horror" as he viewed the party conflicts in fourth-century Greece as typified by Thucydides' account of the sedition at Corcyra; but its relevance for eighteenth-century America was questionable on many scores. Nevertheless Adams, prayerfully hoping that American legislators would repress the "factions and confusions" which threatened the United States, quoted William Smith's translation of this famous passage verbatim in his *Defence:*

> During the few days that Eurymedon [the Athenian general], with his troops, continued at Corcyra, the people of that city extended the massacre to all whom they judged their enemies. The crime alleged was, private enmity; some by the hands of the borrower, on the account of the money they had lent. Every kind of death, every dreadful act, was perpetrated. Fathers slew their children; some were dragged from altars, some were butchered at them; numbers, immured in temples, were starved. The contagion spread through the whole extent of Greece; faction rages in every city; the licentious many contending for the Athenians, and the aspiring few for the Lacedaemonians. The consequence was, seditions in cities, with all their numerous and tragical incidents.

"'Such things will ever be,' says Thucydides, 'so long as human nature continues the same.'" But, John Adams interpolated, "if this nervous historian had known a balance of three powers, he would not have pronounced the distemper so incurable, but would have added—*so long as parties in cities remain unbalanced.*" [25]

To draw even the most tenuous analogy between the events at Corcyra in 427 B.C. and the disturbances in the back country of Massachusetts in 1786-1787 was to miss the most significant characteristic of the Shays' insurrection. For these events were very generally limited by what Jefferson, in Paris at the time, rightly termed "the discretion" of the "malcontents."

The fact that Jefferson was separated from the American scene by three thousand miles of ocean helps to explain why his view of the disturbances was not infected with the alarm which spread among so many of his intelligent contemporaries. In the first place, from the moment of this arrival abroad, he had been exposed to a series of fictitious news stories on American affairs that predisposed him to examine critically all accounts of turbulence in the States. Almost as soon as he was established in Paris in 1785, we find him reporting to Monroe that "the English papers are so incessantly repeating their lies about the tumults, the anarchy, the bankruptcies and distresses of America, that these ideas prevail very generally in Europe."[26] His complaints about "the torrent of lies" published in London, appear at intervals all during the following year; and in August, 1786, two weeks before the Shaysites first gathered in force, he was again denouncing the "false" reports of American "anarchy" current in Europe.[27] Thus when the letters of his correspondents and their enclosed American papers informed him during the last week of December of the actual "tumultuous meeting" in New England he was prepared to discount any wild rumors that pictured them as all-out attacks on the social order and constitutional government.

Historians today in their analysis of the obstreperous activities of Captain Shays, Luke Day, and their followers, generally endorse Jefferson's contemporary estimate of the rebels' aims:

> Their principal demand was a respite in the judiciary proceedings...[Nor are] those people...entirely without excuse. Before the war these States[28] depended on their whale oil and fish... The heavy duties on American whale oil now required in England, exclude it from that market; and the Algerines excluded them from bringing their fish into the Mediterranean. France is opening her ports to their oil, but in the meanwhile, their ancient debts are pressing them, and they have nothing to pay with. The Massachusetts Assembly, too, in their zeal for paying their public debt, had laid a tax too heavy to be paid in the circumstances of their strata.[29]

Jefferson's judgment that "no injury was done...to the person or property of any one" was perhaps too optimistic. Yet George Minot, who wrote a careful account of the insurrections within a year of their occurrence,[30] and Robert A. East, the most recent historian of the rebellion,[31] both support Jefferson's claim as the fundamentally law-abiding spirit with which the vast majority of the so-called incendiaries went about the business of closing the courts to debt cases.[32]

With all their seizing of court houses, loud talk, parading up and down before scandalized judges, Minot points out that "no disorders... of an outrageous nature took place," during any of the early demonstrations.[33] The leaders considered their convocations as petitions-in-boots, and maintained fairly rigid discipline. Only when the Assembly had manifested its "obstinate"[34] determination not to give any legislative relief to the back country in its genuine distress, only when Governor Bowdoin's successful demand for the suspension of the writ of Habeas Corpus indicated that reprisals were to be leveled against mob leaders, did some of the insurgents assume anything resembling a threatening attitude toward law and order as such. But even then, their hearts were not in it. The militia was able, practically by its appearance, to disperse units of the rebels that numbered as high as a thousand men. When one remembers that in the ranks of the Shaysites were hundreds of ex-continental soldiers, well fitted to use the muskets in their hands, the bloodless victories of Shepherd's and Lincoln's citizen army over them is revealing. The severest trial suffered by the forces of law and order was the exhausting pursuit of the rebels. Not the wounds suffered by their bullets.[35] The vicious democrats of Western Massachusetts whom the conservatives were mentally comparing with the blood-crazed citizens of ancient Cocyra, Syracuse, and Megara, had neither the intent, nor the will to social or political revolution.

It is a great misfortune that the historian cannot weigh with the scientific exactitude the different factors in a given historical situation. It would be very pleasant to be able to state that the principles enunciated and the programme followed by the Americans, frightened by the economic and political disorders that culminated in Shays' rebellion, were motivated in precisely nine-tenths of what they did and said by material interests, say, and exactly one-tenth by analogies drawn from their reading of world history. Such percentages can only be a pipe dream. The most that one can claim is that when Madison, Hamilton, and the conservatives marched out to do battle for a stronger national government under banners inscribed with the watchwords "security for property" and "liberty for the individual" they devised these slogans in part at least from the stuff of ideas, beliefs, and aims that had first been enunciated by Greek thinkers in the fourth century before Christ.

*   *   *

If Aristotle had never written a line on politics, if the Greek Republics with their record of violent class struggles had vanished without a trace, it is possible that the history of the critical period in America would still have followed exactly the course that it did. Surely no elaborate corpus of classical learning, nor complex theory of the historic vices of republics was necessary to frighten the propertied classes into some sort of political reform. After all, their pocket books were directly threatened by the demands of the back country debtors. But since Aristotle's writings had been preserved, since the men most responsible for the successful creation of a strong union show their familiarity and indeed, acute consciousness, of the events that had taken place in classical ages, the impact of such knowledge on their thought cannot be denied. Moreover, since they themselves insist time and again on drawing analogies between the problems confronting the American republics and those of antiquity, historical discretion at least requires some notice be taken of the close relationship between their interpretation of ancient history and their theories of the economic basis of politics.

The Constitutional Convention had been in session only eight days before Madison, in an extremely able speech, took the opportunity to present the conclusions of government which he had drawn, in part at least, from his researches into classical history. Mr. Sherman of Connecticut had argued that the primary purpose of the meeting was to grant the existing Congress greater powers over taxes and commerce and foreign affairs; that the Convention should do a job of political tinkering, not a thoroughgoing reconstruction of government. This was what Madison had been waiting for. Agreeing that Mr. Sherman's specification of powers was important,

> he differed from the member from Connecticut...in thinking the objects mentioned to be all the principal ones that required a National Govt. Those were certainly important and necessary objects; but he combined with them the necessity of providing more effectually for the security of private rights, and the steady dispensation of Justice. Interferences with these were evils which had more perhaps than any thing else, produced this convention.[36] Was it to be supposed that republican liberty could long exist under the abuses of it practised in some of the States... All civilized Societies would be divided into different Sects, Factions, & interests, as they happened to consist of rich & poor, debtors and creditors, the landed, the

manufacturing, the commercial interests, the inhabitants of
this district or that district, the followers of this political
leader or that political leader, the disciples of this religious
Sect or that religious Sect. In all cases where a majority are
united by common interest or passion, the rights of the
minority are in danger... These observations are verified by the
Histories of every Country ancient and modern. In Greece &
Rome the rich and poor, the creditors and debtors, as well as
the patricians & plebeans alternately oppressed each other with
equal unmercifulness. What a source of oppression was the
relation between the parent cities of Rome, Athens, &
Carthage & their respective provinces: the former possessing
the power, & the latter being sufficiently distinguished to be
separate objects of it? Why was America so justly apprehen-
sive of Parliamentary injustice? Because G. Britain had a
separate interest real or supposed, & if her authority has been
admitted, could have pursued that interest at our expense...
What has been the source of those unjust laws complained of
among ourselves? Has it not been the real or supposed interest
of the major number? Debtors have defrauded their creditors.
The landed interest has borne hard on the mercantile interest.
The Holders of one species. The lesson we are to draw from
the whole is that where a majority are united by common
sentiment, and have an opportunity, the rights of the minor
party become insecure. In a Republican Govt. the Majority if
united have always an opportunity.[37]

Consideration of Shays and his "desperate debtors," study of the
deadly internecine strife of the Greeks and the Romans, fear of the
threat to republicanism itself from the tyrant-breeding anarchy which
had so often in the past disfigured free states, all these combined to
make Madison rethink the present problems of government in the
light of events long since recorded and made clear.

The Young Virginian's learned mingling of the old and new to
prove the inadequacy of partial remedies for the ills of the Confederation impressed his audience favorably. Pierce of Georgia reporting the
debate noted that "Mr. Madison in a very able and ingenious Speech,
ran through the whole Scheme of Government,—pointed out all the
beauties and defects of ancient Republics; compared their situation
with ours wherever it appeared to bear any analogy..."[38] The
reminders of the bitter contentions of the plebeans and patricians in
Rome, the recalling of the bloody rivalry of rich and poor which had
distracted Greece in the pre-Christian era, did not seem out of place in
the Convention chamber where the Fathers puzzled over the problem
of a new Constitution. Madison's speech in the hot summer of 1787

could stand as a climax to ten months of conservative propaganda, in the course of which Shays' rebellion was transformed into a vicious democratic movement, with frightening Aristotelian overtones.[39]

Such arguments as ran contrary to the ideas held by Madison were at odds with his solutions rather his illustrations from the past. Dickinson of Delaware had already on June 2 suggested that "if antient republics have been found to flourish for a moment only & then vanish forverver, it only proves that they were badly constituted..."[40] From this he went on to argue that the State governments should be preserved with fairly large powers. Four days later Madison rose to refute this and similar arguments: he believed that only by concentrating political power in the hands of the national government could the threat of faction be removed. On June 9th another small state delegate, Paterson of New Jersey, while not denying democracy's turbulence, entered a plan of confession and avoidance against the Virginians indictment. In Paterson's own outline of this speech he set down as a point to elaborate, "Insurrections—So there are in every Govt.—even in England."[41] And he, too, insisted that Madison's political remedy of the class struggle would never do, drew upon historical example to support his conflicting opinion.

It is safe to say that the carping of Paterson, Dickinson, Sherman, and the delegates of thinly peopled states was directed less at Madison's description and diagnosis of the evils of the republican form of government than at certain of his proposed remedies for them. They had little objection to powers which the Virginians proposed to vest in the new Congress. They did have strenuous objections to the selection of that Congress on the basis of proportional representation, for they feared the power newly granted would slide into the hands of the larger states. As Brearly of Delaware put it, "Virga. with her sixteen votes will be a solid column indeed, a formidable phalanx. While Geogie [sic.] with her solitary vote, and other little states will be obliged to throw themselves constantly into the scale of some large one, in order to have any weight at all."[42] So on June 15th, the small state leaders offered a new plan of government of their own; if they could rally their forces in support of it and hold their lines without defections—and it soon appeared that they could—there was every indication that the convention would be deadlocked.

*   *   *

At this juncture Alexander Hamilton marched the Greeks and

Romans into the Convention Hall again in what was in many ways the most remarkable speech delivered during the whole session. Hamilton's situation in the Convention was most unhappy. As one who for six years had steadily been working for a "high-toned government"; as the individual most responsible for the gathering of the Convention in Philadelphia that summer, he was of all the delegates the most disappointed in his expectations and hopes, when the meeting once got down to business. The dissolution of the Convention was threatened by the fight of the small states for some sort of equality of representation in the contemplated Congress. The vote of New York, his own state, was consistently cast on the side of small state pretensions; and his own position in the state delegation was solitary and unsupported. As his son was to write later, "the policy of Clinton [governor of New York] had placed him there to become a cipher and a sacrifice,"[43] for Yates and Lansing the other New York representatives voted as a unit against his dearest desires. The deadlocked convention seemed fated to adjourn with nothing done; but even if some compromise could be worked out between the big partisans of the Virginia plan and the small State advocates of the New Jersey plan, the result was bound to be calamitous from Hamilton's viewpoint. Neither plan contemplated a government strong enough to counteract the evils incident to democracy. So Hamilton, at a crisis of his hopes and fears rose from his chair to try to stave off the threatened defeat which seemed inevitable.

This speech of Hamilton's, lasting several hours, was his major contribution on the floor of the Convention and fully justifies Major Pierce's impression of this persuasive talents. "Colo. Hamilton," he reports, "...enquires into every part of his subject with the searchings of phylosophy, and when he comes forward he comes highly charged with interesting matter, there is no skimming over the surface of a subject with him, he must sink to the bottom to see what foundation it rests on."[44] This thoroughness so commendable in Hamilton is fortified by his wealth of historic examples. Pierce finds it worthy of mention that he is "reputed to be a finished Scholar," and the illustrations from Aristotle, Cicero, Montesquieu, Neckar, in which Hamilton's speech abound, bear out Pierce's best expectations.

Madison reports that Hamilton commenced with diffident statement explaining his silence up to that moment: only the present crisis induced him to voice this disagreement with Colleagues of his own State, and his unfriendliness toward both plans now before the Convention.[45] He then launched into a carefully prepared speech—his own detailed outline with numbered sections, topics, and sub-topics has been preserved and fills eight printed pages in his son's *History*[46]

—which Gouverneur Morris, a finished orator in his own right, called "the most able and impressive he had ever heard."[47]

We are fortunate in possessing not only Madison's report of what Hamilton said, but also the record made by the Robert Yates of New York as he listened to his fellow delegate's arguments. The two accounts, one by the most ardent defender of the Virginia plan, the other by a leader of the small state bloc, complement each other and reveal aspects of Hamilton's speech that a reading of either report singly would obscure. The difference is mainly a matter of stress; but using Hamilton's own outline as a guide and check, one sees that the Virginian delegate took slightly more care to note Hamilton's strictures on the Paterson plan than those leveled against the one he had helped to devise, whereas the New York delegate, missing nothing derogatory that was said of the Virginia scheme, ignored a few of the more brutal attacks on the plan presented by New Jersey. Both agree that Hamilton began his address with an impassioned analysis of the feebleness of the Confederation. His design was to show that salvation of America could be achieved only by "the forming of a new government to pervade the whole, with decisive powers; in short with complete sovereignty."[48] Only thus would a government marked by energy and order be attainable.

After this opening salvo, Hamilton proceeded first to list and compare the defects of both plans, and finally to consider the ultimate roots of political loyalty. These "principles of civil obedience" as this outline phrases it, consistently operated to strengthen the State government at the expense of any national interests.[49] This conflict of loyalties had been the bane of the existing Continental Congress. Nor could either of the new systems proposed by Paterson and Randolph rectify this failing; the whole controversy between the adherents of each of these plans did not touch this vital issue. "The State governments, by either plan will exert the means to counteract it. They have their State judges and militia, all combined to support their State Interests; and these will be influenced to oppose a national government. Either plan is therefore precarious."[50]

Then Hamilton, having marshalled his theoretical arguments and general principles, delved far back into history to drive home his points. These illustrations are preserved in Madison's notes on the speech:

> Theory is in this case fully confirmed by experience. The Amphyctionic Council had it would seem ample powers for general purposes. It had in particular the power of fining and using force agst. delinquent members. What was the

> consequence? Their decrees were signals of war. The Phocian
> war is a striking example of it. Philip at length taking ad-
> vantage of their disunion, and insinuating himself into their
> Councils, made himself master of their fortunes.

This was the lesson of ancient history. Hamilton then proceeded to a
discussion of the Germanic Empire under Charlemagne and his
successors, and the Swiss cantons as "other examples [which] instruct
us in the same truth": that all these evils can be avoided "only by such
a compleat sovereignty in the general Governmt. as will turn all the
strong principles & passions above mentioned on its side."[51]

Hamilton had talked over two hours by this time, and although he
was showing no signs of weariness, both Yates and Madison evidently
began to develop writer's cramp. At any rate, neither of them report
with any degree of fullness Hamilton's presentation of a favorite
theme of his: that war was the normal concomitant of political
independence. Yates indeed takes note of Hamilton's presentation of
the problem of common defense against European powers as one of
"the variety of important objects of which must necessarily engage
the attention of a national government," but he ignores, along with
Madison, Hamilton's even more striking remarks on the relation of
peace to republicanism and of war to commercial development.
Yates' quotation: "You have to protect your rights against Canada on
the North, Spain on the south, and your western frontier against the
savages. You have to adopt necessary plans for the settlement of your
frontiers..."[52] covers only the defensive aspect of Hamilton's topic of
"league[s] offensive and defensive."[53] If his outline is to be trusted he
was even more interested in elaborating on the problem of aggressive
war as the normal instrument of policy wherever independent states
or nations existed.

In the development of this line of reasoning Hamilton had to
examine two propositions that enlightened European publicists had
advanced in the then current attack on eighteenth-century militarism.
The first of these held that republican governments were by their
nature disinclined to warlike aggression; for were not most wars fought
because of the dynastic ambitions of irresponsible Kings? John Jay
summed up in *Federalist* IV, for purposes of refutation, this doctrine
that antimonarchical and antimilitarist theorists had been proclaiming
for a generation: "absolute monarchs will often make war when their
nations are to get nothing by it, but for purposes and objects merely
personal, such as a thirst for military glory, revenge for personal
affronts, ambition, or private compacts to aggrandize or support their
particular families or partisans."[54] Therefore, so the argument ran, if

Kings are removed and the power to make war comes into the hands of the people, their obvious self-interest will lead them to vote against conflicts which their own blood and treasure must pay for. Kings were always willing to fight; for their subjects bore the burden; Kings had no vested interest in peace since it was a case of heads, I win, tails, you lose. Related to this negative deduction of the pacifism of republics was a positive doctrine most authoritatively advanced by Montesquieu: "Peace is the natural effect of trade. Two nations who traffic with each other become reciprocally dependent; for if one has an interest in buying, the other has an interest in selling; and thus their union is founded on their mutual necessities."[55] Each of these plausible doctrines Hamilton considered dangerous and false. With brilliant anticipation of the forces that were to mold the nineteenth and twentieth centuries, he still appealed for proof to Greece and Rome for his demonstration that neither republicanism nor commerce were sufficient to protect a disunited America from the "arms and arts of foreign nations" nor from "frequent and violent contests with each other."[56]

In the outline of his speech set for discussion: "GENIUS of republics pacific.—Answer. Jealousy of commerce as well as jealousy of power, begets war."[57] By considering together the two doctrines of the eighteenth-century pacifists, Hamilton had come to the conclusion that their prophecies were "Utopian speculations"—the "deceitful dream of a golden age"—and he was prepared to let "experience, the least fallible guide of human opinions, be appealed to for an answer to these inquiries."[58] And "experience," as is customary with Hamilton, means the appeal to history—the use of a past even so remote as that of the classical civilizations to guide the practicing statesman.

Boldly turning Montesquieu's thesis upside down, Hamilton asked the assembled convention: "Has commerce hitherto done anything more than change the objects of war?... Sparta, Athens, Rome, and Carthage were all republics; two of them, Athens and Carthage, of the commercial kind. Yet were they as often engaged in wars, offensive and defensive, as the neighboring monarchies of the same times. Sparta was little better than a well-regulated camp; and Rome was never sated of carnage and conquest. Carthage, though a commercial republic, was the aggressor in the very war that ended in her destruction. Hannibal had carried her arms into the heart of Italy and to the gates of Rome, before Scipio, in turn, gave him an overthrow in the territories of Carthage, and made a conquest of the co-mmonwealth."[59] Examples from modern history merely confirmed this obvious lesson. Venice and Holland were republican states that lived by commerce and that had "figured more than once in wars of ambition." England where "the representatives of the people compose one branch of the national legislature" has fought predatory people's wars for generations.

Hamilton had been on his feet for more than three hours and he had still not finished listing the dangers inherent in America's situation—dangers which made it absolutely essential to go beyond the feeble provisions of the New Jersey plan and the half-way measures proposed by the Virginia delegation. Having completed his survey of man's propensity toward external war, he next took up the matter of "domestic faction and insurrection"—the internal wars of classes in the same state. And here again we must depend upon his subsequent treatment of the subject in the *Federalist* for both Madison and Yates seem to have lacked the energy to drive their pens in note-taking as the speech relentlessly continued.

Again Hamilton turned to the past for his theme, reminding his audience of the "sensations of horror and disgust" that all right-thinking men must feel as they contemplated the "distractions" which marked "the history of the petty republics of Greece and Italy," as these swung like pendulums "between the extremes of tyranny and anarchy." Their occasional periods of calm

only serve as short-lived contrasts to the furious storms that are to succeed. If now and then intervals of felicity open to view, we behold them with a mixture of regret, arising from the reflection that the pleasing scenes before us are soon to be overwhelmed by the tempestuous waves of sedition and party rage. If momentary rays of glory break forth from the gloom, while they dazzle us with a transient and fleeting brilliancy, they at the same time admonish us to lament that the vices of government should pervert the direction and tarnish the lustre of those bright talents and exalted endowments for which the favored soils that produced them have been so justly celebrated.

From the disorders that disfigure the annals of those republics the advocates of despotism have drawn arguments, not only against the forms of republican government, but against the very principles of civil liberty. They have decried all free government as inconsistent with the order of society, and have indulged themselves in malicious exultation over its friends and partisans. Happily for mankind, stupendous fabrics reared on the basis of liberty, which have flourished for ages, have, in a few glorious instances, refuted their gloomy sophisms."[60]

We cannot tell if Hamilton mentioned by name on the Convention floor these "few instances" of governments which slightly redeemed the dark pictures of republican faction. If he did call their names, he probably spoke of Carthage and Rome and possibly added Sparta and Crete to the list.[61] But Hamilton was nearing the climax of his oration; and it is quite possible that he left it to his classically-educated audience to translate his allusion for themselves, as he hurried on to even more important matters.

For he was now ready to propose his own scheme of government to the Convention—a constitution which suffered from none of the inadequacies of the two plans before the House. He had in mind a "general government," which would "not only have a strong soul, but *strong organs* by which that soul is to operate," as his italicized outline put it.[62] And as Hamilton launched into the crowning sections of his speech the tired Convention jerked to close attention. Madison and Yates recommenced their rapid note-taking. For Hamilton was boldly praising the excellencies of the British monarchy.

The vast size of America, the strength of the States, the unlovely democratic aspects of the populace, "almost," he declared, "led him to despair that a Republican Govt. could be established" in this country.

> He was sensible at the same time that it would be unwise to propose one of any other form. In his private opinion he had no scruple in declaring, supported as he was by the opinions of so many of the wise & good, that the British Govt. was the best in the world: and that he doubted much whether anything short of it would do in America. He hoped Gentlemen of different opinions would bear with him in this, and begged them to recollect the change of opinion on this subject which had taken place and was still going on... The members most tenacious of republicanism, he observed, were as loud as any in declaiming agst. the vices of democracy. This progress of the public mind led him to anticipate the time, when others as well as himself would join in the praise bestowed by Mr. Neckar on the British Constitution, namely that is the only Govt. in the world 'which unites public strength with individual security.'[63]

From the syllabus that Hamilton held in his hand as he spoke we know that Neckar was not the only authority whose testimony was adduced to prove this point. Other "wise & good" men were quoted by Hamilton: Montesquieu, the illustrious French admirer of the matchless British Constitution; Cicero, lawyer and political theorist of

the dying Roman republic; and the greatest of all political philosophers, Aristotle.[64]

Hamilton then proceeded to an exposition of the ABCs of
political wisdom that also was an echo of Aristotle. "Society," he had
written in his outline, "naturally divides itself into two political
divisions—the *few* and the *many*, who have distinct interests." And
Yates, transcribing his remarks, makes clear the economic doctrine
implicit in this statement for eighteenth-century theorists, by
rendering it, "all communities divide themselves into the few and the
many. The first are the rich and well born, the other the mass of the
people."[65] Acceptance of this absolute dualism in society, which
parallels Aristotle's descriptive analysis of the Greek city states of the
fourth and fifth centuries, was conceived by Hamilton to be the alpha
and omega of political wisdom. Here was the rock of truth upon which
he would build his constitutional temple.

If these two classes into which the political community is divided
differ from each other in the objectively measurable matter of wealth
and poverty, their attitudes toward political power is in each case the
same.

> Give all power to the many, they will oppress the few. Give
> all power to the few, they will oppress the many. Both
> therefore, ought to have the power, that each may defend itself
> against the other. To the want of this check we owe our paper
> money, installment laws &c. To the proper adjustment of it
> the British owe the excellence of their constitution.[66]

Hamilton's remark about the legislation favoring the poverty-
stricken many in America indicates where he felt the real danger of
class oppression lay for this country. Artistic balance, however,
required that the danger from the rich to the "multitudinous poor" be
at least mentioned. His audience expected it. For this rubric of the few
against the many, many against the few, was the key proposition in
one of the most ancient theories of constitutional philosophy—that
of the mixed government. And to this theory, hardened after 2,000
years of repetition into the most banal of political clichés, the
brilliant young New York lawyer subscribed with a burning faith
approached fanaticism.

It is hard to escape the conviction that the mind of Alexander
Hamilton in so far as his political thinking was concerned was held to
an unusual degree in what Leonard Woolf calls "intellectual
mortmain."[67] That all men suffer to a certain extent from intellectual
lag is undoubtedly true. That the other members of the Constitutional

Convention of 1787 besides Hamilton could be charged to a greater or less degree with the same failing is also true. But Hamilton's complete inability to emancipate his mind from this stereotype of long dead political thinkers, from which time had squeezed all the life, the formal dogmatism with which he advocated a mixed government—with rough and ready approximation of King and Patricians—for America, is distinguishable both from the outdated political thinking of the average man in the street and the less outmoded theories held by the far more average group of his fellow delegates in Philadelphia. Comparing Hamilton with the latter, one finds a difference of degree amounting almost to a difference in kind; while all the leading members of the Convention advanced opinions at some stage in the debate which were incongruous, irrelevant, and unmeaning in the American world of 1787, no one of them stiffened into so rigid a system of thought as Alexander Hamilton. The tight and logical coherence of the New Yorker's second-hand theory, with its assumption that there was one and only one form of good government, with its implied acceptance of class struggle as a universal and ultimate truth divorced from social and environmental peculiarities, makes Madison's use of his gleaning from the classics seem positively relativistic in comparison.

One feels that the kingdom with which Hamilton's doctrine was concerned was not of this world; yet his dedicated search for it never flagged throughout his life. As Gouverneur Morris was to note soon after his death:

> Our poor friend Hamilton bestrode his hobby to the great annoyance of his friends, and not without injury to himself. More a theoretic than a practical man, he was not sufficiently convinced that a system may be good in itself, and bad in relation to particular circumstances. He well knew that his favorite form was inadmissable, unless as the result of civil war; and I suspect that his belief in that which he called an approaching crisis arose from a conviction, that the kind of government most suitable, in his opinion, to this extensive country could be established in no other way.[68]

There is something of the knight-errant in Hamilton, the consecrated seeker for the absolute in government; even in the face of death he still refused to accept the verdict of current history that in politics the best is often the enemy of the good.

Hamilton's meeting with Burr was tragically irrelevant to the course that American political development had already taken, long before that July day he rowed to the Jersey shore and the field of honor. So far as his future in public affairs was concerned the train of history had already turned the curved and thrown him off. Yet he offered himself as sacrifice to the *code duello* for fear that failure to do so would ruin hid political chances of saving America ultimately for a mixed government. Hamilton never wavered in his conviction that the catastrophe the civil war between the few and the many was sure to come; nor did he believe that it could be much longer delayed in the United States. And so he gambled on the slight chance that Burr might miss with his pistol; because no stain on his courage or honor must mitigate then against his being called to save the people from themselves.[69] By 1804 Hamilton's "hobby" had become a wild horse that dragged him to his death.

Notes

1. *Federalist*, X, published in the New York Packet, Friday, November 23, 1787.
2. Gillies' *Aristotle*, II:40.
3. Gillies' *Aristotle*, II:42. Gillies' footnote, 41, points out how totally different Aristotle's opinions on bullion and agriculture are from the mercantile writers, Child, Mann, and Locke. With an example from Adam Smith designed to snub Frenchmen as well as to prove that Aristotle's economic theories were up to date even after 2,000 years, he notes: "The poverty and misery of Spain and Portugal not withstanding all their gold and silver, and the riches and happiness of England, a commercial country without mines, as well as the riches and happiness of Switzerland, an agricultural and pastoral country, which disdains working its mines, more strongly fortify Aristotle's conclusions, than a thousand fine spun arguments of the French economists." Gillies, while accepting Aristotle's physiocratic doctrine that all wealth originally derives from agriculture departs from his master to praise commerce, if moderately pursued, as a stimulus to agricultural productivity.
4. "There are few ways in which a man can be more innocently employed than in getting money," March 27, 1775.
5. Gillies' *Aristotle*, II:41.
6. Bernard Mandeville in his *Fable of the Bees* was to include doctors and soldiers among those professional men corrupted in his own day by that "Root of Evil, Avarice."

Physicians valu'd Fame and Wealth
Above the drooping Patients' Health.

Some valient Gen'rals fought the Foe;
Others took Bribes to let them go.
7. Gillies' *Aristotle*, II:42-43.

8. Adams's very rough translation of one of the many bitter complaints of Theognis that "wealth is wont to mix the breed" and corrupt the pure blood of lords, goes as follows: "Nobility in men is worth as much as it is in horses, asses, or rams; but the meanest blood puppy in the world, if he gets a little money is as good a man as the best of them." John Adams to Thomas Jefferson, July 9, 1813. *Writings of Thomas Jefferson* (Memorial ed.), (Washington, D.C., 1903-1904), XIII:306 (hereafter referred to as *Works* [Mem. ed.]).

9. Glotz, *Ancient Greece at Work*, 71-72.

10. See Glotz on the final embodiment of the idea of the State in a divine right King, when contact with barbarians added to the incessant conflicts of city against city, and class against class finally forced reintegration of society on a new level. "For a long time the system-builders, Xenophon, Plato, Socrates, had called in the their writings or looked in real life for the good tyrant who should undertake to make justice reign. They were prophets. Monarchy appeared as a necessity, to hold together the opposing classes; to govern the relations between different races, and to define the rights and mark the place. On the King, the son of God, fell the superhuman mission of arbitrating the destinies of men. The State enjoyed omnipotence in order to organize society." Glotz, *Ancient Greece at Work*, 319.

11. *Federalist*, IX.

12. David Hume, *Essays and Treatises on Several Subjects* (Dublin: 1779), I:423-424. "Of the Populousness of Ancient Nations." The original edition of the *Essays* was published at London, 1752.

13. Hume's footnote BB, *Essays*, I:557. Adams' transcription of it is to be found in *Works*, VI:286-287.

14. John Adams, *Works*, VI:287.

15. Gillies' *Aristotle*, II:282.

16. *Federalist*, X. It should be noted that Aristotle was not the first political writer to stress the interplay of economics and politics. Plato, for example, had the theme in various parts of *The Republic;* see his remark in Book IV that every existing state, for practical purposes, "consists of many states, and is not one...for there are always in them two parties at war with each other, the poor and the rich;" also see the statement in Book VIII that the city containing an oligarchy "is not one, but of necessity two [cities]; one consisting of the poor, and the other of the rich, dwelling in one place, and always plotting against each other." Translation of H. Spens (Glasgow: 1763), 140 and 327.

The earliest economic interpretations of history in the writings of Englishmen seem to be as closely related to Plato's *Republic* as to Aristotle's *Politics*; cf. Thomas More's designation of European states of this day as "conspiracies of rich men" in *Utopia*, and note the title Henry Neville's *Plato Redivivus or Dialogues Concerning Government* (London: 1681), a typical product of the 17th century "balance of property school, best known through the *Oceana* of James Harrington, Neville's close friend and political associate.

17. Gillies' *Aristotle*, II:180. Compare Madison's statement in *Federalist*, X: "...no man is allowed to be a judge in his own cause, because his interest would certainly bias his judgment, and not improbably corrupt his integrity.

18. Madison to James Monroe, Oct. 5, 1786, *Letters*, I:250-251. Both

Madison and Aristotle believed in justice as an attribute of the moral order of the
universe; see the latter's summary of the *Nichomachean Ethics* in *Politics,* II:8,
commencing, "every science and every art proposes to itself some end or
purpose which it considers as absolutely good and ultimately desirable, that is
good and desirable in itself without reference to the attainment of any object
beyond it. Of politics the most comprehensive and the most important of all
sciences, the end and aim is the public good of the community, which can only
be upheld in justice, which, as we said before, forms the great law of the moral
world. To a certain length, the general opinions of mankind coincide, respecting
justice, with the accurate decisions of philosophy." Closely related to this ideal
of justice as a quality of the universe, is the Aristotelian concept of reason: the
means by which men understand and obey the dictates of universal justice.

Roland Bainton has pointed out parallel assumptions that lay back of the
eighteenth century cult of reason (see his "The Appeal to Reason" in *The
Constitution Reconsidered* [New York: 1938]). See also Ralph Gabriel's
discussion of the prevalence of the belief in an overruling moral order in
American history: *The Course of American Democratic Thought*, (New York:
1939), especially Ch. II. Gabriel's book is concerned mainly with the 19th
century when the idea of the moral order in the U.S. was loaded with a
Protestant supernaturalism. The concept as utilized by the Founding Fathers,
who overwhelming took a Deistic view of God and Nature, is in many ways
closer to the naturalistic Rationalism of the Aristotelian order than it is to the
concept Gabriel discusses.

19. Gillies' *Aristotle*, II:171.

20. Gillies' italics.

21. Gillies' *Aristotle*, II:179-180.

22. Certain nineteenth century students found it so illogical, however, that
they insisted on reading into Madison a streamlined dogma of determinism:
Daniel de Leon, *James Madison and Karl Marx* (New York: 1932) for an
extreme example of this (1st ed. in 1889).

23. *Federalist*, X, Madison, always the good republican, makes haste to
add: "it could not be less folly to abolish liberty, which is essential to political
life, because it nourishes faction, than it would be to wish the annihilation of air,
which is essential to animal life, because it imparts to fire its destructive
agency."

In 1829 he was still linking faction to republican governments: "No free
country has ever been without parties, which are a natural offspring of freedom."
Memorandum labeled; "Notes on Suffrage, written at different periods after his
retirement from public life," Madison, *Letters*, IV, 24.

24. *Federalist*, X. The issuance of paper money was considered by many as
a device operating purely and simply as a debt destroyer. See Col. Grayson's
letter to Madison, March, 1786. "The Ancients were surely men of more candor
than We are; they contended openly for an abolition of debts in so many Words,
while we strive as hard for the same thing under the decent & specious pretense
of a circulating medium. Montesquieu was not wrong when he said the
democratical might be as tyrannical as the despotic, for where is there a greater

act of despotism than that of issuing paper to depreciate for the purpose of paying debts, on easy terms." Printed in Madison, *Writings*, II:403 n.

25. John Adams, *Works*, IV:285. The original of the quotation can be found in Thucydides, II:81. The translation is by William Smith, published 1753. Jefferson owned this translation as well as that of Thomas Hobbes.

Adams also included in his quotation the memorable passage beginning: "Words lost their signification; brutal rashness was fortitude; prudence, cowardice; modesty, effeminacy; and being wise in every thing, to be good for nothing; the hot temper was manly valor; calm deliberation, plausible knavery; he who boiled with indignation, was trustworthy; and he who presumed to contradict, was ever suspected. Connection of blood was less regarded than transient acquaintance; associations were not formed for mutual advantage, consistent with law, but for rapine against all law; trust was only communication of guilt; revenge was more valued than never to have suffered an injury; perjuries were master-pieces of cunning; the dupes only blushed, the villains most impudently triumphed."

26. Jefferson, *Writings* (Mem. ed.). To Monroe, August 28, 1785.

27. Jefferson, *Writings* (Mem. ed), V:395. To George Wythe, August 13, 1986.

28. There were mobs and less serious riots in Connecticut and New Hampshire, as well as in Massachusetts.

29. Jefferson, *Writings* (Mem. ed.), VI:30. To Mr. Carmichael, Dec. 26, 1786. Writing to Madison on Jan 30, Jefferson says he is impatient to learn his "sentiments on the late troubles... So far as I have yet seen, they do not appear to threaten serious consequences. Those States have suffered by the stoppage of the channels of their commerce... This must render money scarce, and make the people uneasy. This uneasiness has produced acts absolutely unjustifiable; but I hope they will provoke no severities from their governments. A consciousness of those in power that their administration...has been honest, may, perhaps, produce too great a degree of indignation; and those characters, wherein fear predominates over hope, may apprehend too much from these instances of irregularity. They may conclude too hastily, that nature has formed man insusceptible of any other government than that of the force, a conclusion not founded in truth nor experience... To have an idea of the curse of existence under...[a government of force] they must be seen. It is a government of wolves over sheep." Ibid., VI:64-65.

30. George Richards Minot, *The History of the Insurrections in Massachusetts in the Year MDCCLXXXVI and the Rebellion Consequent thereon* (Boston: 1810). This is the second edition; the first was published in 1788. Minot, while a conservative Boston lawyer, produced an eminently fair and non-partisan study. For this background and career see S. Morison's biography in the D.A.B.

31. Robert A. East, "The Massachusetts Conservatives in the Critical Period," in *The Era of the American Revolution* (New York: 1939), R.B. Morris, ed.

32. They believed that the article in the Massachusetts Bill of Rights— included when John Adams set up that beautifully balanced constitution—

giving "the people...a right in an orderly and peaceable manner to assemble; and to request of the legislative body, by way of addresses, petitions, or remonstrances, redress of the wrongs done them, and of the grievances they suffer" justified their actions. For the closing of the courts was to continue only while they waited for the legislature to act—and constituted a rough and ready substitute for an injunction in equity, freezing the status quo until some sort of legal accommodation could be reached. See Minot, *History*, 24. Their misjudgment lay in supposing that the legislature, dominated as it was by the conservatives, would reconsider its fiscal policy (which undoubtedly aggravated the financial crisis) and do anything to relieve their distress as debtors.

It should be remembered that judgment against a debtor in the eighteenth century put his person as well as his property in jeopardy. As one of the rebel petitioners noted, "the present expensive mode of collecting debts, which by reason of the great scarcity of cash, will thereby a reputable body of people rendered incapable of being serviceable either to themselves or the community." Minot, *History*, 82.

33. Minot, *History*, 81. After the rebellion had been put down there were a few scattered cases of the rick-burning and cattle-maiming.

34. The adjective is from James Truslow Adams' biography of Daniel Shays in the *Dictionary of American Biography*. See the bibliography included there for the movement as a whole. McMaster's *History*, I, contains numerous quotations from contemporary newspaper accounts of the riots.

35. Actually only one real skirmish took place, and this after the back of the rebellion had been broken. Col. John Ashley with 80 militia caught up with an equal number of rebels in Sheffield, Berkshire County, on February 26, 1787. The "rebels began a scattering fire at a distance"; for six minutes, before they fled, the rebels held their ground and succeeded in killing one and wounding another militiaman. "In addition to this loss," Minot continues, "ought to be reckoned, that of two amiable young men and intimate friends, whose habits of body were unequal to enduring the fatigue of the rapid march which this party performed, who after languishing under the effects of their exertions died with peculiar marks of sympathetic grief for each other." Minot, *History*, 149-150.

The "attack" of January 25 on Springfield arsenal by the 800 men led by Shays can hardly be called a skirmish. The rebels marched "to which 250 yards of the arsenal," and announced "that they would have possession of the barraks." General Shepherd, by messenger, warned them "that if they approached nearer they would be fired upon. To this, one of their leaders replied that was all they wanted; and they advanced one hundred yards further." Shepherd then ordered two shots to be fired over their heads, and, this not stopping their advance, opened with his artillery on their column. "A cry of murder arose from the rear of the insurgents, and their whole body was thrown into the utmost confusion." Shays attempted to rally them, but to no avail. They fled to Ludlow, ten miles away, leaving three dead and one wounded on the field. Shepherd's handling of the affair was brilliant. He could have killed many more of the insurgents during their disorderly flight, but his object "was rather to terrify than to destroy." Minot, *History*, 111-112. This description, I feel, applies equally to the purpose of the insurgents.

36. Compare his letter to Jefferson of Oct. 24, 1787, in which he comments on the "encroachments" on property rights by the democratic legislatures the "injustice" of which "were so frequent and so flagrant as to alarm the most steadfast friends of Republicanism. I am persuaded that I do not err in saying that the evils issuing from these sources contributed more to that uneasiness which produced the Convention...than those which accrued to our national character and interest from the inadequacy of the Confederation to its immediate objects." Madison, *Letters*, I:350.

37. Debate of June 6; *Documents*, 161-163.

38. *Documents*, 94.

39. East's study of Shays' rebellion makes it clear that its main significance lay in its use by the conservatives as the basis of a brilliant propaganda program. He insists that "the larger importance of the disturbances...is that they played into the hands of the strong nationalists, who used them as arguments to drive the more complacent conservatives, against their earlier distress and fears, into accepting a plan to reconsider the powers of the Federal union. The drift of the conservative purpose and interest thus affords a study more revealing of the inner meaning of the so-called Critical Period in Massachusetts than do the activities per se of the "Reverend" Samuel Ely, the sturdy Captain Shays, and other colorful disturbers of the peace." *Loc cit.,* 349.

I am inclined to enter one caveat against the conclusions of East's brilliant article. By implication (rather than forthright statement) this stress on the Massachusetts conservatives' "purpose" makes their arguments for stronger government seem consciously cynical and dishonest—a tactically brilliant intellectual frame-up. There is an element of truth in this interpretation; some of the publicists who were screaming about social anarchy in 1787 were indeed deliberate in their manipulating of public opinion with horror stories which they knew were fake. One Benjamin Hickborn, for instance, could write to General Knox stating: "I am afraind the Insurgents will be conquered too soon." (quoted in East, *op cit.*, 384). Also Knox' letters to Washington, the basis of his estimate of the affair, were disingenuous to say the least. Most of the conservatives seem to have honestly misjudged, with erudite stupidity, the limited aims and political impotence of the Shays movement. In a panic for their private property and social peace, they recalled their lessons in the classics, which appeared now to be pointing surely to a repetition of the shambles at Cocyra. Most of their effectiveness as propagandists in fooling others was a result of the fact that they had first fooled themselves.

40. Debate June 2, *Documents*, 143.

41. Outline of a speech delivered June 9, *Ibid.*, 887. Neither Madison or Yates report this point in transcribing Paterson's long speech of that day against the advisability of a consolidated government. The memo continues: "it may shew, that our particular Systems are wrong—that our Instns. are too pure—not sufficiently removed from the state of Nature to answer the purposes of a State of Society—will not militate agst. the democratick Principle when properly regulated and modified.—The democratick spirit beats high—"

42. Debate of June 9th, *Documents*, 181.

43. John C. Hamilton, *History of the Republic of the U.S. of America, as*

Traced in the Writings of Alexander Hamilton and His Contemporaries (New York, 1859), III:275.

44. Pierce's characterization as a whole is most interesting. "Colo. Hamilton is deservedly celebrated for his talents. He is a practitioner of the Law, and reputed to be a finished Scholar. To a clear and strong judgment he unites the ornaments of fancy, and whilst he is able, convincing, and engaging in his eloquence the Heart and head sympathize in approving him. Yet there is something too feeble in his voice to be equal to the strains of oratory—it is my opinion that he is rather a convincing Speaker that [than] a blazing Orator. Colo. Hamilton requires time to think—[then follows the quotation *supra.*]. His language is not always equal, sometimes didactic like Bolingbroke's, at others light and tripping like Sterne's. His eloquence is not so defusive as to trifle with the senses, but he rambles just enough to strike and keep up the attention. He is about 33 years old, of small stature, and lean. His manners are tinctured with a stiffness, and sometimes a degree of vanity that is highly disagreeable." Pierce's "Characters," *Documents*, 98-99.

45. Debate, June 18th, *Documents*, 215.

46. J.C. Hamilton, *History*, III:275-283.

47. J.C. Hamilton, *History*, III:284.

48. "Hamilton's Outline," J.C. Hamilton, *History*, III:276.

49. "The great & essential principles necessary for the support of Government," Hamilton believed were,

I. Interest to support it.

II. Opinion of utility of and necessity.

III. Habitual sense of obligation.

IV. Force.

V. Influence.

Madison reports that Hamilton was careful to explain that by "influence" he did not mean corruption, but a dispensation of those regular honors & emoluments, which produce an attachment to the Govt. *Documents*, 217

50. Yates' report, *Documents*, 778. This is one of the sections of Hamilton's speech where Madison fails to make it clear that the Virginia plan as well as the New Jersey plan is being castigated.

51. Madison's report, *Documents*, 218. Hamilton's outline reads

"Experience corresponds.

"Grecian republics.

"Demosthenes says—Athens seventy three years—

Lacedaemon twenty seven—Thebans after battle of Leuctra.

"Phocians—consecrated ground—Philip &c.

"Germanic Empire.

"Charlemagne and his successors.

"Diet-recesses.

"Electors now seven, excluding others.

"Swiss Cantons.

"Two Diets.

"Opposite Alliances.

"Berne—Lucerne."

An examination of *Federalist*, XVIII, makes it clear that the number of years after Athens, Sparta, Thebes, refers to the period that each of these states dominated the Amphyctonic League: "The more powerful members tyrannized successfully over all the rest. Athens as we learn from Demosthenes, was the arbiter of Greece seventy-three years. The Lacedemonians next governed it twenty-nine years at a subsequent period after the battle of Leuctra, the Thebans has their turn of domination." This number of the *Federalist* was written cooperatively by Madison and Hamilton (as were XIX, XX). It is possible by examining the memoranda in which their research in ancient and modern history have been preserved to attribute with confidence almost every paragraph in these numbers to one or the other's authorship. Use of the same technique makes it possible to show that *Federalist*, LXIII, which was claimed by both Hamilton and Madison, in all liklihood was written by the latter. At some future date I expect to enter that long controverted field of all the disputed numbers of the *Federalist* and show from internal evidence that Madison was probably correct in claiming them.

52. Yates' report, *Documents*, 779.

53. Hamilton's Outline reads: "League offensive defensive, &c.—Particular governments might exert themselves, &c.—But liable to the usual vicissi[tudes] —Internal peace affected.—Proximity of situation—natural enemies.—Partial confederacies from unequal extent.—Power inspires ambition.—Weakness begets jealousy.—Western territory." J.C. Hamilton, *History*, III:279.

54. *Federalist*, IV.

55. Montesquieu, *The Spirit of the Laws*, book, XX, ch. 2. "Of the Spirit of Commerce."

56. *Federalist*, VI. An examination of the middle section Hamilton's outline of his speech and the VI, VII, VIII, IX, XI, numbers of the *Federalist* show that the same points were covered in each. It seems safe to assume that the latter were a reproduction of material he had carefully worked up for his great effort in the convention. It should be remembered, however, that in Philadelphia the purpose was to prove that no Constitution based on the Virginia plan would remedy that situation, while in the Federalist he was arguing that such a Constitution would serve.

57. J.C. Hamilton, *History*, III:279.

58. *Federalist*, VI.

59. *Federalist*, VI. The outline of Hamilton's speech (which agrees with this number of the Federalist in every detail except the latter's discussion of Holland, where the speech treated of the Hanseatic League) reads: "GENIUS of republics pacific.—Answer. Jealousy of commerce as well as jealousy of power, begets war.—Sparta—Athens—Thebes—Rome—Carthage—royal wars.—Lewis XIV.—*Austria*—Bourbons—William and Anne.—Wars depend on trifling circumstances.—Where—Dutchess of Marlborough's glove—Foreign conquest. —Dismemberment—Poland.—Foreign influence.—Distractions set afloat vicious humors.—Standing armies by dissentions." J.C. Hamilton, *History*, 279.

Federalist, VI covers topics through "Duchess of Marlborough's glove"; *Federalist*, VII treats the topics through "vicious humors," developing the idea that the clash of interests of the disunited states will breed war and serve as an opportunity for foreign intervention; *Federalist*, VIII prophecies the inevitable rise of standing armies among the states for protection against each other and foreign nations if a strong union is not set up.

60. *Federalist*, IX.

61. Hamilton's outline reads: "Domestic factions—Montesquieu," and an examination of *Federalist*, IX shows the connection; for the latter half of this number quotes at length from *The Spirit of the Laws*, book IX, ch. I, which is entitled "In What Manner Republics provide for their Safety." Montesquieu points out that "If a republic be small, it is destroyed by a foreign force; if it be large it is ruined by an internal imperfection," but by contriving some sort of "confederate republic" it is possible to combine "all the internal advantages of republican, together with the external force of a monarchical, government." Specifically treating of the question of domestic factions; "Should a popular insurrection happen in one of the confederate states, the others are able to quell it. Should abuses creep into one part, they are reformed by those that remain sound." The main example of a "stupendous fabric" that lasted for ages in spite of its "free principles" adduced by Montesquieu is in this chapter on Rome.

Now as is often the case with Montesquieu's great grab-bag of a book, this chapter from book IX contradicts a statement made five pages earlier that "it is natural for a republic to have only a small territory, otherwise it cannot long subsist" (book VIII, ch. 16). We find moreover that Hamilton uses book IX in the *Federalist* both to make his point about "factions" and to scotch a political heresy which Brearly and Paterson had argued for on June 9th in the convention: that the large states be divided up to make equal republics of small territory. So we can assume that as he worked over this section of his speech with its two-pronged argument Hamilton reread book VIII of Montesquieu which he was attempting to refute. Now chapter 14 of book VIII contains a long discussion of the stability of Carthage and Rome, commencing: "Aristotle mentions the city of Carthage as a well regulated republic."

We cannot be sure that Hamilton went back to Aristotle to check out at the fountainhead on this point: but we know that Madison did. And there, in book II of the *Politics* he discovered that, "Though its origin remounts to a very ancient date, and though for many centuries it has contained within its bosom a numerous and a free people, yet Carthage has never, to the present day, experience any one sedition worthy of record, nor has it ever endured for a moment the cruel yoke of a tyrant" (Gillies' *Aristotle*, 115). Aristotle's detailed description of Carthage is part of a comparison of that state with Crete and Sparta. In Madison's "Memorandum for the Convention of Virginia in 1788" (Madison, *Letters*, I:394-395) is a synopsis of Aristotle's book II, ch. 7-8, with one incidental citation of Polybius added. It commences, "Carthage. 500 years, says Aristotle, without any considerable sedition or tyrant," and includes a careful breakdown of the divisions of government, tenure of magistrates, size of senate, etc., etc., for Carthage and for Sparta. Madison's Memo leaves out Crete; but he adds a long account of the Roman government based on Cicero, Middleton's *Life of Cicero*, Gibbon, Vertot, and Felice's *Code d'Humanité* which Jefferson had sent him from Paris. *Federalist*, LXIII which has been attributed by some commentators to Hamilton, is an obvious elaboration by Madison of his memorandum. Discussing the need for a senate he writes: "It adds no small weight to all these considerations, to recollect that history informs us no long-lived republic which had not a Senate. Sparta, Rome, and Carthage are, in fact, the only states to whom that character can be applied." It is possible that Madison had Aristotle open before him as he wrote this; for Crete, missing in his memorandum, reappears again in the careful six-page analysis of these admirably stable states which had remedied by their constitution the vices of republicanism.

62. Hamilton's outline. J.C. Hamilton, *History*, III:280.

63. Madison's notes, *Documents*, 220-221; Yates reports: "I believe that British government forms the best model the world ever produced, and such has been its progress in the minds of the many, that this truth gradually gains ground. This government has for its object *public strength* and *individual security*. It is said with us to be unattainable. If it was once formed it would maintain itself." *Documents*, 781.

64. "The general government must, in this case, not only have a strong soul, but *strong organs*, by which that soul is to operate.

"Here I shall give my sentiments of the best form of government—not as a thing attainable by us, but as a model which we ought to approach as near as possible.

"British constitution best form.

"Aristotle—Cicero—Montesquieu—Neckar." Hamilton's outline, J.C. Hamilton, *History*, III:280.

Hamilton's quotation from Neckar is given by Madison, above in the text.

Montesquieu's famous description of the British Constitution is to be found in *Spirit of the Laws*, book XI, ch. 6.

Hamilton's citation of Cicero undoubtedly refers to the passage from *De Republica*: "*Statuo esse optime constituam rem publicam, quae extribus generibus illis, regali, optimo, et populari, modice confusa*," II:69. [I hold that the best constituted state is one which is formed by the due combination of the three simple types, monarchy, aristocracy, and democracy, and which does not arouse a wild and untamed spirit (in its citizens) by punishing... Translation by George Holland Sabine and Stanley Barney Smith in *On the Commonwealth* (New York: Macmillan, 1976), 175-176.] This fragment was one of the several known to the eighteenth century through its preservation in Augustine's *City of God*. Hamilton, if he read John Adams' *Defence* would have found it quoted there. *Works*, IV:295.

Aristotle, the inventor of the term "mixed government" appropriated by eulogists of the British Constitution, discusses its form and character in book VI, ch. 9 of the *Politics*. Gillies, in his introduction to book VI, points out that "Nothing can be added to the copiousness and perspicuity with which he [Aristotle] explains under what circumstances democratical and oligarchical laws are to be...blended in one truly political and salutary institution." Gillies as a Briton did not fail to add as a special recommendation to all Britons that, "There is pleasure not be expressed but which every friend to his country must warmly feel," in discovering that Aristotle's criteria of the constitution of a good state "are more applicable to the government established in this island, than to any other which history exhibits." Gillies' *Aristotle*, II:276.

65. Yates' report, *Documents*, 781; cf. Madison's report: "In every community where industry is encouraged, there will be a division into the few & the many. Hence separate interests will arise. There will be debtors & creditors &c."

66. Madison's notes; Hamilton's outline reads: "If government in the hands of the few, they will tyrannize over the many.

"If [*in*] the hands of the many, they will tyrannize over the few. It ought to be in the hands of both; and they should be separated.

"This separation must be permanent." J.C. Hamilton, *History*, III:280.

67. "There used to be, and still is in some countries, a law of mortmain or the dead hand under which it was not the living but the dead who determine the use and ownership of property. The dead man's hand was always being stretched out of the grave to control the holding of land, the sowing of fields, the building of houses. It requires but little knowledge of history to recognize that there is also psychological law of the dead hand.... There can be no understanding of history, of politics, or of the effects of communal psychology which does not take into consideration the tremendous influence of this psychological dead hand, the dead mind. At every particular moment it is the dead rather than the living who are making history, for politically individuals think dead men's thoughts and pursue dead men's ideals. Very often these are not only the thoughts and aims of dead men, but are themselves dead and rotten; they may be the mere ghosts of beliefs, ideals from which time has sapped all substance and meaning." Leonard Woolf, *After the Deluge* (London: 1937), 30.

68. Jared Sparks, ed., *The Life of Gouverneur Morris with Selections from his Correspondence* (Boston: 1832), III: 216-217. To Aaron Ogden, Dec. 28, 1804. Morris added, however, "when our population shall have reached a certain extent, his [Hamilton's] system may be proper, and the people may then be disposed to adopt it; but under present circumstances they will not, neither would answer any valuable purpose." Morris with somewhat startling understatement concludes that even "an absolute, that is, an unmixed monarchy, would hardly last three lives" in America at that time.

69. There appears to be no reason to dispute his biographer Henry Cabot Lodge's conclusion that "his career as a public man had closed before his death"; but Hamilton never realized this. He himself explained in a paper written to justify his meeting with Burr, in spite of his ethical aversion to duelling and premonitions of disaster, his compelling motive; "The ability in to be in the future useful, whether in resisting mischief or effecting good, in those crises of our public affairs which seem likely to happen, would probably be inseparable from conformity with public prejudice in this particular." Quoted in H.C. Lodge, *Alexander Hamilton* (Boston: 1882), 280.

Chapter 5

The High Toned Government

What was this theory of the "balanced government" whose beauties so enchanted the mind of Alexander Hamilton that he would eventually wreck his political career and give his life in unavailing pursuit of it? In his speech of June 18th Hamilton had implied Aristotle's paternity; but in strict accuracy the Greek was only its godparent. Disciples of Aristotle, using materials from the *Politics*, were the first to formulate this theory of balanced government which had come down from antiquity to the eighteenth century. The Stagirites's divisions of government had followed the traditional scheme common in his own day: there were monarchies, aristocracies, and democracies; or governments respectively of the one, the few, and the many. To his threefold division of simple governments, he added as subheads their congruent corrupt forms, in which sovereignty lay either in the hands of the tyrannical one or the lawless few, or the tumultuous many. Aristotle, however, as we have seen, refused to halt his analogies with this catalogue of political forms in which the arrangement of offices formed the main basis for distinction. His concern with the social groups whose political potency made given political institutions work badly or well in a specific case, led him to consider the state not only as a formal legal structure, but also a social structure made up of occupational groups, and—most important of all —of economic classes. This twofold analysis of the state—into political agencies and classes united by economic interests—was used by Aristotle as the basis for an attempt to devise some form of government that would neutralize the unceasing class struggles in Greece between the exploiting and rich oligarchs and the plundering, poverty-stricken democrats. Aristotle's solution was the "mixed constitution," wherein political institutions characteristic of both democracies and oligarchies were judiciously combined, and under which the two social factors that are certain to count for something in every free state—the power of property, and the power of numbers

—could make limited and hence legitimate claims for political power. The principle of Aristotle's "mixed" state was balance, balance between the two great groups or factions in the Greek states, of his day: the rich and the poor whose mutually antagonistic interests, where either monopolized political power, guaranteed a class tyranny basically inimical to its rival.[1]

Aristotle's theory, part diagnosis of the disease which was killing the city-states of his day, and part prescription for it, was not used by contemporaries as a basis for action.[2] A hundred years later, however, Polybius was to seize on Aristotle's discussion, join it to the traditional sixfold classification of the simple governments with their corrupted forms, add a rigid doctrine of cyclical evolution in history and use this hybrid hypothesis to explain in what manner, and through what kind of government almost the whole habitable world, in less than the course of fifty-three years, was reduced to the Roman yoke.[3] And with Polybius mixed government becomes the mixed government that Alexander Hamilton was to argue for: a threefold blend of the one, with the few, and the many.

Those members of the Constitutional Convention who had forgotten the lines of Polybius they had studied in school would have found John Adams' fat volume on government a ready source of reference. For Adams, as intent as Alexander Hamilton in seeing that his country achieved the correct sort of balance, led off the section of his book in which he assembled "the opinions and reasonings of philosophers, politicians, and historians, who have taken the most extensive views of men and societies, whose characters are deservedly revered,"[4] with lengthy excerpts from Polybius' sixth book on peculiar advantages of the Roman Constitution.

In these quotations selected by Adams—they include almost the whole of two chapters from the original—Polybius presents his most important modification of the earlier theory of mixed government. This thesis states that by an iron law of political necessity all three of the simple forms of government must deteriorate from good to bad, to a different form of good, to bad, and so on, through an interminable cycle. From "necessity and the laws of nature...every form of government that is simple, by soon degenerating into that vice that is allied to it, and naturally attends it, must be unstable. For as rust is the natural bane of iron, and worms of wood, by which they are sure to be destroyed, so there is a certain vice implanted by the hand of nature in every simple form of government, and by her ordained to accompany it. The vice of kingly government is monarchy; that of aristocracy, oligarchy; and of democracy, *rage and violence;* into which all of them, process of time, must necessarily degenerate."[5]

This was the law of decay according to Polybius. Hinted at before his time by both Plato and Aristotle, it had never been stated with such precision. And to it Polybius joined the supplementary theory that the degeneration of the simple governments caused one form to run into another in a closed circle of never-ending revolutions.

Nor did John Adams fail to include this interesting hypothesis of the dynamics of revolution in his monitory publication of 1787. Working with scissors and paste-pot he made sure that Americans would take notice of what the *"grave, judicious, excellent"* Polybius had discovered two thousand years earlier, and had presented in his cyclical theory of political history. Polybius had asked, "From whence do governments originally spring? From the weakness of men, and the consequent necessity to associate; and he who excels in strength and courage, gains the command and authority over the rest; as among inferior animals...the strongest are by common consent, allowed to be masters."[6] Here was the origin of kingly government; and for an indeterminate length of time Polybius believed, the royal family would govern with justice and honor. Inevitable decay would eventually do its work, however. Then the King's "posterity, succeeding to the government by right of inheritance...were led by superfluity to indulge their appetites, and to imagine that it became princes to appear in a different dress, to eat in a more luxurious manner, and enjoy without contradiction, the forbidden pleasures of love. The first produced envy, the other resentment and hatred. By which means kingly government degenerated into tyranny." This tyranny in time produced its own cure. The nobility—"persons of the most generous, exalted and enterprising spirit"—drove out the royal family and became rulers in their turn, setting up a just and moderate aristocracy.

The political drama accordingly opened its second act. The sons and grandsons of the original *aristoi*, forgetful of their fathers' public spirit, gradually "giving themselves up to avarice...to intemperance, and...to the abuse of women," are banished or killed in their turn by the outraged people; and the evil oligarchy gives way to the moderate democracy. Then the routine commences again. For a while the people look upon "equality and liberty" as the greatest of blessings. But when a new race of men grows up, these, no longer regarding equality and liberty, from being accustomed to them, aim at a greater share of power than the rest, particularly those of the greatest fortunes, who, grown now ambitious, and being unable to attain the power they aim at by their own merit, dissipate their wealth in alluring and corrupting the people by every method; and when, to serve their wild ambition, they have once taught them to receive bribes and entertainments, from that moment the democracy is at an end and changes to force and violence. For the people, accustomed to live at the expense of others, and to place their hopes of a support in the fortunes of their neighbors, if headed by a man of a great and enterprising spirit, will then have recourse to violence, and getting together will murder, banish, and divide among themselves the lands of their adversaries till, grown wild with rage, they again find a master and a monarch.

"This is the rotation of governments, and this the order of nature, by which they are changed, transformed, and return to the same point of the circle."[7] And this was the Polybian cycle from which there was no escape either in ancient Greece or in modern America, so long as men set up the simple governments, whether monarchy, aristocracy, or democracy.

The belief of Alexander Hamilton and the other educated leaders of 1787 that all men in all ages were driven by essentially the same passions made this theory of Polybius something more than an interesting excursion into dead history. "Human nature," Adams argued in recalling the bloody massacre in the ancient city-states, "is as incapable now of going through revolutions with temper and sobriety, with patience and prudence, or without fury and madness, as it was among the Greeks so long ago... Without three orders, and an effectual balance between them, in every American constitution, it must be destined to frequent unavoidable revolutions; though they are delayed a few years, they must come in time. The United States are large and populous nations, in comparison with the Grecian common-wealths and they are growing every day more disproportionate, and therefore less capable of being held together by simple governments... Countries that increase in population so rapidly...are not to be long bound with silken threads; lions, young or old, will not be bound by cobwebs. It would be better for America, it is nevertheless agreed, to ring all the changes with the whole set of bells, and go through all the revolutions of the Grecian States, rather than establish an absolute monarchy..."[8] But from the conclusions of Polybius, John Adams well knew that America was not limited to the choice between an absolute despot and entrance into the vicious cycle. The one sure way to escape from the endless circle of revolts occurring in simple governments was to set up a mixed government which was compound-ed of all three types.

Polybius gave the credit for the invention of the golden panacea in politics to Sparta's great legislator Lycurgus. For "Lycurgus to avoid the inconveniences [of the change-ringing cycle of revolution in simple constitutions], formed his government not of one sort, but

united in one all the advantages and properties of the best governments; to the end that no branch of it, by swelling beyond its due
bounds, might degenerate into the vice which is congenial to it; and
that, while each of them were mutually acted upon by *opposite
powers*, no one part might incline any way, or *outweigh* the rest; but
that the commonwealth being equally *poised* and *balanced*, like a *ship*
"or a *wagon*,"9 acted upon by *contrary powers*, might long remain in
the same situation; while the king was restrained from excess by the
fear of the people, who had a proper share in the commonwealth;
and, on the other side, the people did not dare disregard the king,
from their fear of the senate, who, being all elected for their virtue,
would always incline to the justest side; by which means, that branch
which happened to be oppressed became always superior, and by the
accessional weight of the senate, *outbalanced* the other."10 This
system of political stations, Polybius believed, had provided the
Spartans with a free and stable state; the Romans, through accidental
development had achieved a like hybrid form.11 In both Sparta and in
Rome the irreconcilable struggles between the classes of the one, and
the few, and the many, had been meliorated. "It is not possible,"
Polybius argued therefore, "to invent a more perfect system," than
this of the balanced government.

There is something so aesthetically satisfying in the logical
neatness of the balanced system by which Polybius extracted a good
government from his vicious cycle of bad constitutions that one can
understand why the theory would find strong partisans from Cicero,12
through Machiavelli,13 down to John Adams and Alexander Hamilton.
The appeal was so great indeed, that practically all the major and
minor prophets of the mixed system overlooked the fact that
Polybius was merely praising the matchless Roman constitution under
pretense of describing it. His analysis of the republican government of
Rome, made in the first century before Christ, was every bit as
superficial as the similar analysis of the peerless British constitution
made by Montesquieu in the mid-eighteenth century.

This formula of Polybius, in comparison with Aristotle's earlier
theory, lacked any genuine insight into social organization as the basis
of politics. He touched, indeed, on a passing phase of the Roman
constitution; yet even there with but little penetration. For such
empirical observation as lay back of his cycle of revolutions was lifted
whole from the history of the Greek city-states, and did not fit the
development of the Roman constitution at all. Even the Polybian
balanced government, while logically far more consistent and tidily
articulated than Aristotle's confused discussion of the form, suffered
from historical inadequacy. The office of the tribune which already in

Polybius' own time had evolved into the most important magistracy of the people, simply could not be fitted into his scheme. Thus, even in throwing over Aristotle's complex version of mixed government[14] for an artificial balance of political powers, Polybius failed to exhibit synthetic ability of a very high order. Nevertheless it was his flashy system or variation of it that was to carry prestige down through the ages.

It is strange that the course of Roman history after the historian's death did not provoke more critical scrutiny of the theory. Cicero's praise of Rome's mixed government was the expression of a forlorn hope. The stability and permanency which the form was supposed to guarantee had already in his day vanished, and this futile discussion fully deserved the sour gibe of Tacitus, with his first hand knowledge of its failure to prevent despotism, that "a constitution compounded of these three simple forms, may in theory be beautiful, but can never exist in fact; or, if it should, it will be but of short duration."[15] Arthur Murphy, eighteenth-century translator of Tacitus, far from throwing over the theory merely insisted on a footnote qualification in accord with contemporary belief. Tacitus' opinion he argued, "has been long since refuted. The government of KING, LORDS, and COMMONS, has been the pride of Englishman, and the wonder of all Europe, during several centuries." The Roman critic of balance was mistaken "probably...because in all the popular governments then known in the world, the people acted in their collective body; and, with Polybius, Tacitus saw the fatal consequences. He had no idea of people acting by representation. It is that circumstance, and the wise regulations of our ancestors, that have made in this country *the according music of a well-mixed state*."[16] Murphy's distinction was the normal device used by eighteenth-century theorists to save the Polybian system as good as new in spite of its failure at Rome. Representation rather than direct participation of the many in government was the modern tonic which had vivified the ancient form and made it even more effectual than it had been in the days of Lycurgus.[17] The British government thus became the great exemplar of the theory's truth. And ironically enough, Tacitus himself was conscripted to show that the English balance, while not the result of the brilliant action of a single legislator like Solon, had a pedigree that stretched back to the day of the Anglo-Saxons and the Germanic hordes that overran Rome.[18]

Stanley Pargellis has brilliantly told the story of the appearance of the theory of balanced government in English politics at the time of the civil wars: its use as a compromise basis for the restoration in 1660, and the general belief prevailing throughout the eighteenth century that the balance achieved in 1688 was the main glory of the

Revolution settlement.[19] Without too much intellectual straining it was possible to equate the estates of King, Nobles, and Commons with classical categories of the one, the few, and the many; but the actual course of English history in the seventeenth and eighteenth centuries was such that it was quite difficult to view the real or fancied conflict between these estates in terms of the struggles between the rich and the poor. More and more as the eighteenth century advanced the tendency was to focus the theory on the governmental balances necessary to keep the tripartite balance of monarch and Parliament in London from destroying the liberty of the Nation. The idea of the balance of social classes so strong in Aristotle, still perceptible in Polybius, almost entirely disappeared in the writings of Bolingbroke, the most famous eighteenth-century English expounder of the system, whose view of the contemporary economic conflict was cast, not in terms of rich against the poor, but the landed versus the moneyed interest. With Montesquieu, the renowned French commentator on the British Constitution, the marvelous equilibrium achieved by the English ceases to be a blending of the forms of simple government necessary to provide social stability, and becomes a balance of the functions necessary in any government where political liberty is to be preserved.[20]

The peculiar elaboration of the theory of balanced power which was developed by admirers of the British Constitution can be explained in part by the political careers of Oliver Cromwell, James II, and John Locke. Cromwell provided Englishmen, in both the mother country and the colonies, with clear proof that a tyranny of self-proclaimed Saints would result from the unchecked dominance of a single branch of the legislature. James Stuart's attempt to establish executive despotism spiced with Popery had been halted, it would seem, in the nick of time. Recent English history seemed to demonstrate beyond question what the age-old theorists had claimed; the Constitution could survive only if government was held in a delicate equipoise by equal powers jealously teetering. The struggle between the few and the many, however, could on the basis of historical experience be translated into the conflict of the few as the rulers against the many as the ruled.

It was "the great Mr. Locke," self-appointed apologist for the glorious Revolution of 1688, who crystallized, with deceptive clarity, the idea held by an increasing number of Englishmen: that every government, whatever its form, tends to operate in an antisocial direction against the real interests of the governed. And it was his argument that the balance necessary to preserve freedom from this antisocial appetite inherent in all government was a constitutional balance—or separation—of legal powers. Dialectical necessity impelled Locke, as he marshalled the arguments which would "maintain" the right of King William on his new throne, to deny the classical assumption for centuries associated with the mixed government theory that "the people" were perpetually intent on aggrandizing themselves at the expense of the one, or the few. The people, he insisted, are not potential revolutionaries; they are characterized by conservation and political inertia.[21] With a bland disregard of recent history, Locke charged the Stuarts with being the sole disturbers of domestic tranquility. The real threat of revolution and disorder in any state was from magistrates forgetful of their trust. Locke was very sure that the magistrate to be especially wary of was the prince; for by his very position every king has "the forces, treasure, and offices of state to employ...he alone is in a condition to make great advances toward such changes [tyranny] under pretence of lawful authority, and has it in his hands to terrify or suppress opposers, as factious, seditious and enemies to the government; whereas no other part of the legislature, or people is capable by themselves to attempt any alteration of the legislative."[22] As Locke did his sleight of hand performance with the concepts of natural rights, contract, government as a trust, the danger of one economic class of people in society invading the property rights of another class, practically disappears; in prose of which the persuasive lucidity concealed many of the ambiguities, Locke set it down that the primary problem of establishing good government was to organize it so the governors were controlled and limited from injuring the governed.[23]

As was inevitable, the Lockian solution of this problem catalogues the expedients by which Englishmen curbed the unlucky Stuarts and established parliamentary supremacy in England. With a glance backward to the days of the Star Chamber and the more recent judicial decisions handed down by Judge Jeffreys it was insisted that the King should not have it in his power to put pressure on the courts to guarantee legal interpretations that were all too specifically in a partisan sense, "the King's justice." Let the judiciary be separated from the executive; keep the judges independent by protecting their tenure in office, no matter how unsatisfactory their decisions are to the crown. Let the executive, also, be separated from [the] Legislature. Efficiency requires that the monarch head the army which can operate only under a hierarchical form; but Parliament must keep control of the purse with the army's wages to insure that the armed forces will be used only to defend the nation, and not to conquer it. To make sure of having a commonwealth in which the state's power would not be turned against its citizens, Bills of Rights and Acts of Settlement must fence off certain areas from government in terference.[24] This triple balance of magistrates, cunningly woven into the very frame of government itself, *should* keep the machine running in such a way that liberty would flourish. If it did not—if the balance was broken sufficiently for any of the magistrates to establish a tyranny—Locke had yet another prescription to guarantee freedom. For if despite all the precautions of setting those who were trusted with political power at each other's throats so they would have little opportunity to turn that power against the people's rights—rulers nevertheless abandoned their trust and over-stepped the limits of their authority. Locke was prepared to justify the most potent of remedies —Revolution. The mild-mannered philosopher was prepared to argue that the majority of the people ought to rebel against any government that threatened their "lives, liberties, and estates," and then re-establish a new government under any form that would protect these natural rights.[25]

In Locke's writing the theory of the balance of power tags along well after the accomplished fact; in Montesquieu's *The Spirit of the Laws*, written half a century later, and based on Locke, the fact of English freedom is ascribed solely to the sovereign-remedy theory. "The British Constitution," as Madison noted, not without sarcasm,[26] "was to Montesquieu what Homer has been to the didactic writers of epic poetry. As the latter have considered the work of the immortal bard as the perfect model from which the principles and rules of the epic art were to be drawn, and by which all similar works to were to be judged, so this great political critic appears to have viewed the Constitution of England as the standard, or to use his own expression, as the mirror of political liberty."[27] Englishmen, so the great French writer believed, by separating the legislative, executive, and judicial powers, and by balancing these powers against each other, had actually achieved the dream of the Utopian legislators of the past. They had made of their island the "one nation there is...in the world that has for the direct end of its constitution political liberty."[28]

Montesquieu's doctrine of the separation of powers came to be accepted as dogma by all liberal constitution makers in the eighteenth century; but nowhere was their influence so great as in the British colonies in North America.[29] Just as in England the controversies between the common law courts and the crown, and the crown and the parliament had given concrete importance to the theory during Locke's lifetime, so the continual controversies between the colonial assemblies and royal governors in the period before 1776 made it possible for the Americans to conceive of it as the palladium of their liberties. As result any number of Bills of Rights and constitutions show unquestioned influence of the Frenchman's famous dictum.[30] And after the treaty of Paris in 1781, Montesquieu himself, if he had been alive, would have been forced to admit that insofar as political liberty was the equivalent of the separation of powers, England had lost her unique distinction of being the "one nation...in the world" where it prevailed. The thirteen American States had unanimously set up constitutions based on this principle; if the theory was correct, liberty would "appear in its highest perfection."

The operation of the American constitutions succeeded almost at once in demonstrating that the separation of powers as Montesquieu described it, and as it has always remained in England, was crossed by a contradictory principle. The powers were not equal powers; sovereignty actually was vested in the legislature.[31] Moreover, in America after the Revolution, the legislatures in many of the States were controlled by representatives of the "people," who behaved in a manner significantly different from "the people's" representatives in the British Parliament. In England the Commons had become the paramount organ of government; but election to that House and control of it had been taken over so exclusively by a hereditary aristocracy that no overt clash could embroil the many with the few.

In the United States, however, the State Legislatures showed a regrettable sympathy for the demands of the debt-ridden small farmer, as the issuance of paper money, passage of the legal tender acts, and stay-laws proved. The "rich and the well-born" could not help being disturbed at this unforeseen by-product of political liberty. They had justified their Independence from Britain on Lockian principles. The logic of their situation had necessitated that the Revolution be fought on the basis of the People's rights, popular sovereignty, and majority rule. They had followed the rules about balancing powers that Montesquieu had listed. Unfortunately now that the people's voice was being heard, its message was both unexpected and singularly unattractive. Perhaps they had not struck a true balance? Perhaps John Locke has been wrong in the use of his ill-defined term, "people."[32] Majority rule was all very well when it came to securing liberty from tyrant George III; but had majority rule actually guaranteed stability as well as liberty in other republican states? These were the questions that increasing numbers of Americans were asking after the depression of 1785. Since the "rich and well born" in America were also "well educated"—they preferred of course the adjective "wise"—and since the obvious republican history to turn to for guidance was to be found in the Greek and Roman authors, it was inevitable that Aristotle and Polybius, Thucydides and Cicero, would be combed for information bearing on the problem. And in the classics they rediscovered the balance of social classes which had lain concealed in such diluted form in the century-old English theory of balanced powers. Here in ancient "mixed government" theory was a balance designed primarily to give security to the rights of minorities as against what Madison termed "a majority...united by a common interest or passion." Here was precept and historical example in the writings of long dead classical authorities in which it would possible to qualify, modify, and redefine Lockian principles of popular sovereignty

Notes

1. Aristotle's own description of a mixed government makes this clear: "The nature of a mixed government, or what for distinction's sake we call a republic, will evidently appear by considering the elements of which it is composed. These are, oligarchy and democracy...[In it] wealth and numbers, that is, the prerogatives of the few, and the rights and liberties of the many, are duly respected and impartially maintained. The laws, therefore, adapted to a republic, must be formed by properly blending those which prevail in democracies and oligarchies. When, with regard to any one object, the respective laws of the distinct forms of polity are not incompatible with each other, both are to be employed, but a new law is to be framed holding a due middle between them; and when the oligarchic and democratic laws regulating any object, are both of them complex, and consist of many articles or clauses, some clauses are to be copied from the one, and some from the other... A well-mixed republic, then... must seem to be both, and neither; and it must subsist by internal vigour... Any form of commonwealth, good or bad, may be kept together by the impression of external force; but that form is good which flourishes by its native energy; for this can only take place, when each component part feels its own benefit intimately connected with the safety of the whole." Gillies' *Aristotle*, II:293-295.

2. Aristotle sadly admits that the mixed state which he praises "is, indeed, a rare phaenomenon. Of all those invested with power, one man alone, as far as history informs us, could be prevailed on to establish such a political arrangement; most other leaders, whether of the nobles or of the people, never contenting themselves with equality, but always aspiring to superiority, and alternately abusing their advantages for giving an undue preponderancy to their respective factions. In this fatal ambition they have been encouraged and confirmed by the leading states of Greece, which have always been solicitous to mould every neighboring republic after their own model. Blinded by passion, contending parties have been unable or unwilling, to perceive anything between the miserable alternative of commanding with insolence, or obeying with servility; and substantial happiness has therefore been almost constantly sacrificed to silly pride." Gillies' *Aristotle*, II:299. It is uncertain whether

Aristotle is referring to Clisthenes or Solon (both of Athens) as the single wise legislator who established a mixed government, Gillies argues for Solon.

3. Polybius, *The General History of the Wars of the Romans*, book I, ch. I. This is the Hampton translation which was owned by Jefferson.

4. John Adams, *Works*, IV:435.

5. John Adams, *Works*, IV:443, quoting from Polybius, VI:1. Adams' was the translation by Edward Spelman which was published as an appendix to his translation of the Roman Antiquities of Dionysius *Halicarnassensis* (London: 1758). Hampton's translation follows the more usual procedure of classifying monarchy as the legitimate form with tyranny its related opposite; but use "government of violence" and "government of the multitude" interchangeably for the opposite of democracy.

6. John Adams, *Works*, IV:441.

7. John Adams, *Works,* IV:441-443, quoting Spelman's Polybius, Book VI, ch. 1. It will be noted that the Polybian theory is untainted by any attempt at economic analysis but assumes as given the party of the many will be poor. There is not attempt on the Roman historian's part to tie his progression from government of the one to the few, to the many, and back to the one, to the rise of capitalism, as Aristotle had done. The cycle ending with the tyrant appeared in Greek history, upon which Polybius based his theory, mainly in the cities along the great trade routes generally at a time when increasing wealth and resulted in a condition of overt or suppressed class war. In the commercially backward areas, such as Arcadia, Boetia, and Thessaly, where such tensions did not arise, for the most part tyrannies did not appear. In Rome the influx of new wealth in the form of tribute rather than as the product of commerce was to operate to the same end.

Alfred Cobban in his *Dictatorship: Its History and Theory* (New York: 1939) while discussing the relationship of the Greek despot to aristocracies and democracies, throws interesting light on the Polybian circle. "Aristocracies were the natural enemies of any ambitious man, whether from within or without their own ranks, who desired to make himself a tyrant... Tyranny does not appear until the traditional monarchic and aristocratic authorities have either disappeared or are so weakened as to have lost their effective hold on the state. The republican principle with its ideal of equality among members of the citizen body, most—at least have become strong enough to challenge the traditional hereditary rulers, before tyranny is possible...it is an alternative to republicanism not to monarchy. This conclusion naturally follows from our earlier argument tracing the rise of tyranny to social instability. The collapse of the prestige of monarchy allows the conflict of interest between different classes in society to develop into a real class war; party strife becomes acute; and the opportunity then exists for ambitious politicians to build up their own power, by putting themselves at the head of one faction, or by making use of the general discontent." (320). Cobban, of course, holds no brief for the theory that dictatorship appears in given "stages" of a state's life, but stresses "conditions" which prevent or make for its appearance.

8. John Adams, *Works*, IV:287-288. Gouverneur Morris in 1804 was to use this same bell-ringing figure to prophesy what he feared to be the future of

America was a result of the Jeffersonian revolution. The election of 1800 had, he believed, brought the United States dangerously near the corruption of democracy, mob-rule, and hence into the cycle. Writing to his Federalist crony Aaron Ogden he argued: "America, my good friend, will at length learn some of those things, which an attentive study of the ancients long since taught you. The people of these United States will discover, that every kind of government is liable to evil. The best is that which has the fewest faults... In short, after ringing round the changes they will find, that there is a single alternative on which they must decide... How far the influence of manners, habits, opinions will permit them to pursue the best road, is a problem of no easy solution." (To Aaron Ogden, Dec. 28, 1804, *Correspondence*, Sparks ed., III:216.) Morris thought it possible that Hamilton's "favourite form," a balanced monarchy, might perhaps be adopted by the people "when our population shall have reached a certain extent." Morris' preferred system would vest "the principal authority in a permanent Senate;" but that too must wait for the cycle to go further for a while. Like Adams, however, and Hamilton, Morris was fearful that in the historical process of education the populace would go too far, and set up an absolute tyrant: "When a general abuse of the right of election shall have robbed our government of respect, and its imbecility have involved it in difficulties, the people will feel, what your friend [Hamilton] once said, that they want something to protect them against themselves. And then, excess being their predominant quality, it may be a patriotic duty to prevent them from going too far the other way." *Correspondence*, III:218.

9. This is Adams' own interpolation. Hampton's translation renders it, "as a vessel when impelled to either side by the wind, is kept steady by a contrary force."

10. John Adams, *Works*, IV:435-436. Quoting Polybius, book VI, ch. 1.

11. "All the three principal orders of government were to be found in the Roman Commonwealth...it was not possible, even for a Roman citizen, to assert positively whether the government, on the whole, was aristocratical, democratical, or monarchical. For, when we cast our eyes on the power of the consuls, the government appeared entirely monarchical and kingly; when on that of the senate, aristocratical; and when any one considered the power of the people, it appeared plainly democratical." John Adams, *Works*, 436.

12. Cicero's "intention," as George Sabine points out, "to sketch a theory of the state in close relationship to Roman institutional history was laudable, but it was not to be realized by a man who took his theory ready-made from Greek sources and grafted it upon an account of Roman history." George H. Sabine, *A History of Political Theory* (New York: 1937), 163.

13. When Madison studied Machiavelli as a text at Princeton, he must have found (in Machiavelli's *Discourses in the First Ten Books of Titus Livus*, book I, ch. 2) a literal translation of sections of Polybius that relate to the cycle and the necessity for mixing the government. John Adams did not omit the Machiavelli quotations, even though they were repetitious in his heavy handbook on balanced states. They are to be found leading off his chapter V, entitled, "Writers on Government," John Adams, *Works*, IV:416-420.

14. Aristotle's *Politics* as a whole has many confusions and shifts in focus.

It was written apparently at two different times and represents two stages in his thought. Books II, III, VII, and VIII, deal in general with the ideal State, while books IV,V, and VI are a study of the actual Grecian oligarchies and democracies of his day. The discussion of the mixed government occurs in this middle section which commentators agree was written last, and is not entirely consistent with discussion of the traditional forms of government discussed earlier. Even Aristotle's analysis of this new form, however, lacks clarity in its organization; possibly due to the fact that Aristotle, the great lover of categories, was unwillingly driven to treat of political life as too infinitely varied for rigid classification. See George Sabine's discussion of Aristotle's analysis of the extreme complexity of the factors which the legislator, who would mix a government would handle. "The use which Aristotle made of this twofold analysis of the state—into political agencies and classes united by a similarity of economic interest—would have been easier to follow if he had always distinguished his use of the one from his use of the other, and if he had discriminated both from the interaction of the one upon the other... But though the treatment is not schematic, it is substantially clear... There are certain political regulations...which are characteristic of democracy and others which are characteristic of oligarchy. There are also economic conditions...which pre-dispose a state toward democracy or oligarchy and determine what kind of political constitution will be most likely to succeed... The way a government actually works depends in part on the combination of political factors, in part on the economic factors, and also on the way both sets of factors tend to produce a lawless state and others a law-abiding state, and the same is true of the political factors. Such a conclusion is hard to state in a formal classification, but it has the merit of recognizing a great mass of political and social complexity." Sabine, 109-110.

15. Arthur Murphy, translator, *The Works of Tacitus* (London: 1793), "The Annals," book IV, ch. 33.

16. Murphys' *Tacitus*, I:499, note to "Annals," book IV, ch. 33. The last sentence refers to Cicero's analogy in the Republic, of mixed government to close harmony in music, which is to be found quoted in John Adams, *Works*, IV:205, with his own variation on the theme. Adams evidently admired Handel for he speaks of the "exquisite" harmonies produced by him out of "the treble, the tenor, and the bass." Compare also Shakespeare's,

> For government, though high and low & lower
> Put into parts, doth keep in one consent,
> Congreeing in a full and natural close
> Like music.
> *Henry the Fifth*
> Act I, sc. Ii, 11. 180, ff.

17. See Montesquieu, *The Spirit of the Laws*, XI:8. "The ancients had no notion of...a legislative body composed of the representatives of the people." Adams cites two other innovations, both them discussed by Montesquieu, as admirably adapted to keep the balanced government free and stable: "Representations, instead of collections, of the people; a total separation of the executive from the legislative power, and of the judicial from both; and a balance in the

legislature, by three independent, equal branches, are perhaps the only three discoveries in the constitution of a free government, since the institution of Lycurgus." John Adams, *Works*, IV:284.

These recent innovations incorporated into a correctly balanced government in the United States promised to produce commonwealths that were practically immortal. "The institutions now made in America will not wholly wear out for thousands of years." John Adams, *Works*, IV, 298. Adams with all his faith in the three discoveries that have made the ancient system of balance practically perfect can give no reason why every state in the world has not adopted them or preserved them; for presumably they were suitable to all people at all times. He does note, however, that "Even these [three discoveries] have been so unfortunate, that they have never spread: the first has been given up by all the nations, excepting one, which had once adopted it; and [the] other two, reduced to practice, if not invented by the English nation, have never been imitated by any other, except their descendants in America." John Adams, 284.

18. The discussion in Tacitus' *Germania* of the "government" of the Germans with its elective war leader, its council of elders, who managed minor affairs, but referred all matters of importance to the collective decision of the tribe was seized on eagerly by enthusiasts of England's balance who wanted an ancient pedigree for the form. Montesquieu made the most famous statement among many writers of this unhistoric history: "In perusing the admirable treatise of Tacitus 'On the Manners of the Germans' we find that it is from that nation the English have borrowed the idea of their political government. This beautiful system was invented first in the woods." *The Spirit of the Laws*, XI:6. The ancient Germanic origin of the British government continued to be accepted even after scholars agreed that it had never been balanced according the eighteenth-century theory. This was partly due to the revulsion, *post* 1789, against all things French (or Norman) plus the rise in prestige of Germany during the later nineteenth century. The theory, buttressed by the concept of biological evolution had half the historians of England debating on the exact form of the old Germanic "hundred" from which in due time had developed the Parliament of Gladstone and Disraeli. It was in violent reaction to this "germ theory" (which naturally explained the origin of U.S. representative institutions as well as the British) that impelled Turner to substitute the "frontier" theory of American democracy. Turner did not object to democracy coming out of the forests; but he did refuse to consider, in a period of rising nationalism, that those forests could be located in ancient Saxony, Brandenburg, or Bavaria.

19. Stanley Pargellis, "The Theory of Balanced Government" in Conyers Read, ed., *The Constitution Reconsidered* (New York: 1938), 37-49. "Begun as a face-saving compromise between Tudor theories of kingship and parliamentary sovereignty, continued as a compromise between the divine right of the Jacobite Tories and the sweeping demands of parliamentary Whigs, it lasted on when those earlier doctrines had died." Pargellis, 43. The theory was practically unchallenged until the middle of the century, and though from that time on increasing numbers of political theorists challenged or qualified it, as recently as 1861 Henry, Lord Brougham could still talk of the British Constitution's perfect mixture of monarchy, aristocracy, and democracy.

20. Since the British theory was a graft on the classical stock, the implication of the few-rich-Lords versus the many-poor-Commons, with the Crown as mediator did color it always to some degree. By the second and third decades of the century, however, the relationship had become quite tenuous in the theory as it was usually presented.

21. "Perhaps it will be said that the people being ignorant and always discontented [Locke significantly does not say 'poor'], to lay the foundation of government in the unsteady opinion and uncertain humour of the people, is to expose it to certain ruin; and no government will be long able to subsist if the people may act up a new legislative [i.e. Government]. To this I answer quite the contrary. People are not so easily got out of their old forms as some are apt to suggest. They are hardly to be prevailed with to amend the acknowledged faults in the frame they have been accustomed to... This slowness and aversion in the people to quit their old constitutions, has in the many revolutions...seen in this kingdom...still brought us back again to our old legislative of Kings, lords, and commons." John Locke, *Second Treatise on Government*, ch. XIX:223. The view that the average man is non-aggressive, amicable, peaceable, in his social relations, that only the marginal man is politically cannibalistic and anarchical, allowed Locke to base government (which is designed to control the few anti-social individuals) on the consent of the majority of the people. This was a direct refutation of Hobbes' thesis that all individuals are heart wolves and will act together in social harmony only when awed into decency by an absolute sovereign: "during the time men live without a common Power to keep them all in awe, they are in that condition which is called Warre; For WARRE, consisteth not in Battell only, or the act of fighting; but in the tract of time, wherein the Will to contend by Battell is sufficiently known... For as the Nature of Foule weather, lyeth not in a showre or two of rain; but in an inclination thereto of many dayes together; so the nature of War, consisteth not in actuall fighting; but in the known disposition thereto, during all the time there is no assurance to the contrary." *Leviathan*, I:13. Hobbes, who had no patience with mixed government theories, gives a description here of the ceaseless conflict between individuals which the classical analyst of the class struggle had attributed to fixed and rigid groups.

22. Locke, *Second Treatise*, ch. XIX:218.

23. The dichotomy between the political state, even when legitimate, and society, which underlies all of Locke's theorizing, was alien to classical thought. As a result, the modern idea of the citizen as an individual to whom certain rights are legally guaranteed does not appear in Greek thought and only to a partial degree in Roman theory. Hobbes quite rightly put his finger on this distinction: "The Libertie, whereof there is so frequent, and honourable mention, the Histories, and Philosophy of the Antient Greeks, and Romans, and in the writings, and discourse of those that from them have received all their learning in the Politiques, is not the Libertie of Particular men; but the Liberties of the Common-wealth... The *Athenians*, and *Romans*, were free; that is free Common-wealths: not that any particular men had the Libertie to resist their own Representative; but that their Representative had the Libertie to resist or invade other people." *Leviathan*, II:21.

24. Separation of the judiciary, while constitutional practice after 1688, was not incorporated into Locke's theory, though it was implied in Locke, and had been discussed by that other Whig paladin, Algernon Sidney. In the *Treatise* the discussion focuses on the balance of the executive (crown) versus the legislature (the two Houses of Parliament); "And because it may be too great a temptation to human frailty, apt to grasp at power, for the same persons who have the power of making laws to have also in their hands the power to execute, whereby they may exempt themselves from obedience to the laws, they make, and suit the law both in its making and execution, to their own private interest... Therefore in well ordered commonwealths...persons who, duly assembled, have...a power to make laws, which when they have done, being separated again, they are themselves subject to the laws, they have made...But because the laws...need a perpetual execution...therefore it is necessary there should be a power always in being which should see to the execution of the laws that are made, and remain in force. And thus the legislative and executive power come often to be separated." Locke, *Second Treatise*, ch. XIII:143-144.

25. Government "being only a fiduciary power to set for certain ends, there remains still in the people a supreme power to remove or alter the legislative, when they find the legislative act contrary to the trust reposed in Them." Locke, *Second Treatise*, ch. XIII:149. This acceptance of majority judgment as Edwin Mims points out, breaks away from the idea of a constitution that has been constituted properly, held by Adams and the mixed government theorists. "Whereas Adams's theory of constitutionalism was based on certain universal and absolute truths divorced from environmental peculiarities, Locke's theory of constitutionalism was relativistic, recognizing the ever present possibility that a majority under new conditions might develop new criteria of good and bad government." Edwin Mims, Jr., *The Majority of the People* (New York: 1941), 62. This perhaps overstates Locke's willingness to accept popular innovations: He apparently expected the right to revolution would be used almost entirely as a defensive measure against the innovating tendencies of governors in the direction of tyranny; but of necessity his discussion of the right to revolution was shot through with ambiguities in regard to what, exactly, justifies revolt. This unclearness, as time was to prove, worked to the advantage of individuals already determined to rebel. See Carl Becker, *The Declaration of Independence* (New York: 1922), chs. 1-2.

26. Madison, while accepting Montesquieu's conclusion on the vital importance of the separation of powers, disliked his British bias. The Virginian was far from being a wholehearted admirer of the British government, which he believed had lost its balance in large part through "corruption" of the legislative by the executive. See his remark on the "vicious ingredients in the parliamentary constitution" (*Federalist*, LII), and his statement on "the experience of Great Britain, which presents to mankind so many political lessons, both of the monitory and exemplary kind" (*Federalist*, LVI).

Though both of these numbers of Federalist have been attributed to Hamilton, this criticism does not square with this admiration of the British government. It does square with Madison's judgments of English political institutions. See especially his remarks on "corruption" in the Convention, June

22, and his comments on the "reproaches & evils which have resulted from the vicious representation in Great Britain." Moreover, as E.G. Bourne has noted in his study, "The Authorship of the Federalist" (*Essays in Historical Criticism*, New York, 1901, 133), the word "monitory" is a favorite of Madison's. He speaks of the "melancholy and monitory lesson of history" (referring to the "imbecility" of the Belgic Confederacy) in *Federalist*, XX. "Monitory lesson" again appears in an essay "On Nullification" written within a year of his death (*Letters*, IV:424) in relation to the weakness of "ancient and modern" confederations. In 1821 he had used the phrase "monitory examples" to refer to the same subject. In 1833 he called attention to the "monitory reflection that no government...can be perfect;...that the abuse of all other governments have led to the preference of republican government as the best of all governments, because the least imperfect; that the vital principle of republican government is the *lex majoris partis*, the will of the majority..." Letter of 1833, lacking superscription. *Letters*, IV:334. Bourne might also have added that on the convention floor itself Madison had remarked that "Experience was instructive monitor" as introduction to a discussion of the "Heroic period of Antient Greece [,] the feudal licentiousness of the Middle Ages." Debate June 28, *Documents* 293.

27. *Federalist*, XLVII.

28. Montesquieu, *The Spirit of the Laws*, book XI, ch. 5 To Montesquieu is due the rigid delineation of the legislative, executive, *and* judiciary. This was implicit rather than expressed in Locke, who depended on the balance of Parliament v. Crown in this theory as expounded. Montesquieu may have been impelled to find three functions of government by Aristotle's claim that sovereignty is divided into deliberative, judicial, and appointive (i.e. executive) powers though the Greek does not relate these to any balance (see L.M. Levin, *The Political Doctrine of Montesquieu's 'Espirit des Lois:' Its Classical Background* [Columbia University Press: 1936], 127). It is clear that Montesquieu did not rely on observation for his grand discovery; for as Sabine notes, "no man who relied on independent observation would have pitched upon the separation of powers as the distinctive feature of the constitution." Sabine, 560.

29. Paul Merril Spurlin, *Montesquieu in America 1760-1801* (Baton Rouge: 1940), shows how common were quotations from Montesquieu (many of which indicate beyond a doubt that *The Spirit of the Laws* was actually read and not just talked about) during the early Republican era. It is unfortunate, however, that Mr. Spurlin has done only half the job promised in his title. Until someone carefully analyzes those sections of Montesquieu which were quoted and those which were ignored, and distinguishes between the use made of the Frenchman's doctrines by conservatives as well as radicals, we shall not have a comprehensive picture of Montesquieu in America.

30. The Virginia Bill of Rights of June 12, 1776 (mainly composed by George Mason), after stating the Lockian theory of the origin and ends of government, pronounced in paragraph V; "That the legislative and executive powers of the state should be separated and distinct from the judiciary; and that the members of the two first may be restrained from oppression, by feeling and participating the burthens of the people, they should at fixed periods, be reduced

to a private station, return into that body from which they were originally taken, and the vacancies be supplied by frequent, certain, and regular elections..." *Doc. American Hist.* #67, Commager, ed.

31. Sabine points out that as a result the doctrine of separation of powers in Montesquieu was "in effect...a dogma supplemented by an undefined privilege of making exception." Sabine, 560.

32. Englishmen started re-defining the term "people" after 1789. See the statement in the Hammonds' classic volume on the British worker: "The shock of the French Revolution had brought with it a new way of looking at the mass of the nation. When Bacon wrote on the dangers to which Kings are exposed, he had treated the danger of popular insurrection as very slight, 'except it be where they have Great and Potent Heads, or where you meddle with the Point of Religion or their Customs or Means of Life.' This was the light in which the rank and file of the nation appeared to the ruling class down to the day when France destroyed their peace of mind. In English history for two centuries rebellion had been the business of aristocrats, churchmen, yeomen, squires, Puritans, in fact of everybody but the poor... We have only to recall the key in which Burke himself wrote before 1789 to appreciate the depth of the change in upper-class thinking that followed the French Revolution. 'When popular discontents have been very prevalent,' he wrote in 1770, 'it may well be affirmed and supported, that there has been generally something found amiss in the constitution or in the conduct of government. The people have no interest in disorder. Where they do wrong it is their error, not their crime...' There was no presentiment here of the 'swinish multitude.' After the French Revolution the tone was very different. The poorer classes no longer seemed a passive power; they were dreaded as a Leviathan that was fast learning its strength." J.L. and Barbara Hammond, *The Town Labourer*, 1760-1832 (London: 1918), 93-94.

Chapter 6

The Extended Republic

For nearly a generation American political thinkers had shared Locke's exclusive concern with curbing the powers of kings. But now in the summer of 1787, the Convention delegates were almost unanimously agreed that the people themselves presented an additional problem. The will of the majority, as they had seen it in action since 1783, called to memory frightening pictures out of the classics; the rule of the many too closely resembled descriptions of the interested, ruthless, overbearing *demos* party, which in ancient times had licentiously conceived of governmental power as the short and easy way to seize the wealth of their betters. Almost all of the Fathers were prepared to argue that the "anarchy of mob-rule" existing in States like Rhode Island was so vicious that a single "despot" would probably be a welcome relief as had been foretold by the Polybian cycle.[1] Yet few of them were entirely prepared to throw over republicanism with its principle of majority rule, if only some system could be worked out that would secure the blessings of liberty by insuring domestic tranquility.[2]

Madison put the problem neatly in a letter to Washington the month before the delegates met at the Convention. "The great desideratum, which has not yet been found for Republican Governments, seems to be some disinterested and dispassionate umpire in disputes between different passions and interests in the State. The majority, *who alone have the right of decision*, have frequently an interest, real or supposed, in abusing it."[3] That fractious majority: Unfortunately there was no way to escape the fact that, "According to Republican Theory, right and power, both being vested in the majority, are held to be synonymous."[4] Madison, like most the Fathers, was too candid to deny that the frightening many, with all their abuses of the natural rights of the few, were still the bedrock on which Republicans must build. It posed a ticklish problem, and there appeared to be no honest way to get around it. The Lockian principle that governors must be kept responsible by the participation in government of the many who were governed could not be thrown over. Locke's scheme required, on the other hand, some supplementary principle to guarantee security. This was the general consensus of opinion among the fifty-five men who arrived at Philadelphia in the hot summer of 1787 to help balance a new Government for the United States. This was the goal which the Virginia Plan was designed to attain. And this was what Alexander Hamilton, speaking on the Convention floor June 18, claimed was impossible, under conditions prevailing in America.

Hamilton was prepared to go farther toward throwing over entirely Locke's majority principle than was any man in the Convention. Whereas Madison argued "the majority have *frequently* an interest, real or *supposed*, in abusing their right of decision in republican government, Hamilton believed that they would *always* have an interest that was real, concrete, and obvious. The majority, as he saw it, was an external threat to the entire edifice of government; *lex majoris partis* could not be distinguished in the smallest degree from the principle of tyranny. And on Hamilton's cherished assumption that society was divided eternally into two, and only two parties of the rich and the poor, his conclusion was understandable.

Alexander Hamilton's criticism of the Virginia plan as too democratic was completely logical if his original premise is granted. If a state "naturally divides itself into two political divisions—the *few* and the *many*, who have distinct interests,"[5] a government in the hands of either group will naturally take action looking to its own interests, which by definition are inimical to the other. It was logical and also traditional to argue that political power "ought to be in the hands of both; and they should be separated." The crux of Hamilton's program, however, lay not simply in separation; for even the reprobated Virginia plan attempted to do this. His point of departure came in the degree and type of separation which he advocated for his Senate. "The aristocracy ought to be entirely separated; their power should be permanent, and they should have the *caritas liberorum*. They should be so circumstanced that they can have no interest in change—as to have an effectual weight in the constitution. Their duration should be the earnest of wisdom and stability." And then with a final argumentative thrust that evicted Locke from the Convention Hall and called in old Thomas Hobbes: "'Tis essential there should be a permanent will in a community."[6] Here was a flat refusal to identify the will of majority with the will of the commonwealth. The "permanent will" of the society was to be found in the few, set off in sharp contradistinction from the many. Hamilton's Senate holding office during good behavior would be as irresponsible—"there ought to be a principle in government capable of resisting the popular current"—to the electorate as a whole, as it was humanly possible to make it without a hereditary order.

The Virginia plan's failure to provide for a Senate that would be "permanent" in this sense was enough to damn it for the New Yorker. Its Senate was to be elected by the State legislatures—populist tendencies had already appeared—and they were expected to hold office for only seven years. Hamilton considered it pure fantasy that the convention could expect this feeble upper chamber with its quasi-aristocratic features would be an effective check on the lower house.

> No temporary Senate will have firmness eno' to answer the purpose... Gentlemen differ in their opinions concerning the necessity checks, from the different estimates they form of the human passions. They suppose seven years a sufficient period to give the Senate an adequate firmness, from not duly considering the amazing violence & turbulence of the democratic spirit. When a great object of Govt. is pursued, which seizes the popular passions, they spread like wildfire and become irresistible. He appealed to the gentlemen from the N. England States whether experience had not there verified the remark.[7]

So much for the Virginia plan's sorry excuse for a Senate. There was as great a weakness in another of its triple organs.

The "amazing violence & turbulence" of the ravening *demos* of New York, Jersey, Delaware, and the other states required, or so Hamilton believed, still a further check, beyond a Senate elected for life. "As to the Executive, it seemed to be admitted that no good one could be established on Republican principles. Was not this giving up the merits of the question: for can there be a good Govt. without a good Executive. The English model was the only good one on the subject.[8] The Hereditary interest of the King was so interwoven with that of the Nation, and his personal emoluments so great, that he was placed above the danger of being corrupted from abroad—and at the same time was both sufficiently independent and sufficiently controlled, to answer the purpose of the institution at home... Let the Executive also be for life."[9] And here again that significant phrase appears for the second time in Hamilton's own notes. "The principle chiefly intended to be established is this—that there must be a permanent *will*.[10] Gentlemen say we need to be rescued from the democracy. But what the means proposed? A democratic assembly is to be checked by a democratic senate, and both these by a democratic chief magistrate."[11]

As Hamilton pled the necessity of a strong-souled general government with "*strong organs*," to domesticate the untamed proletariat of America into a semblance of law and order, he granted in full John Adams' wish that "the history of Greece" should serve as a mirror for his countryman in their task of making a Constitution. In his speech Hamilton was depending on terms whose validity as empiric observation applied almost entirely to the class struggle of the rich and the poor in classical antiquity. Hamilton was not really talking of the British constitution for all his praise of it by name; his discussion of its virtues was as remote from its actual institutional development as it was from contemporary commentators' praise of its mythical balance of power. Whether he realized it or not, Alexander Hamilton was really extolling a Platonic philosopher king, powerful enough to awe or coerce into quietude an Aristotelian *hoi polloi*. His "republican" executive bore as little resemblance to George III as his projection of the term "people" from antiquity did to the actual population inhabiting the thirteen young American republics. Hamilton, so brilliant and precocious in certain fields of analysis, so clear-sighted and efficient when faced with any administrative job, was obsessed with the phantasy that the independent farmers composing ninety per cent of the population in eighteenth-century America were identical counterparts of the poverty-stricken many who had mas-sacred the opulent few in Corcyra, 427 B.C.[12]

Alexander Hamilton had read his classical authors widely but not too well. The fact was obvious to shrewd Gouverneur Morris[13] whose admiration and close personal relations did not blind him to this fantastic intellectual aberration in the mind of the man who moved with such sure realism in the realm of economics and administration. In reply to a letter of Robert Walsh requesting information in 1811 about the intentions of Hamilton and the other delegates in framing the Constitution, he wrote,

> General Hamilton had little share in forming the Constitution. He disliked it, believing all republican government to be radically defective...
>
> General Hamilton hated republican government, because he confounded it with democratic government, and he detested the latter, because he believed it must end in despotism, and be, in the meantime, destructive to public morality... In short, his study of ancient history impressed on his mind a conviction, that democracy ending in tyranny is, while it

lasts, a cruel and oppressive domination.

> One marked trait of the General's character was the per-
> tinacious adherence to opinions he had once formed... In
> maturer age his observation and good sense demonstrated, that
> the materials for an Aristocracy did not exist in America;
> wherefore...he considered the fate of Rome, in her meridian
> splendor, and that of Athens from the dawn to the sunset of her
> glory, as the portrait of our future fortune.[14]

In fine, Alexander Hamilton was a victim of his Plutarch and his
Tacitus. "More a theoretic than a practical man," as Morris had noted
earlier, Hamilton could not turn his reading of ancient history at all
toward the clarification and ordering of the American world in which
he lived; on the contrary, his classical learning operated to distort and
becloud so many political phenomena lying under his very eyes that
he could never deal with them realistically, except in minor matters
of technique. Here is the kernel of truth in Woodrow Wilson's dictum
that Hamilton was "a very great man, but not a great American."[15]
His foreignness consisted not in the fact that he was born in Nevis
rather than in Boston or Norfolk: it was a foreignness of time rather
than of geographical space, that made him call himself "exotic."
Alexander Hamilton could hardly fail to appear slightly alien and
archaic since the conception of political reality upon which his whole
career was based had vanished with the pagan civilization of the
ancient Mediterranean world.

Here lies the paradox of Hamilton's contribution to American
nationalism. The most indefatigable worker for a stronger Union
during the critical period, he was profoundly dissatisfied with the
Constitution which went into effect in 1789. Its paper provision
would be but frail and illusory bulwarks against the debauched and
murderous *demos* his mind's eye saw about him. In a memorandum
written immediately after the Convention had ended and while
ratification was still extremely doubtful, he noted with gloomy
foreboding.

> If the government be adopted, it is probable General
> Washington will be the president of the United States. This
> will ensure a wise choice of men to administer the govern-
> ment, and a good administration. A good administration will
> conciliate the confidence and affection of the people, and
> perhaps enable the government to acquire more consistency
> than the proposed constitution seems to promise for so great a
> country. It may then triumph altogether over the state

governments, and reduce them to an entire subordination,
dividing the larger states into smaller districts. The *organs*[16]
of the general government may also acquire additional strength.

If this should not be the case, in the course of a few years, it is
probably that the contests about the boundaries of power
between the particular governments and the general government, and the *momentum*[17] of the larger states in such
contests, will produce a dissolution of the union. This, after
all seems to be the most likely result.[18]

As the event turned out, the government was adopted; Washington
did appoint wise men to his cabinet; and among those appointees was
Hamilton, with his *idée fixeabout* fortifying the organs of government. As Secretary of the Treasury his knowledge of the history of
British administrative techniques served him as well as his ignorance
of contemporary social history was to serve him badly. With a
creative touch which was nothing short of genius, Hamilton adapted
to American conditions the English banking and financial devices by
which the Revolutionary Settlement of 1688 had been stabilized and
the Whig party made supreme.[19] Building on economic appetites that
flourished in direct proportion to their cultivation, the New Yorker
was well on his way to creating a solid, cohesive interstate "party of
the few" whose loyalty tied it fast to the political agency that
guaranteed its pecuniary privileges. Dextrous management—Hamilton's opponents screamed "corruption"—resulted in a subservient
Congress in which even the lower House, the people's representatives
in the balance, seemed forgetful of their duty to the many. Hamilton's dream had come true; he had the chance to rectify the mistakes
made at Philadelphia, and organize for the United States a government with a strong soul.

Unfortunately this magnificently managed coup created an
increasingly cohesive party of the many also, although not exactly in
the Aristotelian sense. Hamilton's search for a check against the
suspected *hoi polloi* was successful; but he soon found that his balance
had ceased to be a theorem in social statics and had become a problem
in political dynamics.[20] Instead of producing "domestic tranquility"
his system divided the American people into a sharper cleavage than
had existed since 1776. Members of the party of the many, produced
simultaneously with his party of the few, as they saw the strength of
the organs of Hamilton's leviathan taking shape under his fiscal wand,
could claim with a strong element of truth that the Constitution had
become a government of the many, by the few, for the few. And
every action that helped to build up the support of the few tended to

erode the loyalty of the many.[21] They disliked the monster's strong soul. And they disliked even more the brazen claws of its tax collectors, for the whole system was bottomed upon a moderate but continual squeezing of the pocketbooks of the general public for the advantage of special interests.

And then the circle had made a complete turn: Hamilton had created his oligarchy on too narrow a base. There were far too many politically and socially important interests excluded from the benefits of his national system for it to win the popular assent necessary for its stability; of the five "great and essential principles necessary for the support of the government" which he himself had listed on the convention floor, consent—"opinion of utility and necessity" he had called it—by 1800 had assumed a paramount position. Nationalism had endured a critical period in 1786 because too few individuals had a vested interest in supporting the general government, nationalism went through a second critical period in 1800 because Hamilton's policies had succeeded in convincing sizable groups that they had a vested interest in opposing it. By that time the only support of government that appeared to the Federalist to promise safety was "Force." Scarcely a decade after the Constitution had gone into effect the last resources that Hamilton could draw on for balancing the few against the intemperate many were fraud, suppression, and fomenting a foreign war. Hypnotized with fright as it became apparent that the ignorant people were about to vote his party out of power, the New Yorker became unwilling to await the "crisis" he anticipated; and so took the very action most apt to produce it. As the century drew to an end the United States was very close to civil war.

In this final phase as always Hamilton's tactics, political technics, and his operational skills, were brilliantly rational; but as always they were directed toward an irrational end. His fear of the *demos*, accordingly, which had always been a monomania, now became an obsession. The French Revolution gave him a recent reign of terror to set besides those described in Diodorus Siculus and Aristotle. Only his tragic death would free that brilliant, bold mind from the antique demons which possessed it.[22]

All this was hidden in the future, however, as Alexander Hamilton pled with the Convention on June 18th. His cry then was to cast aside as mere palliatives the two plans proposed by Randolph and Paterson, and to embrace [the] strong government that the nation required if domestic tranquility was to be assured. It was not to be. In spite of Hamilton's impressive deductive reasoning; in spite of his enormously effective emotional appeal to a group nervously prepared to believe the worst of the people, neither his logic, nor his aristogoguery could quite overcome common sense, vested interests and Madison's competing theory embodied in the Virginia plan. The Constitution, based on that more flexible plan, was ratified by a narrow margin. Though Hamilton's speech, as Johnson of Connecticut put it, "has been praised by every body, he has been supported by none."[23] This was not entirely true. Read of Delaware frankly confessed that Hamilton's was the only scheme that would satisfy him; Rufus King and Dr. McClurg were converted to the idea of a President elected for life; and Gouverneur Morris was at least fortified in his demand for a permanent Senate. Nevertheless Johnson's remark reflected the general sense of the meeting. The members as a whole felt it would be inexpedient even to consider a system that could not possibly be ratified.

The Virginia plan with its "excess of democracy" might, as Hamilton contemptuously put it, be "*pork still, with a little change of the sauce*";[24] but the dish he had cooked up would surely be spit out after the first taste by the people of the thirteen states. The young New Yorker had done his best and no one knew better than he that it had not been enough. With one last despairing warning against certain democratic fallacies enunciated by Mr. Sherman on June 26, "he acknowledged himself not to think favorably of Republican Government; but addressed his remarks to those who did think favorably of it, in order to prevail on them to tone their Government as high as possible." Then on June 30th he left the convention.[25] A month and a half later he was to return to Philadelphia, assist in putting the last touches on the body of the Constitution that the assemblage had blocked out during his absence, and finally sign it with the hope that it would be that the first step toward his idea of a well-balanced government.

If the common sense of expediency had not been fatal to Hamilton's plan the vested interests of the states would have killed it. It was clear both before and after Hamilton spoke that no new system would be acceptable that did not preserve the existing states with enough sovereignty to guarantee protection to local interests. Hamilton had argued that the one great source of social insecurity lay in the clash between those who owned property and those that did not. He had contended that the democratically controlled state governments had neither the desire nor the ability to control this clash in the interest of justice. On the contrary since the State Legislatures represented the many, they would be always tend to oppress the few. Therefore destroy the States, he had begged, transfer *all* of their sovereignty to a newly-created national organism so balanced that the nonpropertied mob cannot use its powers to harry the rich. Let the propertied classes everywhere throw all their capital of political sovereignty into a new state where it will be utilized to secure their present income and their expectation of future profits.

The catch in this neatly presented Hamiltonian scheme was that while all the delegates were anxious to erect new guards for the security of property, they were not equally agreed upon the kinds of property most deserving of protection. Income and profits depended in different states upon different types of economic organization and activity. Georgia's profits were based on agriculture and Massachusetts' on trade, South Carolina's income came from slaves where Connecticut's labor was free. Pennsylvania had embryo manufactures, North Carolina had none, Virginia was deeply concerned with the navigation of the Mississippi, while to New York it was unimportant. Here were vertical rifts in American society which already cut across Hamilton's great divide. If the more perfect union was armed with enough power to awe the *demos* into seemly behavior there was always the chance that such power could be used by traders to exploit farmers, by abolitionists to free slaves, and by one section to depress the vital interests of another. A few of the large state delegates at Philadelphia were not concerned by the disappearance of state sovereignty; after all they would have, under proportional representation, safeguards for their parochial interest. Not the men from the small states: Hamilton's scheme or any scheme that abolished state sovereignty would leave their local and peculiar institutions unprotected. As a result, the majority of the delegates, even if they had considered it possible to get "high toned" government ratified, were still not prepared to put all the eggs of local sovereignty into the single basket of a consolidated union. However, rejection of Hamilton's plan as visionary was but a negative triumph for common sense and local jealousy. The problems that he had unsatisfactorily resolved remained as manifest as ever, crystallized by his vibrant oratory.

The Convention of 1787 faced a pair of interlocking dilemmas, pointing across both the field of practical politics and the field of political theory. In the first place, the members sincerely desired to retain a republican government with its Lockian concomitant of the people's ultimate sovereignty; yet they were determined that the property rights of the minority must be protected lest anarchy produce a theoretical king, and lest they be robbed by the masses in the meantime. Madison's statement in the thirty-seventh *Federalist* put it neatly: "Among the difficulties encountered by the convention, a very important one...[lay] in combining the requisite stability and energy in government, with the inviolable attention due to liberty and to the republican form." Madison's phrase, "stability and energy in government" serves to conceal only partially the delegates' preoccupation with the dilemma of minority rights in a governmental system whose dynamic principle was majority rule.[26] Second, there was the dilemma of the "interfering pretensions of the larger and smaller States" which pivoted on the problem of the majority and minority rights of the states as corporate beings. In this instance Delaware, Jersey, and the other less populous members of the confederation demanded on equality of representation in the new Senate as security for the minority interests encompassed in their existing bounds, while spokesmen of Virginia, Pennsylvania, and Massachusetts contended that this equal participation would plumb depths of injustice by allowing the smaller part of the Union to control the larger whole. This, they protested, flew in the face of sound republican doctrine. If these thorny issues were to be solved, a plan was needed that would serve as the basis for compromise and accommodation; a scheme of government was needed whose institutional framework could satisfy distinguished antidemocrats and still not outrage ardent republicans. This plan would have to promise stability, of course, but without sacrificing the liberty to which the United States was committed. Above all, the new government could not depart too drastically either in structure or theory from the systems to which old habits and customs had devoted to the American people.

The Virginia plan served this purpose remarkably well. As a "middle ground"—to use Madison's description of it written before the Convention met—it promised a due supremacy to the national authority while still preserving the states as functioning units; and thus was a satisfactory system to bargain over in the Convention Hall. The bicameralism which was one of its salient features was also admirably adapted to compromise. As C.M. Walsh has stated, the main advantage of bicameralism seems to be its capacity to satisfy clashing claims and to quiet distracted minds. For the essence of bicameralism is compromise. It conciliates opposing theories by making room for both, giving a place to each in each of the halves into which it divides the legislature. The number of diversities that may in this way be reconciled, is truly surprising.[27]

Out of the malleable provisions which Randolph read to the Convention on the opening day of the session it was possible to hammer out the large-small state compromise on representation. The separation of the Senate and the House which had always been the traditional guard of liberty, also served after a little thought to satisfy those of the Fathers who were so torn between the respective merits of the few and the many. Archaic elements lifted from the ancient "mixed governments" were woven into the very structure of the new state. It has been truly said that the completed Constitution was a "bundle of compromises"; so too was the Virginia plan from which it developed. In fact, the main virtue of that plan was its capacity for evolution in terms of the middle way.

From this viewpoint it is not unfair to say that the completed Constitution in practically every clause reflects prudential motives as well as principles. Too many blocs in the Convention had to be satisfied for the members to hew to the line of strict theory. The shadow of the gauntlet of the state ratifying conventions which the constitution must run hung over the deliberations throughout. Inevitably the government that the delegates evolved under the pressure of these circumstances was a hybrid form the like of which had never before been seen. Hamilton was to sneer at its "motley" characteristics, and Dayton of New Jersey on June 30th had frankly dubbed it an "amphibious monster."[28] Hindsight tells us today that this was the greatest virtue of the American Constitution which, though written in 1787, still operates to this day. Only because its chiseled phrases were replete with anomalies and ambiguities could it continue to serve as a living instrument of national development during the century and a half that was to destroy the world of the Fathers with such revolutionary, social, economic, and intellectual changes.

Since, however, the members of the Convention were not seers, since their eighteenth-century minds were so completely preoccupied with the past as the guide to the future, the fact that so much of their Constitution was unique and unprecedented gave them cause for uneasiness. The hybrid Constitution that they wrote, loaded with compromises, was right for the America they lived in because it was the only charter of government that could be subscribed to by all the Convention and ratified by the people. The delegates, nevertheless, had a psychological need to be reassured that their charter squared with the "experience" of all ages. The flouting of so many accepted dogmas gave them a feeling of uneasiness; some sort of compromise theory was needed to justify the Convention for doing what it had to do. Accepted principles accordingly had to be juggled and rearranged to buttress the actions they had to take with the authority that classical authority alone could give. James Madison furnished that compromise theory.

A suggestive description of James Madison was sent about this time by the French Ambassador to his superiors in Paris. The young Virginian is characterized as, "*Instruit, sage, modéré, docile, studieux; peut être plus profond que M. Hamilton, mais moins brillaint... C'est un homme qu'il faut étudier longtemps pour s'en former une idée juste.*"[29] ["Learned, wise, moderate, docile, studious; perhaps more profound than Hamilton, but less brilliant...This is a man whom one must study for some time in order to form an adequate opinion of him."] These qualities of mind, especially his moderation, studiousness and sober intelligence, helped him to see the weakness in the Polybian theory that the precocious genius of Hamilton leaped over at one bound. Madison, as he carefully read his books on ancient confederations during the winter and spring of 1787, and cautiously tried to square his authorities with the facts as he saw them, had come to the conclusion that the basic theorem of the doctrinaire advocates of mixed monarchy didn't stand up under examination. All history had not been just the struggle of the rich and the poor trying to devour each other. The problem of faction did not pivot entirely upon the conflict of haves and have-nots. Madison challenged the basic postulate upon which the ancient mixed government depended for its justification; and in so doing he exploded the justification for a permanent will in the community to keep the immutable strife of the few and the many within bounds.

The best known statement of Madison's theory is to be found in the tenth number of the *Federalist*, but he had worked it out in detail at least a month before he journeyed to Philadelphia.[30] The Convention had been in session hardly a week before he took the opportunity to present it in detail to the delegates, who were considerably impressed.[31] The hypothesis therein stated has proved to be Madison's most original contribution to political theory.

It is significant that Madison's first complete formulation of his new idea written in April, 1787 in preparation for the Philadelphia meeting occurs in his "Notes on the Confederacy" under the heading, "Injustice of the Laws of the States." Like Hamilton and so many of the leading men of America he had been badly frightened by the Shays' Rebellion and disturbed to only a slightly less degree by the "itch" for paper money in his own Virginia.[32] It was this sort of injustice he was convinced that "brings...into question the fundamental principle of republican Government, that the majority who rule in such Governments are the safest guardians both of public good and of private rights."[33] This was exactly the question that Hamilton and Adams had asked and then answered with a flat negative. Madison, however, did not hasten so quickly to his conclusions.

Part of the "evil," he admitted, proceeded from the age-old tendency of rulers to forget their obligations to the majority. Madison was echoing Locke when he attributed part of the trouble to corrupt rulers who with "interested views, contrary to the interest and views of their constituents, join in a perfidious sacrifice of the latter to the former." But this was not the maine evil. "A still more fatal, if not more frequent cause, lies among the people themselves." Madison and Hamilton were still following parallel trails.

They parted at this point, for the young Virginian could not be satisfied with the deceptive neatness of the theory which divided all society through all history into the paired categories of the struggling rich and poor. He could not deny that society and politics did exhibit continual strife and conflict. The "Theoretic politicians...have erroneously supposed that by reducing mankind to a perfect equality in their political rights, they would, at the same time, be perfectly equalized and assimilated in their possessions, their opinions, and their passions,"[34] were demonstrably wrong. The fact of class conflict was basic in republican governments, but this conflict was not solely between the rich and poor. On the contrary, a wide variety of economic and noneconomic factors were involved in class antagonisms. Madison in 1788 was prepared to argue that society was to a large degree pluralistic, not dualistic as the ancient mixed government theorists had insisted.

This wider view did not alter the fact that "party" was still the greatest bane of republicanism. Madison still considered "the violence" generated by these multitudinous factions as "the mortal diseases under which popular governments have everywhere perished."[35] But since his analytical insight showed that the problem of faction was not necessarily the death grapple of the rich and the poor, both the causes of faction and the cures for it were due for re-examination.

The causes of faction Madison traced to the "nature of man" whose latent dispositions are "everywhere brought into different degrees of activity, according to the different circumstances of civil society. A zeal for different opinions concerning religion, concerning government, and many other points, as well of speculation as of practice; an attachment to different leaders ambitiously contending for pre-eminence and power; or to persons of other descriptions whose fortunes have been interesting to the human passions, have, in turn, divided mankind into parties, inflamed them with mutual animosity and rendered them much more disposed to vex and oppress each other than to cooperate for their common good. So strong is this propensity of mankind to fall into mutual animosities, that where no substantial occasion presents itself, the most frivolous and fanciful distinctions have been sufficient to kindle their unfriendly passions and excite their most violent conflicts."[36] Here were a whole series of antagonisms; here were dozens of clusters of special interests, entirely outside the field of economics, that must be taken into account by the statesman who would attempt to promote the general welfare.

While Madison refused to accept the theory that the state was divided simply into the two classes of the rich and the poor, he was never prepared to argue that the conflicts of the haves and the have-nots were unimportant. His mind was too saturated with the classical authors for that. In fact he was willing to concede that "the most commone and durable source of factions has been the various and unequal distribution of property."[37] But the important word here is "various." Granting that "those who hold and those who are without property have ever formed distinct interests in society," nevertheless "property holding" itself, when examined closely, takes on a multiplicity of meaning that complicates the picture enormously. There are various "degrees and kinds of property," and these also have been "common and durable" reasons for class conflict. "A landed interest, a manufacturing interest, a mercantile interest, a moneyed interest, with many lesser interests, grow up of necessity in civilized nations, and divide them into different classes, actuated by different sentiments and views. The regulation of these various and interfering interests forms the principle task of modern legislation, and involves the spirit of party and faction in the necessary and ordinary operations of the government."[38] This analysis put a new complexion upon the immutable class struggle that had figured for so long in political theory. It was no longer an affair of two classes, one set against the other in sharp relief, but a teeming galaxy of class struggles. The Polybians had been wrong in their major premise; could they also have been mistaken in their monarchical conclusion? Perhaps this new light on the "*causes*" of faction could show a new way "of controlling its *effects*."[39]

The difficulties were obvious. A small economic faction or a tiny splinter group of crack-pots, offered little trouble: "relief is supplied by the republican principle, which enables the majority to defeat [the minority's] sinister views by regular vote." But what if a ruthless and overbearing party included 60 or 70 percent of the electorate?

> When a majority is included in a faction, the form of popular government...enables it to sacrifice to its ruling passion or interest both the public good and rights of other citizens. To secure the public good and private rights against the danger of such a faction, and at the same time preserve the spirit and the form of popular government, is then the great object to which our inquiries are directed. Let me add that it is the great desideratum by which this form of government can be rescued

from the opprobrium under which it has so long labored, and
be recommended to the esteem and adoption of mankind.[40]

Needless to say, James Madison had become convinced that he knew
how this "great desideratum" was to be achieved.

The importance for republican theory of his discovery of the wide
variety of different types of factions had dawned on him. If society is
polarized into two clashing groups, violent conflict is inevitable and
the strongest of the two will arrogate to itself supreme power after
crushing its rival; realistically speaking, the poorer members of a state
will rob the rich by their voting control of the government, with such
devices as paper money, stay laws, and unequal taxes. But what
happens, Madison asked, if some of the poor are Baptist and some are
Anglicans; and both fear each other for religious reasons; what if some
blame their poverty on rack-renting landlords and some on grasping
bankers; what if the rabble from Massachusetts will follow only New
England demagogues, while the poor white from Georgia will listen
only to a leader with a Southern accent? Will not the very fragmenta-
tion of society into a complex swarm of self-interested units serve to
guarantee all minorities their rights by their very multiplicity? Is
there a possibility of establishing a commonwealth where functional
checks and balances in the very body of society itself will protect
"the opulent few" from the grasping many? Madison was certain from
reading and from experience that such a government was possible; he
was further convinced that the Constitutional Convention had the
ideal chance of establishing it in the United States.

A slighting remark of Mr. Sherman's about Rhode Island—in
1787 everybody who was rich, or wise, or well born was making such
remarks about Rhode Island—gave Madison his cue for presenting his
theory to the Convention. Sherman had said that Rhode Island was
faction ridden because it was so small. All the states, Madison cried in
rebuttal, are too small. Had not "faction & oppression...prevailed in
the largest as well as the smallest tho' less than in the smallest; and
were we not thence admonished to enlarge the sphere as far as the
nature of the Govt. would admit. This was the only defence agst. the
inconveniencies of democracy consistent with the democratic form of
Govt."[41] So long as government was limited to a small area a
homogenous, cohesive, majority faction would inevitably arise to
threaten the local minority.[42] "In all cases where a majority are
united by a common interest or passion, the rights of the minority are
in danger." Neither conscience nor honor will serve to keep them
from passing unjust laws in a popular state; "religion itself may
become a motive to persecution & oppression." Madison did not fail

to drive home his point with observations from "the Histories of every Country antient & modern." The conclusion he felt that the Convention must draw from the evidence should impel them to institute a national government comprehending as wide a variety of economic, religious, and social interests as was possible. This sovereign cure for faction would leave any strong single-minded minority in a comparatively advantageous position among a welter of divergent and mutually incompatible regional factions. To "enlarge the sphere" would "thereby divide the community into so great a number of interests & parties, that in the 1st place a majority will not be likely at the same moment to have a common interest separate from that of the whole or of the minority; and the 2nd place, that in case they shd. have such an interest, they may not be apt to united in the pursuit of it."[43] Madison was understandably proud that he had discovered "a republican remedy for the diseases most incident to republican government."[44]

The importance of Madison's theory for his distinguished fellows at the Philadelphia convention did not lie in its economic interpretation of history, nor yet in its jaundiced prophecy of what a popular majority might do if ever it became conscious of its strength. These were political clichés that all the delegates knew by heart.[45] What Madison had done that was noteworthy in 1787 was to devise a new formula which could be substituted for the weighty authority of the mixed monarchy theorists. He had ignored none of the traditional elements that they had used to erect their crowned pyramid. Yet he had exploded the theoretical argument for a hereditary aristocracy whose political privileges were claimed to be a necessary adjunct of their natural right to property. The theory was therefore able to give doctrinal respectability to the Virginia plan, with its innovations and anomalies.[46] In a very real sense, Madison's brain child must be credited with moderating the tendency of the Convention to push matters too far and "tone" their new government too high.

It cannot be argued that the Constitution that was to emerge from behind the closed doors of the Convention Hall was democratic in spirit or form. It was a candid attempt to limit the sphere of popular rule. Nor was the Convention content to do this merely by trusting to Madison's assurance that factions could be neutralized by enlarging the sphere of government. The only democratic organ it was intended that the new government should possess was the House of Representatives; and it was carefully checked and balanced by a quasi-aristocratic (or plutocratic) senate, the electoral college, the presidential veto, and by judicial review. Nevertheless with the tide of reaction as it was in 1787 under the combined impetus of Captain Shays and the classical writers on democracy it was of incalculable significance that the only organ of government that was constituted with a permanent and irresponsible will was the Supreme Court. If the Constitution had gone beyond an indirect denial of popular rule in its institutional structure it is hard to see how it could have survived the democratic upsurge kindled all over the world by the French Revolution.

Since the Constitution was "pork, still" even with all of its oligarchic features, it was possible to transform it by interpretation into an instrument for direct popular rule.[47] Its ambiguities, both deliberate and unconscious, were its saving feature.[48] In time the American people came to believe, under Jefferson's tutelage, that it was a genuine expression of democracy. This may have been "a great conservative fiction" as Walter Lippman claims,[49] but it is a fiction that it would have been impossible to propagate if the Constitution had not been on its face almost "purely republican" as James Madison described it without the least conscious hypocrisy.

There can be no question that Madison himself valued his new theory primarily because it solved the paradox of liberty and security within the frame of republican institutions. Hamilton proposed that the people's rulers, if drawn automatically from the ranks of the rich, the wise, and well-born, would be purged of passion, ambition and self-interest. He accepted unhesitatingly Locke's dictum that it would be ridiculous to put yourself in the power of a lion in the hope that he would protect you from "polecats or foxes."[50] As Madison was to recall in a letter to Jefferson: "It has been remarked that there is a tendency in *all* Governments to an augmentation of power at the expence of liberty... Power, when it has attained a certain degree of energy and independence, goes on generally to further degrees."[51] Hamilton had sadly complained to the Convention as it listened unconvinced to his great speech that "Gentlemen differ in their opinions concerning the necessary checks from the different estimates they form of human passions." He was mistaken, however, in thinking that these different estimates were solely a question of sentimentality about the people. In part they sprang from the convictions of men like Madison that the New Yorker's concept of the few was overly romantic. As Madison was to remark, government itself "was the greatest of all reflections on human nature. If men were angels no government would be necessary." But he was quick to continue in the next breath, "If angels were to govern men, neither external nor internal controls in government would be necessary. In framing a government which is to be administerd by men over men, the great difficulty lies in this: you must first enable the government to control the governed, and in the next place, oblige it to control itself."[52] Madison was far less exclusive than Hamilton in his estimate of where passion could be expected to appear. All groups or interests required watching lest they do harm.

It is easy to imagine, therefore, the satisfaction with which James Madison of Virginia contemplated his new departure in political theory. As he wrote to Jefferson the month after the Convention adjourned, the new Constitution did not depart very drastically from the type of government that the people of America had set up and lived under since independence.[53] This was possible, he was explicitly to claim, because his theory of the extended republic provided a stable alternative to mixed government; the doctrine of the "expanded sphere" made all the ancient arguments for a permanent executive and a permanent Senate obsolete and inapplicable for America.

There are but two methods, Madison noted in the fifty-first *Federalist*, for securing the rights of minorities in states where the people are given political power:

> the one by a creating a will in the community independent of the majority—that is, of the society itself; the other, by comprehending in the society so many separate descriptions of citizens as will render an unjust combination of a majority... impracticable. The first method prevails in all government possessing an hereditary or self-appointed authority. This, at best, is but a precarious security; because a power independent of the society may as well espouse the unjust views of the major, as the rightful interests of the minor party, and may possibly be turned against both parties. The second method will be exemplified in the federal republic of the United States... In a free government the security for civil rights must be the same as that for religious rights. It consists in the one case in the multiplicity of interests, and in the other in the multiplicity of sects... In the extended republic of the United States, and among the great variety of interests, parties, and sects which it embraces, a coalition of a majority of the whole society could seldom take place on any other principles than those of justice and the general good; whilst there being thus less danger to a minor from the will of a major party, there must be less pretext, also, to provide for the security of the former, by introducing into the government a will not dependent on the latter, or, in other words, a will independent of the society itself.[54]

It is not strange that certain commentators hastily reading the fifty-first *Federalist* felt certain that Hamilton had written it. Some of its interminably long but neatly rounded phrases assuredly have the Hamiltonian ring. Some of them are, in fact, Hamilton's very words, known to have been spoken on the Convention floor in June, and probably repeated innumerable times in more intimate surroundings to his friends and associates. They were not written in this number of the Federalist, however, by Alexander Hamilton. They were being quoted by James Madison as he dispassionately hammered nail after nail in the coffin of Hamilton's theory of the "high toned" government.

*   *   *

If anyone had interrogated the members of the Constitutional Convention about the origins of James Madison's modified theory of the class struggle, they would probably have dismissed the question with a raised eyebrow. The answer was, in their day, obvious. Madison had a brilliant and inquiring mind; he had taken a prominent part in both State and Confederation politics for twelve of his thirty-six years.[55] Personality and background combined to make him a "profound politician." This combination in itself was enough to explain to his contemporaries the clarity and keenness of his insight into the political process. It is the duty of the historian, however, to keep repeating impertinent questions; for the answers are not so obvious a hundred and fifty years after the event. Pierce of Georgia noted that beside being a "profound politician" Madison was also "the scholar." Did this fact have any bearing on his theory of the "extended republic"? Did Madison's reading of history and political theory in any way mould his conclusion that "the opulent few" in American could eat their republican cake and have their property too? The evidence seems clear that it did.

"Let us consult experience, the guide that ought always to be followed whenever it can be found," counseled Madison in the fifty-second *Federalist*.[56] And the problem he is working on here, as elsewhere, most consistently in his writings and throughout the events of his life, depends for its solution on a mass of historical material. For Madison did, as indeed most of his contemporaries, take it for granted that the experience of Greece, the experience of Rome, the experience of England, as revealed in their history, would provide guiding lights to present-day problems. As a result, James Madison's brilliant and undeniably original contributions to the theory and practice of politics in America, rise on a staircase of example and analogy quarried from all the strata of the past.

A highly characteristic use of guiding analogy is seen in the technique Madison devises for securing property rights. If a multiplicity of sects proved the best method for securing religious toleration, might not a multiplicity of interests well secure civil rights? Madison, of course, had in mind the history of toleration in England since 1688. The means of securing religious toleration was a special interest of his all during his life. Pious persecution was one of the few things that could always throw the normally cool and composed Mr. Madison into a fervor of anger; and liberty of conscience was the first issue that he had conspicuously identified himself with on entering Virginia Politics.[57] Madison knew well enough that both minority and majority sects, when they had the power, had been every bit as ruthless toward their opponents as economic factions. Bishop Burnet's *History* gave him documentary evidence of the persecuting violence of Whig and Tory at the beginning of the century; and we know he used this work while pursuing his researches on the problems of the Union.[58] The injustice and harshness of Anglicans toward dissenters, and of Puritans toward Anglicans, when they gained power in the seventeenth century, was so well remembered a hundred years later that Hume, in writing on the unbelievably cruel party strife of ancient Greece and Rome could find no comparison that would explain it to this enlightened contemporaries except in the field of religious fanaticism. "To exclude faction from a free government, is very difficult, if not altogether impracticable; but such inveterate rage between the factions [of the nobles and people], and such bloody maxims, are found in modern times amongst religious parties alone."[59] Madison knew Hume's *Essays* exceedingly well. The Scot's juxtaposition of class struggle and denominational strife may well have stimulated his thought on the subject.

Madison knew, moreover, that freedom of conscience in England had not come about by arming any one sect with disproportionate power. William C. Rives, his first biographer, who knew Madison intimately from 1809 until his death, reports that he "was accustomed to quote with great approbation, as full of wisdom and truth, an observation made by Voltaire...on the sources of religious freedom and security in that country. 'If one religion only were allowed in England,' said the French philosopher, 'the government would possibly become arbitrary; if there were but two, the people would cut each other's throats; but as there are such a multitude, they all live happy and in peace.'"[60] Undoubtedly the analogy of the clashing economic factions and the persecuting sects was extremely suggestive to the young Virginian.

It is probable, however, that Madison found his theory with its positive receipt for a stable republic while searching for a negative rebuttal to Montesquieu's theory of the small republic. After the War for Independence had ended the external pressure of Britain on the thirteen American states, the centripetal tendencies which sprang from their different economic and geographic situation immediately became manifest. There was much talk about the possibility and the advantage of a break-up of the Confederation into several homogeous regional units. Whether this suggestion came from Southerners interested in a wholly agrarian commonwealth, or New Englanders, who took the promotion of commerce to be the equivalent of liberty and independence, all proponents of dividing the union could fortify their arguments with Montesquieu's pronouncement that a large republic was unworkable. Montesquieu's authority was at its height in America just then; so most of the advocates of disunion seized upon the Frenchman's theory as a god-send.

Montesquieu's flat dictum that "it is natural for a republic to have only a small territory; otherwise it cannot long subsist,"[61] was as plausible on its face as it was superficial. The hypothesis indicates the difficulty of basing a large commonwealth upon consent and common ideals in a society where means of communication and transport are primitive. Nor could Americans struggling with this very problem deny its importance. The theory was based mainly, however, the *ex post facto* argument that most of the republics Montesquieu had read about were small and most of the large empires in ancient history had been despotically administered from the center. Consequently, for nationalists intent on erecting "a common roof" over inhabitants of a territory that stretched north and south from Vermont to Georgia, and extended westward past the wilds of Vincennes, it presented a great ideological barrier. It is significant that both Madison and Hamilton felt it necessary to devote an entire essay in the *Federalist* to specific refutation of the French philosopher's dogmatic statement.[62]

Alexander Hamilton was content to comb Montesquieu's own work and to pull out of its eclectic mass a remark that favored a confederated republic in a sizable area; but Madison, the thorough scholar, wanted to do more than bandy quotations from different chapters of the same book. The problem of the correct area of a republic was part of his research project on Confederations. We can be sure at any rate that while reading his eye was sharpened to discover any hint that would illuminate this unacceptable proposition of Montesquieu.

In Aristotle's *Politics*, as part of book VI, from which Madison was to draw the distinction between a republic and a democracy which appears in the tenth *Federalist*, there was a discussion in point. Aristotle saw with clarity that if any state was divided sharply into two groups of the rich and the poor bitter strife was inevitably the result. "It is plain, therefore, that the best commonwealth is that in which middling men most abound; and prove, if not more powerful than both, at least superior to either of the extremes. When this does not take place, the commonwealth necessarily degenerates either into oligarchy or into democracy... Such a republic is not only less liable to be subverted: it subsists unagitated by sedition; the great intermediate mass restraining the activity of the two hostile extremes; for this reason, democracies are found to be more durable than oligarchies, because in the former, the middling class is more numerous than in the latter; and large communities enjoy more tranquility than small ones, which, from the paucity of their members, have few citizens of an intermediate condition between riches and poverty."[63] Madison, if this passage caught his eye, must have paused thoughtfully over the last sentence. If the causes of faction could not be obviated, nevertheless, their effect might at least be controlled by compounding their number. The thing to be avoided was a social organization where two and only two groups were pitted against each other. Increase the size of the community and functional balances may be found in the larger body of society itself, to offset the extremes of the rich and the poor.

It was David Hume's speculations on the "Idea of a Perfect Commonwealth" however that most stimulated James Madison's thought on factions.[64] In this essay Hume disclaimed any attempt to substitute a political Utopia for "the common botched and inaccurate governments" which seemed to serve imperfect men so well. Nevertheless he argued the idea of a perfect commonwealth "is surely the most worthy curiosity of any the wit of man can possibly devise. And who knows, if this controversy were fixed by the universal consent of the wise and learned, but in some future age, an opportunity might be afforded by reducing the theory to practice, either by the dissolution of some old government, or by the combination of men to form a new one, in some distant part of the world." At the very end of Hume's essay was a discussion that could not help being of interest in Madison. For here the Scotchman casually demolished the Montesquieu small-republic theory; and it was this part of his essay, contained in a single page, that was to serve in new-modeling a "botched" Confederation "in a distant part of the world."

Hume concluded his subject with some observations of "the falsehood of the common opinion that no large state, such as France or Great Britain could ever be modeled into a commonwealth, but that such a form of government can only take place in a city or small territory." The opposite seemed to be true, decided Hume. "Though it is more difficult to form a republican government in an extensive country than in a city; there is more facility, when once it is formed, of preserving it steady and uniform, without tumult and faction."

The formidable problem of first unifying the outlying and various segments of a big area had thrown Montesquieu and like minded theorists off the track, Hume believed. "It is not easy, for the distant parts of a large state to combine in any plan of free government; but they easily conspire in the esteem and reverence for a single person, who by means of this popular favor, may seize the power, and forcing the more obstinate to submit, may establish a monarchical government."[65] Historically, therefore, it is the great leader who has been the symbol and engine of unity in empire building. His characteristic ability to evoke loyalty has made him in the past a mechanism both of solidarity and of exploitation. His leadership enables diverse peoples to work for a common end, but because of the temptations inherent in his strategic position he usually ends by crowning himself King.

And yet, this last step is not a rigid social law as Montesquieu would have it. Hume was a fervent believer in the classical idea of the great legislator. There was always the possibility that some leader with the virtue of a Solon or of a Lycurgus would suppress his personal ambition and found a free state in a large territory "to secure the peace, happiness, and liberty of future generations."[66] In 1776—the year Hume died—a provincial notable named George Washington was starting on the career that was to justify Hume's penetrating analysis of the unifying role of the great man in a large and variegated empire. Hume would have exulted at the discovery that his deductive leap into the dark of prophecy was correct: all great men did not necessarily desire crowns.

Having disposed of the reason monarchies had usually been set up in big empires and why it was a matter of free will rather than of necessity, Hume then turned to the problem of the easily-founded, and unstable, small republic. In contrast to the large, "a city readily concurs in the same notions of government, the natural equality of property favours liberty,[67] and the neatness of habitation enables the citizens mutually to assist each other. Even under absolute princes, the subordinate government of cities is commonly republican... But these same circumstances, which facilitate the erection of commonwealths in cities, render their constitution more frail and uncertain. Democracies are turbulent. For however the people may be separated or divided into small parties, either in their votes or elections; their near habitation in a city will always make the force of popular tides and currents very sensible. Aristocracies are better adapted for peace and order, and accordingly were most admired by ancient writers; but they are jealous and oppressive."[68] Here of course was the ancient dilemma that Madison knew so well, restated by Hume. In the city where wealth and poverty existed in close proximity the poor if given the vote might very well use the power of government to expropriate the opulent. While the rich, ever a self-conscious minority in a republican state, were constantly driven by fear of danger, even when no danger existed in fact, to take aggressive and oppressive measures to head off the slightest threat to their property.

It was Hume's next two sentences that must have electrified Madison. "In a large government, which is modeled with masterly skill, there is compass and room enough to refine the democracy, from the lower people, who may be admitted into the first elections or first concoction of the commonwealth, to the higher magistrates, who direct all the movements. At the same time, the parts are so distant and remote, that it is very difficult, either by intrigue, prejudice, or passion, to hurry them into any measure against the public interest."[69] Hume had stood the small-territory republic theory upside down: if a free state could once be established in a large area it would be stable and safe from the effects of faction. Madison had found the answer to Montesquieu. He had also found in embryonic form the theory of the extended federal republic.

Madison could not but feel that the "political aphorisms" that David Hume scattered so lavishly in his essays were worthy of his careful study. He reexamined the sketch of Hume's perfect commonwealth; "a form of government, to which," Hume claimed, "I cannot in theory discover any considerable objection." Hume suggested that Great Britain and Ireland—"or any territory of equal extent"—be divided into a hundred counties, that each county in turn be divided into one hundred parishes, making in all ten-thousand minor districts in the state. The twenty-pound freeholders and five hundred-pound householders in each parish were to elect annually a representative for the parish. These hundred parish representatives in each county would then elect out of themselves one "senator" and ten county "magistrates." There would thus be in "the whole commonwealth, 100 senators, 1100 county magistrates, and 10,000...representatives." Hume then would have vested in the Senators the executive power: "the power of peace and war, of giving orders to generals, admirals, and ambassadors, and, in short all the prerogatives of the King, except his negative." The county magistrates were to have the legislative power; but they were never to assemble as a single legislative body. They were to convene in their own counties, and each county was to have one vote; and although they could initiate legislation, Hume expected the Senators normally to make policy. The ten-thousand parish representatives were to have the right to a referendum when the other two orders in the state disagreed.

It was all very complicated and cumbersome but Hume thought that it would allow a government to be based on the consent of the "people" and at the same time obviate the danger of factions. He stated the "political aphorism" which explained his complex system.

> The lower sort of people and small proprietors are good judges enough of one not very distant from them in rank or habitation; and therefore, in their parochial meetings, will probably chuse the best, or nearly the best representative: But they are wholly unfit for county meetings, and for electing into the higher offices of the republic. Their ignorance gives the grandees an opportunity of deceiving them.[70]

This carefully graded hierarchy of officials therefore carried the system of indirect elections to its ultimate conclusion.

Madison quite easily traced out the origin of Hume's idea. He found it in the essay entitled "Of the First Principles of Government,"[71] Hume had been led to his idea of fragmentizing election districts by his reading of Roman history and his contemplation of the evils incident to the direct participation of every citizen in government. The Scotchman had little use for "a pure republic," that is to say, a direct democracy. "For though the people, collected in a body like the Roman tribes, be quite unfit for government, yet when dispersed in small bodies, they are more susceptible both of reason and order; the force of popular currents and tides is, in a great measure broken; and the public interest may be pursued with some method and constancy."[72] Hence Hume's careful attempts to keep the citizens with the suffrage operating in thousands of artificially created electoral districts. And as Madison thought over Hume's suggested techniques and explanations, it must suddenly have struck him that in this instance the troublesome corporate aggressiveness of the thirteen American states could be used to good purpose. There already existed in United States local governing units to break the force of popular currents. There was no need to invent of a system of counties in America. The States themselves would serve as the chief pillars and supports of a new constitution.

Here in Hume's *Essays* lay the germ for Madison's theory of the extended republic. It is interesting to see how he took these scattered and incomplete fragments and built them into an intellectual structure of his own. Madison's first full statement of this hypothesis appeared in his "Notes on the Confederacy" in April, 1787, eight months before the final version of it was published as the tenth *Federalist*.[73] Starting with the proposition that "the majority in a republican government, however composed, ultimately give the law," Madison then asks what is to restrain an interested majority from unjust violations of the minority's rights. Three motives might be claimed to meliorate the selfishness of the majority: they are "prudent regard for their own good, as involved in the general...good," second, religious scruples, and finally "respect for character." After examining each in its turn Madison concludes that they are but a frail bulwark against a ruthless party.

In his discussion of the insufficiency of "respect for character" as a curb on faction Madison borrows heavily from Hume. The Scotchman had stated paradoxically that it is "a just *political* maxim *that every man must be supposed a knave*: Though at the same time, it appears somewhat strange, that a maxim should be true in *politics*, which is false in *fact*...men are generally more honest in their private than in their public capacity, and will go greater lengths to serve a party, than when their own private interest is alone concerned. Honour is great check upon mankind: But where a considerable body of men act together, this check is in a great measure, removed; since a man is sure to be approved of by his own party...and he soon learns to dispose the clamours of adversaries."[74] This argument seemed to Madison too just and pointed not to use, so under "Respect for character" he set down: "However strong this motive may be in individuals, it is considered as very insufficient to restrain them from injustice. In a multitude its efficacy is diminished in proportion to the number which is to share the praise or the blame. Besides, as it has reference to public opinion, which, within a particular society, is the opinion of the majority, the standard is fixed by those whose conduct is to be measured by it."[75] The young Virginian readily found a concrete example in Rhode Island, where honor had proved to be no check on fractious behavior. In a letter to Jefferson explaining the theory of the new constitution, Madison was to repeat his category of inefficacious motives,[76] but in formally presenting his theory to the world in the letters of Publius he deliberately excluded it.[77] There was a certain disadvantage in making derogatory remarks to a majority that must be persuaded to adopt your arguments.

In April when Madison was writing down his first thoughts on the advantage of an extended government he had still not completely integrated Hume's system of indirect elections. The Virginian had not dismissed the subject from his thoughts, however. He had taken the subsidiary element of Hume's "Perfect Commonwealth" argument and developed it as the primary factor in his own theorem; but he was also to include Hume's major technic of indirect election as a minor device in the new American state. As the last paragraph of "Notes on the Confederacy" there appears a long sentence that on its face has little organic relation to the preceding two-page discussion of how "an extensive Republic meliorates the administration of a small Republic."

> An auxiliary desideratum for the melioration of the Republican form is such a process of elections as will most certainlyextract from the mass of the society the purest and noblest characters which it contains; such as will at once feel most strongly the proper motives to pursue the end of their appointment, and be most capable to devise the proper means of attaining.[78]

This final sentence, with its abrupt departure in thought, would be hard to explain were it not for the juxtaposition in Hume of the material on large area and indirect election.

All of Hume's speculations on the ideal government are paralleled in Madison's "Notes." In time the Scot's panacea of indirect elections was to be tried in the Electoral College designed to choose the President of the United States. The weakness of the method has been manifest in all elections since Washington's. The breakdown began when James Madison and his friend Thomas Jefferson organized a majority party that coalesced across state lines and so was able to force its will on electors even twice removed from the people. How a situation arose in which Madison was forced to subvert his own electoral method must be discussed later. In theory, at least, he never refuted the ideal he shared with Hume, of sifting the popular will.

When Madison was called on to formally present his thesis to the world in the tenth *Federalist*, Hume's *Essays* were to offer one final service. Hume had written a paper on "Parties in General" in which he took the position independently arrived at by Madison concerning the great variety of factions likely to agitate a republican state. The Virginian, with his characteristic thoroughness, therefore turned to Hume again when it came time to parade his arguments in full dress. Hume had already made his major contribution to Madison's political philosophy. Now he was to help in the final polishing and the effect was to achieve the most effective possible presentation.

Madison had no capacity for slavish imitation; but a borrowed word, a sentence lifted almost in its entirety from the other's essay, and above all, the exactly parallel march of ideas in the two papers, show how congenial he found the Scot's way of thinking, and how invaluable Hume was in the final moulding of Madison's own convictions. "Men have such a propensity to divide into personal factions," wrote Hume, "that the smallest appearance of real difference will produce them." And the Virginian takes up the thread to spin his more elaborate web: "So strong is this propensity of mankind to fall into mutual animosities, that where no substantial occasion presents itself, the most frivolous and fanciful distinctions have been sufficient to kindle their unfriendly passions and excite their most violent conflicts."[79] Hume, in his parallel passage presents copious examples. He cites the rivalry of the blues and the greens at Constantinople, and recalls the feud between two tribes in Rome, the Pollia and the Papira, that lasted three hundred years after everyone had forgotten the original cause of the quarrel. "If mankind had not such a strong propensity to such divisions, the indifference of the rest of the community must have suppressed this foolish animosity [of the two tribes] that had not any aliment of new benefits and injuries." The fine Latinity of the word "aliment"[80] apparently caught in some crevice of Madison's mind, soon to reappear in his statement, "Liberty is to faction what air is to fire, an aliment without which it instantly expires."[81] So far as his writings show he never used the word again; but this year of 1787 his head was full of such words and ideas culled from David Hume.

When one examines these two papers in which Hume and Madison summed up the eighteenth century's most profound thought on party, it becomes increasingly clear that the young American used the earlier work in preparing a survey on faction through the ages to introduce his own discussion of faction in America. Hume's work was admirably adapted to this purpose. It was philosophical in the best tradition of the Enlightenment. The facile damnation of faction had been a commonplace in English politics for a hundred years, as Whig and Tory vociferously sought to fasten the label to each other. But the Scotchman, very little interested as a partisan and very much so as a social scientist, could treat the subject therefore in psychological, intellectual, and socioeconomic terms. Throughout all history he discovered mankind has been divided into factions based either on personal loyalty to some leader or upon some "sentiment or interest" common the group as a unit. This latter type he called a "Real" as distinguished from a "Personal" faction. Finally he subdivided the "real factions" into parties based on "interest," upon "principle," or upon "affection." It took the Scot well over five pages to dissect these three types; but Madison, while determined to be inclusive, had not the space to go into such minute analysis. Besides, he was more intent now on developing the cure, than on describing the malady. He therefore consolidated Hume's two-page treatment of "personal" factions, and this long discussion of parties based on "principle and affection" into a single sentence. The tenth *Federalist* reads: "A zeal for different opinions concerning religion, concerning government, and many other points, as well of speculation as of practice,[82] and attachment to different leaders ambitiously contending for pre-eminence and power;[83] or to persons of other descriptions whose fortunes have been interesting to the human passions,[84] have, in turn, divided mankind into parties, inflamed them with mutual animosity, and rendered them much more disposed to vex and oppress each other than to cooperate for their common good." It is hard to conceive of a more perfect example of the concentration of idea and meaning than Madison achieved in this famous sentence. It is one of the prime cases of political writing, achieving an intensity blended with richness of form and content that comes close to carrying the impact of great poetry.

It is noteworthy that while James Madison compressed the greater part of Hume's essay on factions into a single sentence, he greatly expanded the quick sketch of the faction from "interest" buried in the middle of [the] Scotch philosopher's analysis. This reference, in Madison's hands, became the climax of his treatment, and is the basis of his reputation in some circles as the progenitor of the theory of economic determinism. Hume had written that factions from interest "are the most reasonable, and the most excusable. Where two orders of men, such as the nobles and people, have a distinct authority in a government, not very accurately balanced and modeled, they naturally follow a distinct interest; nor can we reasonably expect a different conduct, considering that degree of selfishness implanted in human nature. It requires much skill in a legislator to prevent such parties; and many philosophers are of opinion, that this secret like the *grand elixir* or *perpetual motion*, may amuse men in theory but can never possibly be reduced to practice."[85] With this uncomfortable thought Hume dismissed the subject of economic factions as he fell to the congenial task of sticking sharp intellectual pins into priestly parties and bigots who fought over abstract political principles.

Madison, on the contrary, was not satisfied with this cursory treatment. He had his own ideas about the importance of economic forces. All that Hume had to say of personal parties, of parties of principle, and attachment, was but a prologue to the Virginian's discussion of "the various and unequal distribution of property," throughout recorded history. "Those who hold and those who are without property have ever formed distinct interests in society. Those who are creditors and those who are debtors, fall under a like discrimination. A landed interest, a manufacturing interest, a mercantile interest, a moneyed interest,[86] with many lesser interests, grow up of necessity in civilized nations, and divide them into different classes actuated by different sentiments and views." Here was the pivot of Madison's analysis. Here in this multiplicity of economic factions was "the grand elixir" that transformed the ancient doctrine of the rich against the poor into a situation that a skillful American legislator might model into equilibrium. Compound various economic interests of a large territory with a federal system of thirteen semi-sovereign political units, establish a Humian scheme of indirect elections, which will functionally bind the extensive area into a unit while "refining" the voice of the people, and you will have a stable republican state.

This is the glad news that James Madison carried to Philadelphia. This is the theory which he claimed had made obsolete the necessity for the "mixed government" advocated by Hamilton and Adams. This was the message he gave to the world in the first *Federalist* paper he composed. His own reading of history, ancient and modern, and above all his knowledge of the works of David Hume, ablest English historian of his age, had served him and his country well. "Of all men, that distinguished themselves by memorable achievements, the first place of honour, seems due to Legislators and founders of states, who transmit a system of laws and institutions to secure the peace, happiness, and liberty of future generations."[87]

As Edwin Mims with his usual perspicuity remarks, "It is always an ungrateful task to apply 'the learned knife' of analysis to the tissue of a system of living thought... *The Federalist* papers, like all literary masterpieces, lose immeasurably when broken up into major and minor categories."[88] One regrets particularly the sacrifice of artistry and vitality in this breaking-up of the tenth *Federalist*. But the loss is only temporary—nothing that an uninterrupted rereading will not abundantly restore.

The dissection of Madison's mental processes does make clear that a great deal of his thought was derivative. The ideas that he manipulated were all more or less current in eighteenth-century America; and the particular theory with which his name has been indelibly associated has been shown above to owe much to David Hume. But for all of that, Madison's was essentially an original mind. Whoever thinks that the Virginian's borrowings show him to be a mere dealer in the second-hand should read Hume's scattered remarks and then reread entirely the *Federalist* paper into which they were incorporated. Madison's close-knit reasoning has turned fragmentary bits and pieces into a "system of living thought" as functional as it is coherent. No amount of research can make the smooth flowing paragraphs of the tenth *Federalist* stale. Madison, like all great men who have been intellectual borrowers, could re-forge old ideas into a tool indisputably his own.[89] His consciousness had to feed on ideas, theories, assumptions, and value-schemes current in his own day; but he did not re-issue this medley of thoughts without recreating them. The tenth *Federalist* bears the mark of James Madison's own mind on every page. The positive side of its originality is to be seen in its extraordinary impact, a century after Madison's death, upon all Americans who are still wrestling with the problem of majority rule and minority rights.

Notes

1. "It can be little doubted that if the State of Rhode Island was separated from the Confederacy and left to itself, the insecurity of rights under the popular form of government within such narrow limits would be displayed by such reiterated oppressions of factious majorities that some power altogether independent of the people would soon be called for the voice of the very factions whose misrule had proved the necessity of it." Madison, *Federalist*, LI.

2. Madison, writing to Jefferson on March 19th, 1787, just as the last sporadic flickers of the Shaysite resistance was being stamped out, speaks of the mortal diseases of the existing constitution. "These diseases need not be pointed out to you, who so well understand them. Suffice it to say, that they are at present marked by symptoms which are truly alarming, which have tainted the faith of the most orthodox republicans, and which challenge from the votaries of liberty every concession in favor of stable Government not infringing fundamental principles, as the only security against an opposite extreme of our present situation." Madison, *Letters*, I:285. To Thomas Jefferson, March 19, 1787.

3. Madison, *Letters*, I:288-289. To George Washington, April 16, 1787, [Italics mine]. Madison was clearly fretted by this dilemma of how to establish a republican state dedicated to justice on the basis of a majority that like as not would be inclined to injustice. It is significant that despite his disillusioned suspicions about the many, he never denied the *lex majoris partis* was the fundamental law of republicanism.

4. Madison, *Letters*, I:322, from "Notes on the Confederacy." This memorandum which Madison subheaded "Vices of the Political system in the U. States" was written in April, 1787.

5. Hamilton's outline of his speech of June 18. J.C. Hamilton, *History*, III:260.

6. Hamilton's outline. J.C. Hamilton's *History*, III:281.

7. Madison's report, June 18th. *Documents*, 221. Cf. Yates, 781. "Can a democratic assembly, who annually revolve in the mass of the people, be supposed steadily to pursue the public good? Nothing but a permanent body can

check the imprudence of democracy. Their turbulent and uncontrolling disposition requires checks. The senate of New York, although chosen for four years, we have found to be inefficient. Will, on the Virginia plan, a continuance of seven years do it?"

8. Madison's rendering [of] Hamilton's statement here while roughly accurate conceals a most important aspect of the function he visualized for his elective monarch. Hamilton's outline reads, "It is said a republican government does not admit a vigorous execution. It is therefore bad; for goodness of government consists in its vigorous execution." J.C. Hamilton, *History*, III:282. Hamilton believed in a "positive state" along mercantilist lines (see Walton Hamilton and D. Adair, *The Power to Govern*, New York: 1937, 175-177) and it was to the executive that he looked for dynamic planning and energetic administrative decisions. It was all very well to speak of "checks" and static equilibrium when it came to keeping the mob in place, but good government according to Hamilton required an active program that was not to be hampered by the clumsy triune apparatus that he praised in theory. One beauty of the English system in Hamilton's eyes was that the convention of the Constitution (brought to perfection by Walpole) whereby the King's chief minister "corrupted" the theoretically separated legislature with places and pensions, provided a technique for insuring a steady and dynamic executive policy, although it operated behind the facade of separation of powers.

9. Madison's report, June 18th, *Documents*, 221-222.

10. Hamilton's italics.

11. "Hamilton's outline," J.C. Hamilton, *History*, III:282. "What even is the Virginia plan, but *pork still with a little change in the sauce*." Yates' Notes; the italics are his. *Documents, 783*.

12. This combination of analytical insight and ability in one line of endeavor matched by fatuous blindness in others is not uncommon in prominent men; although it is often slurred over by their biographers. Henry Ford's dangerous conception of "the Jews," and S.F.B. Morse's ugly obsessions about "Catholics" are other obvious examples of this contradictory characteristic.

13. Morris, who still awaits a good biographer, was undoubtedly one of the most brilliant members of the Convention and one of the most capable leaders of the Federalist party. Madison, who was at odds with him politically after 1792, comes close to using eulogistic terms in estimating his contribution at Philadelphia. When Jared Sparks asked for information and anecdotes concerning Morris' share in the Convention, he wrote: "...it may be justly said that he [Morris] was an able, an eloquent, and an active member, and shared largely in the discussion succeeding the last of July... The *finish* given to the style and the arrangement of the Constitution fairly belongs to the pen of Mr. Morris... A better choice could not have been made."

It is but due to Mr. Morris to remark, that, to the brilliancy of his genius, he added, what is too rare, a candid surrender of his opinions, when the lights of discussion satisfied him, that they had been too hastily formed, and a readiness to aid in making the best of measures in which he had been overruled." To J. Sparks, April 8, 1831. Max Farrand, ed. *Records of the Federal Convention of 1787* (New Haven: 1911), III:499-500 (hereafter referred to as Farrand, *Records*).

14. G. Morris, *Correspondence* (Sparks ed.), II:260-261, to Robert Walsh, Feb. 15, 1811. Morris explains that: "He [Hamilton] heartily assented, nevertheless, to the Constitution, because he considered it as band, which might hold us together for some time, and he knew that national sentiment is the offspring of national existence. He trusted, moreover, that, in the changes and chances of time, we should be involved in some war, which might strengthen our union and nerve the executive."

Morris felt that Hamilton "was of all men the most indiscreet. He knew that a limited monarchy, even if established, could not preserve itself in this country...because there is not the regular gradation of ranks among our citizens, which is essential to that species of government. And he very well knew, that no monarchy whatever could be established by the mob. When a multitude of indigent, profligate people can be collected and organized, their envy of wealth, talents, and reputation will induce them to give themselves a master, provided that in so doing they can humble and mortify their superiors... Fortunately for us, no such mass of people can be collected in America. None such exists.

"But although General Hamilton knew these things from the study of history, and perceived them from the intuition of genius, he never failed on every occasion to advocate the excellence of, and avow his attachment to, monarchical government. By this course he not only cut off all chance of rising into office, but singularly promoted the views of his opponents, who, with the fondness for wealth and power which he had not, affected a love of the people, which he had and they had not. Thus meaning very well, he acted very ill, and approached the evils he apprehended by his very solicitude to keep them at a distance" (Morris, *Correspondence*, 262).

15. Wilson's remark refers specifically, of course, to Hamilton's recognition of this fact. "Mine is an odd destiny," he wrote to Gouverneur Morris in 1802. "Perhaps no man in the United States has sacrificed or done more for the present Constitution than myself; and contrary to all my anticipations of its fate, as you know, from the very beginning. I am still laboring to prop the frail and worthless fabric. Yet I have the murmers of its friends no less than the curse of its foes for my reward. What can I do better than withdraw from the scene? Every day proves to me more and more, that this American world was not for me... You, friend Morris, are by birth a native of this country, but by *genius* an exotic. You mistake if you fancy that you are more of a favorite than myself, or that you are in any sort upon a theatre suited to you." Quoted in Henry Cabot Lodge, *Alexander Hamilton* (Boston: 1882), 265-266.

16. Hamilton's italics.

17. Hamilton's italics.

18. J.C. Hamilton, *History*, III:359. Apparently ratification of the Constitution would merely act up to delay dissolution of the union, *unless* administrative devices could be found to so strengthen the Federal government that it could abolish the states. Mere ratification without speedy renovation of the new system would, therefore, be the equivalent of rejecting the Constitution, whose only virtue consisted in being a precarious *temporary* platform in the raging democratic sea. Refusal to ratify the Constitution (and presumably ratification without innovation) would result, Hamilton thought, in civil war.

"Should this happen, whatever parties prevail, it is probable governments very different from the present in their principles, will be established. A dismemberment of the union, and monarchies in different portions of it, may be expected. It may however happen that no civil war will take place, but several republican confederacies be established between different combinations of the particular states."

"A reunion with Great Britain, from universal disgust at a state of commotion, is not impossible, though not much to be feared. The most plausible shape of such a business would be, the establishment of a son of the present monarch in the supreme government of this country, with a family compact." Hamilton, *History*, 358-359.

Hamilton always repudiated the conclusions drawn from certain of his propositions by a few of his fellow Federalists after 1800: that since the union was so precarious and so near simple democracy it would be better deliberately to break off a New England bloc and form a correctly balanced government. See his letter to Theodore Sedgwick, July 10, 1804. "I will here express but one sentiment, which that dismemberment of our empire will be a clear sacrifice of great positive advantages without any counter-balancing good, administering no relief to our real disease, which is *democracy* [italics by A.H.], the poison of which by a subdivision will only be the more concentrated in each part, and consequently the more virulent." This was Hamilton's last statement on public affairs; within a week he was dead.

19. Since I intend to treat of this problem in detail later on, it may suffice here to give a quotation from Bolingbroke to indicate the obvious parallel. "Few men at that time [1688] looked forward enough to foresee the necessary consequences of the new constitution of the revenue...nor of the method of funding that immediately took place... Few people, I say, foresaw how the creation of funds, and the multiplication of taxes, would increase yearly the power of the crown, and bring our liberties...into more real, though less apparent danger, than they were in before the revolution... The notion of attaching men to the new government, by tempting them to embark their fortunes on the same bottom [i.e. invest in the public debt] was a reason of state to some: the notion of creating a new, that is a moneyed interest, in opposition to the landed interest, or as a balance to it, and of acquiring a superior influence in the city of London at least by the establishment of great corporations, was a reason of party to others: and I make no doubt that the opportunity of amassing immense estates by the management of funds, by trafficking paper, and by all the arts of jobbing, was a reason of private interest to those who supported and improved this scheme of iniquity, if not to those who devised it." Bolingbroke, *Letters on the Study and Use of History*, letter II. Bolingbroke's use of "the separation of powers" theory to fight Walpole's use of the funding, debts, etc. to corrupt and manage Parliament set the pattern for the Jeffersonian opposition to Hamilton.

A charmingly naive use of the identification of "sound" fiscal measures and payment of the National Debt with the Hanover succession is to be found in Addison's Spectator #3, where the author dreams of the "beautiful virgin," Public Credit, who "fainted and dyed away" when the young Pretender appeared with a sword in one hand and "a Spunge" for wiping out debts in the other.

This *Spectator* was quite possibly Madison's first introduction to this thorny problem which was to figure so importantly in his political career. His father's library was heavily weighted with books on home medication and theology; and the discovery there of Addison's essays opened a new and delightful world to him. See his letter to his nephew, presenting him with a copy, Jan. 4, 1829. Madison, *Letters*, IV:1.

20. See Madison's sarcastic comment in the essay on "Parties" published in Freneau's *National Gazette*, Jan., 1792. "From the expediency, in politics, of making natural parties mutual checks on each other, to infer the propriety of creating artificial parties in order to form them into mutual checks, is not less absurd than it would be in ethics to say that new vices ought to be promoted, where they would counteract each other, because this use may be made of existing vices." Madison, *Letters*, IV:469.

21. It can be argued that one of Madison's greatest contributions to American nationalism full equal to his yeomen work in the Philadelphia and Virginia conventions, was his keeping the main body of the opposition to Federalism within the framework of the Constitution itself. His invention of "strict construction" and his indoctrination of Jefferson on this point focused criticism not on the Document itself, but on the men who were torturing new powers and interpretations out of its clauses. The opposition to the Hamiltonian system because of Madison's leadership was firmly bottomed on a demand for absolute loyalty to the Constitution. This in effect cut the ground out from under the root-and-branch reformers like John Taylor of Caroline. In like manner Madison's conspicuous position in the ranks of the opposition gave pause to any Federalist designs of suppressing with Constitutional sanction all malcontents as outright traitors. Like the numerous parties formed in England during the 18th century around the Hanoverian Princes of Wales he was a guarantee, too conspicuous for comfort perhaps to some of the Federalists, that criticism of their policy was legitimate. Madison's services were invaluable for creating in the United States that indispensable branch of every free government: the loyal opposition. For a penetrating discussion of this point see A.E. Smith, *James Madison: Builder* (New York: 1937), 214-216.

22. Hamilton's most scholarly biographer, Henry Cabot Lodge (the need is great for a careful modern study of his life and intellectual development in eighteenth-century terms), while arguing for the irrationality of Hamilton's last phase ascribes it entirely to "the effect upon Hamilton of the French Revolution and the dangers which he came to believe threatened the country" (Lodge, *Alexander Hamilton*, 252). Lodge explains "that 'crisis' which had haunted Hamilton for years, which had grown to be his deepest conviction and his first thought" in the following terms: "Hamilton believed the constitution to be unequal to the burdens imposed upon it, and he considered the government too weak. At any moment, as it seemed to him, there might be a general upheaval, and that then the elements [sic.] which had desolated France and swept Europe might here engage in a conflict for supremacy... Then the salvation of the country and the preservation of constitutional liberty would demand a party of order, an army, and a leader ready to play the part of a saviour of society... That great part, Hamilton felt, would fall to him, and if the contingency had been

possible, there can be no doubt that he was the man to whom the party would have turned. He could not do this, he could not stand at the head of the army, if were possible for any man to cast even the most groundless imputation upon his courage. [Hence his acceptance of Burr's challenge]. He was utterly at fault in supposing that there were in the United States the same elements and the same forces as in France. Both race and history made their existence impossible." Lodge, 270.

I agree entirely with the later Senator's analysis, but would insist that Hamilton was hypnotized by the "elements" of anarchy from 1785 on, when the combination of his classical readings and Shays' rebellion set his mind in a mold that remained rigid for the rest of his life insofar as his over-all view of the "reality" of the political process was concerned. The French Revolution and the successful opposition of the American "Jacobins" like Madison, and Jefferson, to his system, merely accentuated his illusion that he could feel the hot breath of the jacquerie on the back of his neck. To Lodge's striking statement that Hamilton's death was "a result of the opinions bred by the French Revolution" I would merely add: and by viewing the American common man through "optic glasses" focused on antiquity.

23. Debate of June 21 (Yates), *Documents*, 781; this remark is not reported though it is implied in Madison's notes. Rufus King's rendering of Johnson's remark is: "The Gentleman from N. York is praised by all, but supported by no Gentleman." Yates, *Documents*, 862.

24. Hamilton's speech of June 18th (Yates' report), *Documents*, 783.

25. Hamilton continued to propagandize for his strong organized government by mail. In his letter to Washington, from New York, July 3, 1787: "I have conversed with men of information not only of this City but from different parts of the state; and they agree that there has been an astounding revolution for the better in the minds of the people. The prevailing apprehension among thinking men is, that the Convention from a fear of shocking the popular opinion, will not go far enough—They seem to be convinced that a strong well mounted government will better suit the popular palate than one of a different complexion.

"A plain but sensible man, in a conversation I had with him yesterday, expressed himself nearly in this manner—The people begin to be convinced that their 'excellent form of government' as they have been used to call it, will not answer their purpose; and that they must substitute something not very remote from what which they have lately quitted." Farrand, *Records*, III:53.

26. "Energy in government is essential to that security against external and internal danger... Stability in government is essential to national character... On comparing, however, these valuable ingredients with the vital principles of liberty, we must perceive at once the difficulty of mingling them together in their due proportions." *Federalist*, XXXVII.

27. Correa Moylan Walsh, *The Political Science of John Adams, A Study in the Theory of Mixed Government and the Bicameral System* (New York: 1915), 336. This stimulating and thorough work which is one of the very few satisfactory studies of the background and theoretical complexity of the Founding Fathers' political philosophy, apparently fell still born from the press.

In spite of Walsh's conclusive evidence of the influence of Adam's writings during the critical period and during the early years of the republic, it has received little notice from historians who have treated of the evolution of the constitution. Walsh's obscure and lonely grandeur in the field is probably the result of the enormous impact of Charles Beard's economic interpretations upon the historical guild. Published at the same time as Walsh's work, these volumes (*The Economic Interpretation of the Constitution*, 1912; *The Economic Origins of Jeffersonian Democracy*, 1915) pre-empted the field of constitutional interpretation for a generation of scholars.

28. Debates of June 30th, *Documents*, 314.

29. "Liste des Membres et Officiers du Congrés, 1788." Farrand, *Records,* III:237. The characterization of Hamilton is also relevant. "*Grand orateur; intrépide dans les débate publics. Partisan zélé et même outré de la nouvelle Constitution... C'est un de ces hommes rares, qui s'est distingué égalment au champ du bataille et au barreau. Il doit tout à ses talens... Il a un peu trop des prétentions et trop peu de prudence.*

"*Voici ce que M. Le chev[lier] de L[a] L[uzerne] dit de lui en 1780. 'M. H.[amilton], un des aides, de camp du Gal. Wash[ington] a le plus d'ascendant sur lui; homme d'ésprit, d'une médicre probité; éloigné des Anglais parce qu'étant d'une tréa basse extraction dans une de leurs colonies, il craint de rentrer dans son ancien Etat... M. Conway pense qu'Hamilton haît les François, qu'il est absolument corrumpu et que les qu'il paroitra avoir avec nous ne seront jamais que trompeuses.'*

M. Hamilton n'a rien fait qui puisse justifier cette dernière opinion; il est seulment trop impétuex, et à force de vouloir tout conduire, il manque sont but." Farrand, *Records*, 234.

["List of the members and Officers of Congress, 1788." The characterization of Hamilton is also relevant. "Great orator; intrepid in public debates. Zealous and even excessive partisan of the new Constitution... This is one of these rare men, who was just as distinguished on the field of battle and at the bar. He owes everything to his talents...He has a bit too many pretensions and too little prudence."

"This is what M. Le Chev. De Luzerne says of him in 1780. 'M. Hamilton, one of the aides de camp of General Washington has the most ascendenacy upon himself; man of spirit, of mediocre probity; estranged from the English because of his being of very low birth in one of their colonies, he fears returning to his former State. M. Conway thinks that Hamilton hates the French, that he is thoroughly corrupt and that the relations he appears to have with us will never be anything but misleading.'

"M. Hamilton has done nothing that would justify this last opinion; he is only too impetuous, and by dint of wishing to direct everything, he misses his mark."]

30. The theory forms the climax of "Notes on the Confederacy" written in April, 1767, Madison, *Letters*, I:325-327; for other elaborations see letter to Jefferson, Oct. 24, 1787, I:350-353; "Notes on Suffrage," written in 1829, IV:22ff; and Federalist, LI.

31. This was the speech that Pierce reports was an "able and ingenious"

survey of "the beauties and defects of ancient Republics; [which] compared their situation with ours wherever it appeared to bear any analogy, and proved that the only way to make a Government answer all the end of its institution, was to collect the wisdom of its several parts in aid of each other wherever it was necessary." *Documents*, 94. Madison also dealt with the problem in Debates of June 26th and Aug. 7th from [a] slightly different focus.

32. Madison had hesitated even after the Annapolis Convention about the practicability of a stronger Union. After he heard about the Shays outbreak all hesitation ceased. A letter of Nov. 1, 1786, recounting the first reports of that affair had reached him, declares that an "amendment of the confederacy" is necessary to its continuance. Madison's report of the "rebellion" is instructive: "We learn that great commotions are prevailing in Massachusetts. An appeal to the Sword is exceedingly dreaded. The discontented, it is said, are as numerous as the friends of Government, and more decided in their measures. Should they get the uppermost, it is uncertain what may be the effect. They profess to aim only at reform of their Constitution...but an abolition of debts, public and private, and a new division of property, are strongly suspected to be in contemplation." To James Madison, Sr., *Letters*, I:253-254.

33. "Notes on the Confederacy," *Letters*, I:325.

34. *Federalist*, X.

35. *Federalist, X.

36. *Federalist, X

37. Madison believed that the inequality of property also resulted from the "nature of man." After discussing the "fallibility of reason" which influences the "self-love" of different individuals in different ways and this explains the variety of noneconomic conflicts in society, he continues: "The diversity in the faculties of men, from which the rights of property originate, is...an insuperable obstacle to a Uniformity of interests. The protection of these faculties is the first object of government. From the protection of different and unequal faculties of acquiring property, the possession of different degrees and kinds of property immediately results; and from the influence of these on the sentiments and views of the respective proprietors, ensues a division of the society into different interests and parties." Madison, of course, as is commonly the case with a member of a privileged class attaches too great a significance to inequality of faculty as the basis for inequality of privilege.

38. *Federalist*, X.

39. "The inference to which we are brought is, that the *causes* of faction cannot be removed, and that relief is only to be sought in the means of controlling its *effects*." *Federalist*, X.

40. *Federalist*, X.

41. Debate of June 6th, *Documents*, 162.

42. "The smaller the society, the fewer probably will be the distinct parties and interests composing it; the fewer the distinct parties and interests, the more frequently will a majority be found of the same party; and the smaller the number of individuals composing a majority, and the smaller the compass within which they are placed, the more easily will they concert and execute their plans of oppression." *Federalist*, X.

43. Debate of the June 6th, *Documents*, 163. Cf. "Extend the sphere and you take in a great variety of parties and interests; you make it less probable that a majority of the whole will have a common motive to invade the rights of other citizens; or if such a common motive exists, it will be more difficult for all who feel it to discover their own strength and to act in unison with each other. Besides other impediments, it may be remarked that, where there is a consciousness of unjust or dishonorable purposes, communication is always checked by distrust in proportion to the number whose concurrence is necessary." *Federalist*, X.

44. *Federalist*, X.

45. See Edwin Mims' illuminating comment: "The significance of the tenth *Federalist*, about which so much has been written, does not lie in the fact that it propounds a theory of class struggle. For thousands of years prior to Madison the masters of constitutional science had been expatiating on the immutable fact of class struggle between the few and the many. Nor does its significance lie, as is so often stated by slapdash columnists, in a denial of the principle of majority rule. For Madison declares forthrightly, in so many words, that the principle of republican government is synonymous with majority rule. The significance of the tenth *Federalist* lies rather in the accuracy of its predictions as to the workings of this fundamental republican principle in a republic composed of a wide variety of regional and sectional interests.

"In almost verbatim echo of Madison, historians of American party government have described the bargaining process by which the majority party pieced together its so-called program out of a welter of minority interest-group demands... And to the same extent the will of the majority became, in the Madisonian sense, merely a lowest common denominator of heterogeneous minority wills." *The Majority of the People*, 287-288.

46. Madison's comments in *Federalist*, XIV are instructive on this point: "Hearken not to the voice which petulantly tells you that the form of government recommended for your adoption is a novelty in the political world; that it has never yet had a place in the theories of the wildest projectors; that it rashly attempts what it is impossible to accomplish... But why is the experiment of an extended republic to be rejected, merely because it may comprise what is new? Is it not the glory of the people of America, that, whilst they have paid a decent regard to the opinions of former times and other nations, they have not suffered a blind veneration for antiquity, for custom, or for names, to overrule the suggestions of their own good sense, the knowledge of their own situation, and the lessons of their own experience? To this manly spirit, posterity will be indebted for the possession, and the world for the example, of the numerous innovations displayed on the American theatre, in favor of private rights and public happiness."

47. By 1811 Gouverneur Morris, who had insisted at the Convention that the Senate must be entirely "aristocratic," was to bemoan this transformation. "The Senate, in my poor opinion, is little if any check, either on the President or the House of Representatives. It has not the disposition. The members of both Houses are creatures, which, though differently born, are begotten in the same way and by the same sire. They have of course the same temper. But their

opposition, were they disposed to make any, would be feeble. They would easily be borne down by the other House, in which the power resides. The President can indeed do what he pleases, provided always it shall please him to please those who lead a majority of the Representatives." To Robert Walsh, Feb. 5, 1811. Morris, *Correspondence*, III, 266. Cf. "The complete sovereignty of America is substantially in the House of Representatives. The Senate forms no check, because (hopeful theories notwithstanding) they are like the other branch." Morris, 186.

48. Morris, who was appointed to draft the Constitution's final form, claimed only one clause was deliberately ambiguous. "Having rejected redundant and equivocal terms, I believed it to be as clear as our language will permit; excepting nevertheless a part of what relates to the judiciary. On that subject, conflicting opinions had been maintained with so much professional astuteness, that it became necessary to select phrases, which expressing my own notions would not alarm others, nor shock their selflove, and to the best of my recollection, this was the only part which passed without cavil." To Timothy Pickering, Dec. 22, 1814. Morris, *Correspondence*, III:323. The judiciary was the one organ of government on which Hamilton's "permanent will" was bestowed.

49. Walter Lippman, *Public Opinion* (New York: 1922), 263. The "myth" of republicanism was fully as important in unifying the nation as was Hamilton's cement of pecuniary privilege. Around it clustered a whole series of symbols that joined the heroic Revolutionary past with the idea of a common glorious future. From 1776 on "republicanism" conceived of as a peculiarly American attribute seemed to distinguish the American in-group from all the rest of the unenlightened world. The doctrine that men are capable of ruling themselves was being proved in America; and Americans were probably quite right in considering the enhancement of human dignity implied in the dogma was their greatest contribution to Western civilization. See Ralph Gabriel's discussion of the "Mission of America" in his *The Course of American Democratic Thought in the Nineteenth Century* (New York: 1940), ch. 2.

50. "For he that thinks absolute power purifies men's blood, and corrects the baseness of human nature, need read but the history of this, or any other age, to be convinced to the contrary... This is to think that men are so foolish that they take care to avoid what mischiefs may be done them by polecats and foxes, but are content, nay, think it safety, to be devoured by lions." Locke's *Second Essay*, VII:92-93.

51. To Thomas Jefferson, Oct. 17, 1788. *Letters*, I:426. Italics by J.M. Madison also felt that too little power in government was fatal. He continued: "But when below that degree, the direct tendency is to further degrees of relaxation, until the abuses of liberty beget a sudden transition to and undue degree of power... It is a melancholy reflection that liberty should be equally exposed to danger whether the Government have too much or too little power, and that the line divides these extremes should be so inaccurately defined by experience."

52. *Federalist*, LI

53. "...the General Government...[and] the State Governments, since they

are both founded on the republican principle which refers the ultimate decision to the will of the majority...are distinguished rather by the extent within which they will operate, than by any material difference in their structure." To Thomas Jefferson, Oct. 24, 1787, *Letters*, I:350. Madison then proceeded to explain to Jefferson how "private rights will be more secure under the Guardianship" of the new Union by expounding in detail his idea of the "extended sphere."

54. *Federalist*, LI. This number has been attributed by some historians to Hamilton.

55. "Mr. Madison is a character who has long been in public life; and what is very remarkable every Person seems to acknowledge his greatness." William Pierce, "Characters in the Convention," *Documents*, 105.

56. This number has on occasion been attributed to Hamilton; but its highly critical discussion of "the vicious ingredients in the parliamentary representation" is completely out of character for Hamilton. Madison, on the other hand, held these sentiments strongly, all of his life.

57. See Irving Brant, *James Madison the Virginia Revolutionist* (Indianapolis: 1941), 128-130, 242-250.

58. "Additional Memorandum for the Convention of Virginia in 1788, on the Federal Constitution." Madison was interested in the union of England with Scotland in 1707. His outline reads: "Many had despaired of Union, as Burnet himself.—In Scotland opposed violently, particularly by those who were for a new revolution, as Union fatal bar to it... The presbyterians brought into opposition by persuasion that religious rights would be in danger; this argument used most by those known to be the most adverse to that Religion." *Letters*, I:390.

59. David Hume, "Of the Populousness of Ancient Nations," in *Essays and Treatises on Several Subjects* (Dublin: 1779), I:425. This is one of Hume's introductory remarks to the section of this essay which discussed all the "butcheries and banishments" in the classical republics that John Adams found so convenient to draw upon in writing his *Defence*.

60. William Cabell Rives, *History of the Life and Time of James Madison* (Boston: 1870), II:220, note. The quotation is from *Lettres sur les Anglais*. Madison could also have the like observation of Voltaire from his article on "Tolérance," in the *Dictionaire Philosophique*, which Jefferson had so helpfully obtained for him in Paris. "Si vous avez deux religions chez vous, elles se couperont la gorge; si vous en avez trente, elles vivront en paix."

61. Montesquieu, *The Spirit of Laws*, VIII:16.

62. *Federalist*, IX and XIV; the former by Hamilton, the latter by Madison.

63. Gillies' *Aristotle*, II:298.

64. Hume, *Essays*, I:523.

65. Hume, *Essays*, I:538.

66. This quotation is not from Hume's essay on the "Perfect Commonwealth," but from essay VIII, "Of Parties in General," *Essays*, I:55-56.

67. Hume seems to be referring to the development in cities of a specialized product, trade, or industrial skill, that gives the small area an equal interest in a specific type of economic activity. All the inhabitants of Sheffield from the lowly artisan to the wealthiest manufacturer had an interest in the steel industry; every

dweller in Liverpool had a stake in the prosperity of the slave trade. It was this regional unity of occupation that Hume was speaking of, not equality of income for the occupation, as is shown by the latter part of his analysis.

68. Hume, *Essays*, I:538-539.

69. Hume, *Essays*, I:539.

70. "Perfect Commonwealth," Hume, *Essays*, I:532. Hume elaborated his system in great detail—working out a judiciary system, the methods of organizing and controlling the militia, etc.

71. "Of the First Principles of Government," Hume, *Essays*, I:29-33.

72. Hume, *Essays*, I:33.

73. *Federalist*, X appeared in the New York Packet, Friday, November 23, 1787.

74. "Of the Independency of Parliament," Hume, *Essays*, I:41-42.

75. "Notes on the Confederacy," Madison, *Letters*, I:326.

76. To Thomas Jefferson, Oct. 24, 1787. Madison, *Letters*, I:352. Where the proposition is stated, "Respect for character. This motive is not found sufficient to restrain individuals from injustice, and loses its efficacy in proportion to the number which is to divide the pain or the blame."

77. In Madison's earliest presentation of his thesis certain other elements indicating his debt to Hume appear that have vanished in the *Federalist*. In the "Notes of the Confederacy" the phrase "notorious faction and oppressions which take place in corporate towns" (Madison, *Letters*, I:327) recalls the original starting point of Hume's analysis in Perfect Commonwealth." Also the phraseology of the sentence: "The society becomes broken into a greater variety of interests...which check each other." ("Notes on the Confederacy, Madison, I:327) varied in the letter to Jefferson to: "In a large society, the people are broken into so many interests" (Madison, I:352), is probably a parallel of Hume's "The force of popular currents and tides is, in a great measure, broken" ("First Principles of Government," Hume, *Essays*, I:33).

78. "Notes on the Confederacy," Madison, *Letters*, I:328.

79. All quotations in the next four paragraphs are either from Hume's essay "On Parties in General" or from *Federalist*, X.

80. *Alimentum,* fr. *Alere* to nourish. Food; nutriment; hence sustenance, means of support.—SYN. See PABULUM. This word is not a common one in 18th century political literature. Outside of the *Federalist* and Hume's essay I have run across it only in Sir Francis Bacon's works. Since the man of the 18th century lacked the modern American's preoccupation with his digestive organs, so brilliantly inculcated by the laxative manufacturers, also since divorce was not easy or frequent in the 18th century, even the cognate forms "alimentary" (canal), and "alimony," so familiar to us in common speech, were still highly technical terms of medicine and law.

81. Compare Hume's remarks: "In despotic governments, indeed, factions often do not appear; but they are not the less real; or rather, they are more real and more pernicious, upon that very account. The distinct orders of men, nobles and people, soldiers and merchants, have all a distinct interest; but the more powerful oppresses the weaker with impunity and without resistance; which begets a seeming tranquility in such governments." Also see Hume's

comparison of faction to "weeds...which grow more plentifully in the richest soil; and though absolute governments be wholly free from them, it must be confessed, that they rise more easily, and propagate themselves faster in free governments, where they always infect the legislature itself, which alone could be able, by the steady application of rewards and punishments, to eradicate them"; and notice Madison's, "The regulation of these various and interfering interests forms the principal task of modern legislation, and involves the spirit of party and faction in the necessary and ordinary operations of the government."

82. This clause of Madison's refers to Hume's "parties from *principle*, especially abstract speculative principle" [italics D.H.] in the discussion of which he includes "different political principles" and "principles of priestly government...which has...been the poison of human society, and the sources of the most inveterate factions." Hume, in keeping with his reputation as the great sceptic, feels that while the congregations of persecuting sects must be called "factions of principle," the priests, who are "the prime movers" in religious parties, are factious out of "interest." The word "speculation" that appears in Madison is rendered twice as "speculative" in Hume.

83. Here is Hume's "Personal" faction, "founded on personal friendship or animosity among such as compose the contending parties." Hume instances the Colonesi and Orsini of Modern Rome, the Neri and Bianchi at Florence, the rivalry between the Pollia and Papiria in ancient Rome, and the confused maze of shifting alliances that marked the struggle between Guelfs and Ghibellines.

84. This phrase of Madison's which is quite obscure in the context, making a separate category of a type of party apparently just covered under "contending leaders," refers to the loyal bitter-end Jacobites of 18th-century England. These sentimental irreconcilables of the Squire Western ilk made up Hume's "party from *affection*" [italics D.H.]. Hume explains: "By parties from *affection*, I understand those which are founded on the different attachments of men towards particular families and persons, whom they desire to rule over them. These factions are often very violent [Hume was writing only six years after Bonnie Prince Charles and the clans had frightened all England in '45]; though I must own, it may seem unaccountable, that men should attach themselves so strongly to persons, with who they are no wise acquainted, whom perhaps they never saw, and from whom they never received, nor can ever hope for any favour."

The fact that Madison includes this category in his paper satisfied me that when he came to write the tenth *Federalist* for publication he referred directly to Hume's volume as he reworked his introduction into its final polished form. One can account for the other similarities in the discussion of faction as a result of Madison's careful reading of Hume's works and his retentive memory. But the inclusion of the "party from affection" in the Virginian's final scheme where its ambiguity indeed detracts from the force of the argument, puts a strain on the belief that it resulted from memory alone. This odd fourth classification was included because Hume's book was open on the table beside him, and because James Madison would leave no historical stone unturned in his effort to make a comprehensive summary.

85. The italics are Hume's.

86. Hume does comment on the burning pamphlet controversy between the

proponents of agriculture and commerce that figured so largely in eighteenth-century English economic theory, and which had been seized upon by Bolingbroke in the fight against Walpole. Hume insisted that this traditional economic cleavage, though sanctified by classical precept, was not a true conflict. "There has been an attempt in England to divide the *landed* and *trading* part of the nation; but without success. The interests of these two bodies are not really distinct, and never will be so, till our public debts encrease to such a degree, as to become altogether oppressive and intolerable." The politic-economic assumptions on which Hume bases this judgment can only be indicated here. Commerce, the handmaid of agriculture, raises agricultural prices and stimulates agricultural production by furnishing a vent for farm products. The debts of the parasitic political state must ultimately be borne by the farmer, and thus have a depressing effect on agriculture, the original source of consumable wealth. A gingerly use of debt funding and kindred schemes by Parliament is therefore essential from a purely economic point of view; but Hume did not believe that the moneyed interest in Parliament had yet been so "corrupted" by sharing in the profits of the rising national debt as to carry it too far.

87. Hume, *Essays*, "Of Parties in General," I:55.

88. Mims, *The Majority of the People*, 68.

89. A short but extremely pertinent statement of this problem of originality in thinkers who admittedly were great borrowers is to be found in the introduction to F.B. Kaye's edition of Bernard Mandeville's *Fable of the Bees* (Oxford: 1924), I, CXI ff.

Chapter 7

The Virtuous Farmer

We have seen the background of certain of the doctrines presented by James Madison in the Constitutional Convention, and his earliest letters of Publius. There was another doctrine assumed but unexpressed in the tenth *Federalist* which was basic to Madison's faith that a purely republican government could be set up in America. This was the doctrine of the virtuous farmer.

One quality clearly distinguishing James Madison's paper republic from that of Hume is the former's burning faith shining through every sentence that his scheme could and would be put into successful practice. Hume's system throughout has the flavor of an intellectual *jeu d'esprit*: the shrewdness of his analysis is always tinged with a wry delight in taking an unpopular position and proving it to be theoretically sound. Madison, on the other hand, clearly composed his hypothesis out of his heart as well as his head.[1] We can understand the pride of James Madison in his brain child: we can allow for the intoxicating wine of national self-consciousness which induced him to view his Constitution as an event affecting "the whole human race." There was still an additional factor to account for Madison's triumphant sense of accomplishment. His ideal commonwealth would operate among a nation of husbandmen; and according to the weightiest authorities of political philosophy the firmest foundation for republicanism was an agricultural society. And only on the basis of this unexpressed postulate is it possible to explain how Madison could believe that the Constitutional apparatus fashioned at Philadelphia would work in the miraculous way he predicted.

There was the system of indirect elections, of course, which was to sift the will of the people as Hume had advocated. There was the State-appointed quasi-aristocratic Senate, which Madison was to call "an anchor against popular fluctuations."[2] There was the executive elected by an especially constituted body of delegates, once removed from the people. Nevertheless it could not have escaped the notice of a realist like Madison that the United States Senate would be chosen by the self-same legislatures whose executive democracy had resulted in the call for a strong national government. Neither had Madison overlooked the fact that the one man executive was a "precarious security" for aristocracies, natural or otherwise. Even the monarchs of mixed government history had showed a tendency to lead the people against the nobles rather than to protect the *aristoi* from the *demos*. And Madison in the fifty-first *Federalist* took explicit note of this datum of past experience. Moreover, even if James Madison had not been independently aware of these circumstances, Alexander Hamilton had called them to his attention. This was the gist of Hamilton's charge that the Constitution was "still pork" for all its change of theoretical sauce.

There was still the hopeful theory of the extended republic; but Alexander Hamilton put his finger on the weakness of this safeguard, too. From the New Yorker's viewpoint Madison's analysis of society contained a basic error. The checks of a multitude of contending interests would not leave the general government in a position of neutrality, Hamilton insisted. Among all the interests that Madison listed only one or two could be called of vital importance to the American people. Inevitably, therefore a paramount interest would swallow up minor differences, and would appear with increased strength in the national Congress. Religious persecution had ceased in England, as much from the slow atrophy of the religious impulse in Britons' mind as from the multiplicity of sects. For in recent years Englishmen had become less interested in saving their souls than in saving their money. The young New Yorker sensed more clearly than any man of his generation the growing importance everywhere of the pecuniary instinct in social relations, and knew that it betokened a pursuit of material gain by all Americans, with what might become a religious intensity.

We know what Hamilton's reactions were to "Madisons Theory," because he scribbled them down after he had heard the Virginian present it to the Convention on the sixth of June. "There is truth in both these principles [indirect elections and large area]," he wrote, "but they do not conclude so strongly as he supposes—The Assembly when chosen will meet in one room if they are drawn from half the globe—and will be liable to all the passions of popular assemblies." Besides, the Representatives produced by a system of numerous electoral districts would be infected at the source. "Paper money is capable of giving a general impulse—It is easy to conceive a popular sentiment pervading the E[astern] states—" Even the large area offered no substantial bulwark against the *demos*. "An influential demagogue will give an impulse to the whole—Demagogues are not always *inconsiderable* persons—Patricians were frequently demagogues."3 Mr. Madison's milk-sop willingness to compromise was leading the Convention along a dangerous path, Hamilton concluded.

It is understandable, therefore, why on the basis of this perception Hamilton would work so hard to prepare his speech of June 18th blasting the Virginia plan that embodied Madison's theory. The Virginian's specious plausibility must be counteracted lest a feeble, indirectly elected Senate and Executive be established as a substitute for the "independent will" that Hamilton desired. And we may be sure too that he privately told Madison that his ingenious paper theory simply would not obviate the struggle between those who had property and those lacked it.

James Madison did not need Hamilton to convince him of the continual threat of class struggle. There is a sufficiency of evidence to show that he believed neither indirect elections nor large area would serve to prevent violent strife between plutocrats and a proletariat. Indeed, when factions of the very rich and the degraded poor appeared in America, Madison fully expected the "unmixed" Constitution which he had worked so hard to attain would become impractical. But in the meantime there was always the hope that such extremes of poverty and wealth would not flourish in America; that the country would not give itself over to the evils of manufacture and commerce. The unexpressed assumption upon which the arguments of the tenth *Federalist* paper rest is that the United States remain predominantly agricultural. Indirect elections and the extensive area of the United States guarantee a purely republican form because the people whose will ultimately prevails are virtuous farmers. In large part, Madison's passionate faith in a workable republican government sprang from his agrarianism.

An able attack made by Charles Pinckney upon the mixed government theory of Alexander Hamilton was the occasion for James Madison to explain what the never-ending struggle of the rich and the poor meant for the future of America. From Madison's answer to this speech it is obvious that he accepted the fatalistic view that the class struggle would eventually wrack the United States. In the meanwhile—and Madison before he died was to measure the respite in actual years—because of the agrarian basis of American society it was possible to rear "the fabrics of governments which have no model on the face of the globe."4

Charles Pinckney with several other members of the Convention had been outraged by Hamilton's reasoning when he pled for a "mixed government" for the United States. On June 25th Pinckney rose, therefore, and begged the delegates to "examine the situation of this country more accurately than it has yet been done. The people of the U. States are perhaps the most singular of any we are acquainted with. Among them are fewer distinctions of fortune & less of rank, than among the inhabitants of any other nation." The South Carolinian was sure that this peculiar blessing would continue for a long period because of the "immense tracts of uncultivated lands" to the west which would guarantee that "there will be few poor, and few dependent." With a nod in Hamilton's direction, Pinckney confessed that he believed the British constitution was the best in existence; "but at the same time I am confident that it is one that will not or cannot be introduced into this country, for many centuries." As for Madison's and Hamilton's learned disquisitions from the classics, the situation of the American people "is distinct from either the people of Greece or Rome, or of any State we are acquainted with among the antients."[5] The inhabitants of America "have very few rich among them,—by rich men I mean those whose riches may have a dangerous influence, or such as are esteemed rich in Europe—perhaps there are not one hundred such on the Continent...it is not probable that this number will be greatly increased."

Mr. Pinckney, while denying any split between the rich and the poor in America, did feel that the people of the United States might be divided into three classes. These were the professional men, the commercial men, and finally "the *landed interest*, the owners and cultivators of the soil, who are and ought ever to be the governing spring in the system." He believed furthermore that though their occupation differed, all these groups "have but one interest" because of their interdependence. This unity of interest would continue "in a Country which must be a new one for centuries."[6]

The following day, June 26, James Madison took notice of Pinckney's analysis.[7] And in this speech he revealed to what extent he believed the theory of the class struggle applicable to America's future history. Madison pounced upon the fallacy in Pinckney's harmony-of-interest idea and in his argument that social equality in the United States would last for centuries. And as he developed his rebuttal Madison made it clear that he thought the irreconcilable conflict between the rich and the poor would burst upon America long before Charles Pinckney expected.

Madison, who had just spent several months studying and pondering on the history of factions through the ages had little patience with Pinckney's identity of interest argument. He answered therefore with the familiar pessimistic refrain, "In all civilized Countries the people fall into different classes have a real or supposed difference of interest. There will be creditors & debtors, farmers, merchts. & manufacturers." His next sentence was even stronger: "There will be particularly the distinction of rich & poor." Nothing could be more unequivocal than that remark. In addition, the Virginian agreed with Hamilton entirely on the political importance of this distinction of have and have-not. How was it, then, that he could still take such an optimistic view of the stability of his extensive republic?

Having acknowledged the dangers of class strife, Madison now disagreed with both Pinckney and Hamilton concerning when the struggle would break into open social war in America. Pinckney airily estimated "centuries" hence; Hamilton argued that the fight was already on. Madison said not yet, but perhaps fairly soon. "It was true," Madison told the Convention, "as had been observed (by Mr. Pinckney) we had not among us those hereditary distinctions, of rank which were a great source of the contests in the ancient Govts. as well as the modern States of Europe, nor those extremes of wealth or poverty which characterize the latter. We cannot, however, be regarded even at this time, as one homogenous mass, in which every thing that affects a part will affect in the same manner the whole." So much for Pinckney, who supposed that Massachusetts debtor and a Carolina grandee had identical interests. As trade and industry developed in the United States the day of conflict was steadily brought nearer. Already the commercial development of New England had produced seismographic shocks warning of future convulsions.

> An increase in population will of necessity increase the proportion of those who will labor under all the hardships of life, & secretly sigh for a more equal distribution of its blessings.[8] These may in time outnumber those who are placed above the feelings of indigence. According to the equal laws of suffrage, the power will slide into the hands of the former. No agrarian[9] attempts have yet been made in this Country, but symptoms, of a leveling spirit...have sufficiently appeared in a certain quarter to give notice of the future danger.[10]

In 1787 Madison believed that the extended republic and such supplementary checks as indirect elections and State-appointed Senators could overcome any danger of share-the-wealth revolt. There is evidence to show, however, that he believed the struggles of the rich and poor would become so fierce within two—or at most three—generations that even the skillfully modeled Constitution might be endangered.

In part the pessimism expressed by James Madison on June 26, was due to Alexander Hamilton's persistent warnings and dire prophecies of impending anarchy. For all Madison's justified pride in his proposed theory, he was impressed by the New Yorker's passionately presented public arguments and persuasive private discussions about the necessity of "toning" the government far higher than the Virginian wished. It was undoubtedly Hamilton's criticism of his plan that induced Madison in this speech of June 26 to advocate a nine instead of a six year Senate, for which he had originally spoken when the Convention met.

Hamilton, however, could not budge him from his stand against a Senate or an Executive with an "independent will." Madison had too great a faith in the mass of the American farmers for that. We are fortunate in possessing several written statements by Madison in which this faith is firmly expressed. For two years Madison had been carrying on a correspondence with John Brown of Kentucky about a model constitution for that state. Madison foresaw the dangers of the increasing commercial spirit in Kentucky and admonished Brown to keep agriculture the dominant interest there. In one letter of particular interest he includes a series of remarks annotating the "Draught of a Constitution for Virginia," written by Jefferson in 1783, a model which Brown was considering for Kentucky, In these notes written a year after the Convention ended, Madison made it clear how closely related his republican theory was to a clearly developed agrarian doctrine.

James Madison advised Brown that the citizens who were to vote for Senators in Kentucky should possess a freehold estate in land, while voters for State Assemblymen should be free from any property qualification. Madison, living up to his reputation for compromise that Hamilton had sneered at, called this "a middle way...which corresponds at once with the theory of free government and the lessons of experience";[11] a "middle mode" that also "reconciles and secures the two cardinal objects of government, the rights of persons and the rights of property." The Virginia Statesman then digresses a moment to recall the history of the writing of the first State Constitutions when independence from Britain was proclaimed. "The necessity of thus guarding the rights of property was, for obvious reasons, unattended to in the commencement of the Revolution. In all the governments which were considered as beacons to republican patriots and lawgivers, the rights of persons were subjected to those of property. The poor were sacrificed to the rich." And with this sentence Madison shows that he too accepted, though with reservations, Pinckney's contention in the Philadelphia meeting that the problem of government in America was in many ways unique. The Virginian's study of all the governments of ancient and modern times had not revealed to him a single political establishment where the many were not ground down by the few. Madison nevertheless believed that in 1776 the American reaction from this historically universal oppression of the poor by the rich had carried the political pendulum too far in the opposite direction.

"In the existing state of American population and of American property," Madison continues, "the two classes of rights were so little discriminated [following independence] that a provision for the rights of persons was supposed to include of itself those of property; and it was natural to infer from the tendency of republican laws, that these different interests would be more and more identified." The laws against entail and primogeniture, which in Virginia had been forced through by Jefferson with Madison's aid, are the "republican laws" that Madison here refers to. With Jefferson, he always justified them as necessary devices to guarantee that the equality of political power essential to a free government would not be overborne by disproportionate social power accruing to a few individuals as result of swollen property holdings.[12] In 1788 Madison no longer believed that these republican laws would automatically produce an identity of the two types of rights. The democratic extravagances of the populist controlled legislatures during the postwar depression had been a "monitory" example. "Experience and investigation have," he explains to the Kentuckian, "however, produced more correct ideas on this subject. It is now observed in all populous countries the smaller part only can be interested in preserving the rights of property, It must be foreseen that America, and Kentucky itself, will by degrees arrive at this state of society; that in some parts of the Union a very great advance is already made towards it." Here, again, as in the Debate of June 26th, 1787, the ominous appearance of the eighteenth-century theory of a large population with the concomitant necessity of supporting it by trade and commerce induced a dark pessimism in the Virginian. How fatalistic was the view Madison took of this impending industrial development, with its crop of paupers, can be appreciated when one remembers that the Indian and the buffalo were still ranging through large parts of Kentucky's area.

When the people of a "populous" country lived by manufacturing and commerce they formed the materials for the most implacably interested and overbearing majority possible. The common misery of their pauperism—which in eighteenth-century terminology was the equivalent of their occupation—would not be meliorated by a large territory or breaking their suffrage into small districts, or by indirect elections. Abject poverty would be the cement uniting an interstate faction of the have-nots. Therefore,

> The time to guard against this danger is the first forming of the Constitution... When the bulk of the people have a sufficient interest in possession or in prospect to be attached to the rights of property, without being insufficiently attached to the rights of persons. Liberty, not less than justice, pleads for the policy here recommended [a Senate elected by landowners]. If all power be suffered to slide into hands not interested in the rights of property, which must be the case whenever a majority fall under that description, one of two things cannot fail to happen, either they will unite against the other description, and become the dupes and instruments of ambition, or their poverty and dependence will render them the mercenary instruments of wealth. In either case liberty will be subverted: in the first, by a despotism growing out of anarchy; in the second, by an oligarchy founded on corruption.[13]

Here in Madison's statement to John Brown of Kentucky lies the concealed assumption, which validated Madison's tenth *Federalist* theory. The husbandmen of the United States who were called upon in 1788 to ratify the Constitution were sufficiently interested in both personal rights and property rights to consent in the establishment of the new government. The farmers as the "bulk" of the population would be the mainspring of the constitutional machine when it commenced operation. The danger of the sharp division of the community into the many envious poor and the few oppressive rich, would not yet become the one supreme issue obliterating the multitude of minor, self-checking interests. In the Virginia ratifying Convention some four months earlier James Madison had estimated that this temporary respite would continue for little over twenty-five years.[14]

The acquisition of the Louisiana Territory during Jefferson's Administration, while Madison was Secretary of State, forced him to make an upward revision of this pessimistic prophecy of 1788. Among Madison's papers found after his death was a statistical study of American population growth written in the winter of 1829-30. At the time he composed this estimate Madison commented on the "precious advantage" in "the actual distribution of property, particularly of landed property, and in the universal hope of acquiring property "possessed by the United States. This latter peculiarity is among the happiest contrast in their situation to that of the Old

World... There may be at present a majority of the nation who are even freeholders, or the heirs and aspirants to freeholds." But Madison knew this could not continue forever even with the magnificent empty spaces extended to the west. The population of the United States in twenty-five years would double from twelve millions to twenty-four millions. If this increase continued, and Madison took it for granted that it would, in one hundred years the United States would contain within its borders approximately one hundred and ninety-two million persons.

By 1930, predicted Madison, the prodigious numbers of inhabitants of his extensive republic would press together as thickly in their expanded area as the crowded and turbulent citizens of the ancient republics. David Hume's writings might perhaps be forgotten in that distant age, but the "near habitation" of citizens in this teeming commonwealth would cause deep disturbances in the will and inclinations of the mob, as Hume had foretold. Moreover, the majority of these citizens could be supported only by trade and commerce. By a "law of nature" in 1930 the surplus population would be "necessarily reduced by a competition for employment to wages which afford them the bare necessaries of life. The proportion being without property...cannot be expected to sympathize sufficiently with its right to be safe depositories of power over them."[15]

Madison had no satisfactory remedy for this future danger. Obviously this "unfavored class" would threaten the stability of the Constitution in direct relation to their participation in politics. On the other hand, it would be impossible to base a republican government on a minority, without creating "a standing military force, dangerous to all parties and to liberty itself." Madison feared deeply for the American republic once its agricultural base had disappeared. He saw clearly that to "these changes, intellectual, moral, and social," incident on the disappearance of the independent farmer, "the institutions and laws of the country must be adapted; and it will require for the task all the wisdom of the wisest patriots."[16] So far as he could discern, however, no amount of intellectual effort could supply that only sure basis for republicanism—an independent people living on their own farms.

Although Madison was always extremely dubious about the long-run chance of preserving a free government in a society devoted to commerce and manufactures, in 1787, he was optimistically certain that a stable republic could be set up in America for at least a generation. The United States Constitution was a novel but sound device for staying clear of the Polybian cycle. It offered a state based on the people's consent that would not be wracked with the class struggle, because in all parts of its large area for some time yet to come the most important social group was neither rich nor poor, but safely and moderately agricultural. Massachusetts had already been infected by trade, and social war had broken out; other sections would slowly but steadily be corrupted. In the meantime it was possible for the legislator to build on America's "precious advantage" to the end of securing a republican government equally solicitous of the rights of persons and the rights of property.

The vision that offered itself to the American Solon was that of a society different from any hitherto seen in the world.

> It is not composed, as in Europe, of great lords who possess everything, and of a herd of people who have nothing. Here are no aristocratical families, no courts, no kings, no bishops, no ecclesiastical dominion, no invisible power giving to a few a very visible one; no great manufacturers employing thousands, no great refinements of luxury. The rich and poor are not so far removed from each other as they are in Europe. Some few towns excepted, we are all tillers of the earth... We are a people of cultivators, scattered over an immense territory, communicating with each other by means of good roads and navigable rivers, united by the silken bands of mild government, all respecting the laws, without dreading their power, because they are equitable. We are all animated with the spirit of an industry which is unfettered and unrestrained, because each person works for himself.[17]

This was "the true and only philosophy of an American farmer." It was also the philosophy of the man who composed the tenth *Federalist*. Without this faith in the American farmer as an honest and stable citizen, Madison's strenuous intellectual labors to preserve a government based on popular sovereignty are not understandable. Probably the wisest thing that James Madison said during the whole period that the new Constitution was under advisement was his statement made in the Virginia Convention in 1788. "I go," he declared, "on this great republican principle, that the people will have virtue and intelligence to select men of virtue and wisdom. Is there no virtue among us? If there be not, we are in a wretched situation. No theoretical checks, no form of government can render us secure. To suppose that any form of government will secure liberty or happiness without any virtue in the people, is a chimerical idea."[18]

Notes

1. See especially the final paragraphs of *Federalist*, X and XIV.

2. *Federalist*, LXIII; cf. Letter to Jefferson, Oct. 24, 1787, "the great anchor of the government," Madison, *Letters*, I:346.

3. "Notes for June 6 and 8, 1787" found among Hamilton's papers after his death, given in *Documents*, 916-917.

4. *Federalist*, XIV.

5. One can detect a trace of sarcasm in Franklin's remark on this point. "We indeed seem to feel our own want of political wisdom, since we have been running about in search of it. We have gone back to ancient history for models of Government, and examined the different forms of those Republics which having been formed with the seeds of their own dissolution now no longer exist. And we have viewed Modern States all around Europe, but find none of their Constitutions suitable to our circumstances." June 28th, *Documents*, 295. Franklin was probably the only delegate in Philadelphia who had emancipated himself from the clumsy balance theory.

6. This speech of Pinckney's undoubtedly the most penetrating general analysis of American social conditions delivered on the Convention floor is to be found in *Documents*, 267-273.

7. Hamilton did also with the expected argument that "inequality of property constituted the great & fundamental distinction in Society."

8. This is a euphemistic description of the industrial proletariat. In this sentence is contained the typical economic and population theory of the eighteenth century. This doctrine held that only by employing a numerous population in manufacture could they be supported; a large birth rate required development of industry. On the other hand, it was believed that manufactures could not compete with foreign products if the workers were paid anything above starvation wages. Every populous industrial country of necessity, then, was sharply divided into classes of the rich and poor. This mixed demographic and economic dogma has an important relation to all eighteenth-century agrarian theory, as I hope to show at some later date.

9. Madison is using agrarian in the classical sense of a type of laws modeled after Tiberius Gracchus, which divided up the wealth of the rich.

10. Debate of June 26th, *Documents*, 280.

11. Madison, *Letters*, I:187.

12. Cf. Charles Pinckney's argument in the Constitution that this type of "republican law" would keep America from ever having many rich men. "The destruction of the right of primogeniture & the equal division of property of the Intestates will also have an effect to preserve this mediocrity; for laws invariably affect the manners of a people." Debate of June 25th, *Documents*, 270.

13. "Remarks on Mr. Jefferson's 'Draught of a Constitution for Virginia' sent from New York to Mr. John Brown, of Kentucky, October, 1788." In *Letters*, I:185-195, at pages 187-188. Compare his letter to Brown of Oct. 23, 1785, outlining his earliest ideas for a Kentucky constitution.

A thorough analysis and comparison of Jefferson's and Madison's views in this period is to be found in Brant's *Madison*, ch. XIII, where he discusses the Jefferson "draught" of a substitute for the Virginia Constitution of 1776 and Madison's strictures on both the constitution and the suggested reform. Brant shows that both Jefferson and Madison were in substantial agreement insofar as constitutional doctrine was concerned. "Viewed as whole Madison's attitude toward the Constitution of 1776 indicates an original acceptance of most of its provisions as conforming to republican principles, followed by a rapid reappraisal in which his tendency was toward a more democratic form of government mixed with more effective checks and balances for the protection of property. Jefferson took the lead, and undoubtedly influenced Madison in his swing toward democracy, but Madison showed a better understanding of the political materials they were dealing with," 270.

14. "The period cannot be very far distant when the unsettled parts of America will be inhabitated. At the expiration of twenty-five years hence, I conceive that, in every part of the United States, there will be as great a population as there is now in the settled parts. We see, already, that in the most populous parts of the Union, and where there is but a medium, manufactures are beginning to be established." Jonathan Elliot, ed., *The Debates in the Several State Conventions on the Adoption of the Federal Constitution* (Philadelphia: 1861), III:309; Debate in the Virginia Convention of June 12, 1788.

It should be remembered that the area of the United States at this time as Madison estimated it in *Federalist*, XIV was "not a great deal larger than Germany...or than Poland before the late dismemberment." This relationship of republicanism with the population spread out on farms helps explain the urge toward the "agricultural imperialism" of the Jeffersonians that culminated in the Louisiana Purchase and the abortive attempt to seize Canada in 1812. Land hunger, it is true, was the dynamic inner spring of this expansive drive; but some importance must be allotted to the obsessive fear lurking in the minds of both Madison and Jefferson that without this new agricultural domain republicanism was doomed. When the majority of Americans became piled up in cities forced to subsist on the pauper wages of artisans, America would re-enact the bloody tragedy of class struggle.

15. Madison at this time had read Malthus; but an examination of his own earlier writings show that the political economist merely substantiated theorems Madison had already subscribed to. See Madison's complaint after conceding Malthus' ability that "he has not all the merit of originality which has been allowed to him. The principle was adverted to and reasoned upon long before him..." To Edward Everett, Nov. 26, 1823. Madison, *Letters*, III:350.

16. "Notes on Suffrage," Madison, *Letters*, IV:21-30. Written in preparation for and during the session of the Virginia Convention of 1829-30, which rewrote the State Constitution. Attendance at this Convention was the last public act of Madison's life.

17. Hector St. John Crevecoeur, *Letters of an American Farmer* (London: 1782). The quotation is to be found in the Everyman edition at 39-40.

18. Elliot's *Debates*, III:536. Debate in Virginia ratifying Convention of June 20, 1788

Epilogue

Thus ends our reconnaissance-in-force into the alien intellectual territory in which Thomas Jefferson and James Madison planned their political campaigns.[1] We have roughly mapped the ideological area in which the battle for Jeffersonian democracy was fought and eventually won. We have also examined the professional training of these field marshalls of the people, that was to serve them so well in planning and carrying out their major operations. We have seen too that the conceptual tactics that they almost instinctively have used, and above all the grand strategy that they adhered to in winning the field for popular sovereignty, stood in precise relationship to a vast and ancient body of maxims that dated back two thousand years to the time of Aristotle and Thucydides.

It is clear beyond question that our Virginians in their writing and thinking did not feel that they were either spokesmen for the frontier or defenders of an economic bloc of farmers. They always considered themselves as political philosophers of the most traditional sort. And it was as *political* philosophers, above all, that they spoke and wrote. Their sociology of occupations, with its sharp hierarchy of adhering values, was conceived of in *political* terms. Their economic theory was *political* economy. The Jeffersonian system was a system of politics. To forget this fact inevitably distorts any judgment of what they were attempting to do, and why they took the actions they did to achieve their goal, at any given stage of their public lives.

Their theories and ideals of the good state were solidly grounded in their own experience as eighteenth-century Americans. The "experience" of the educated eighteenth-century American under examination, however, in Santayana's words, explodes like a shrapnel shell into a thousand pieces. One fragment of "experience" that scarred the mind of Madison and many another of his enlightened contemporaries was the visual impression of corpses rotting under the hot Mediterranean sun in the gutters of Corcyra, in 427 B.C. A great book[2] had made the scene as real, and as immediate to Madison, as the pictures painted by his correspondent of Shays' men parading with evergreen twigs in their hats, and curses on their lips for lawyers and courts. The newspaper reports of the slum-dwelling mob that sacked and burned so much of London during the Gordon riots in 1780 was no more and no less an "experience" for Jefferson than the ugly accounts of the Roman rabble received from Tacitus' morbid anatomy of that state's social and political degeneracy.

Of equal weight as elements in the Virginians' agrarian concept were the yeoman farmers they had known in Orange and Albemarle Counties, and Aristotle's identification of the husbandman's occupation with the golden mean of political virtue. No analytic knife has yet been fashioned that can divide this type of paired "experiences" into separate entities. The conclusions that the Virginians reached about the political process were strands of fact and theory-before-the-fact that served to weave the phenomena that passed before their eyes into a meaningful pattern.

Certainly the doctrines expounded by Jefferson and Madison were much more than "rhetorical defense mechanisms." It is indeed true that they used their ideas as weapons in the seizure of political power. The linking of the farmer's interest with America's mission to propagate republicanism was in one sense a magnificent coup in the field of practical propaganda. It was matched in effectiveness only by their successful identification of the commercial and financial policies of Hamilton with the dangers of monarchy. But if the ideas so successfully used by the Virginians were offensive weapons in the game of power it should not be overlooked that Jefferson and Madison were as much victims of the intellectual concepts they used as were the Federalists against whom they used them. The leaders of the Republican party did not consciously check over the mental stereotypes in their armory and draw out this one or that one to be utilized in winning political friends and gaining electoral influence. Their effectiveness as propagandists resulted in large part from their complete and unquestioning belief in their own propaganda.

The charges of opportunism that have been leveled against the Jeffersonians, especially Madison, fall to the ground as soon as their political careers are viewed in terms of the eighteenth-century background. Few American statesmen have been as consistent in squaring their policy with their ideas as were the Virginians throughout their whole career. Madison did not box the ideological compass in opposing Hamilton. In 1792 he took exactly the same position in regard to defending purely republican principles as he did in 1787. During the Convention itself the grounds of potential opposition between Madison and Hamilton were manifest. In 1787 and 1788, however, though disagreeing as to the form and spirit of the new government they could cooperate effectively on the shared conviction that a new and stronger government was needed.

Madison's opposition, however, was foreordained as soon as the brilliant New Yorker took it upon himself to "administer"—the term is Madison's—the new state into something approximating his favored mixed form. James Madison, if he was to remain consistent to the ideals and concepts of republicanism that permeate every speech he made in the Convention and every number of the *Federalist* papers he wrote, had to form a party himself to preserve "the permanent and aggregate interests" of the whole community from the faction which had seized the state. His collaboration with Jefferson, whose passion for republicanism burned with a flame higher even than Madison's, was a foregone conclusion.

We end with no simple explanation of the origins of Jeffersonian democracy. There is no golden key that opens all of the doors to our understanding of the Virginians as political leaders and builders of America. In fact it must be admitted that discussion of their intellectual system raises far more questions than it can cope with. It supplements Turner's theory of the frontier. It supplements Beard's economic interpretation. In so doing, however, it makes it apparent that the crude frontier theory of Jeffersonian democracy hitherto accepted must be entirely rewritten. The facts that Beard laid open for a generation of historians to echo must also now be re-examined. None of these three elements—frontier influence, economic bias, or intellectual habit—can be ignored if we would understand Jeffersonian democracy. Yet so far not one of these elements has been treated in just relation to the others. Only a wise perception and combination of all three of these historical methods can give a clear cartogram of that obscure terrain—the "origins" of a political philosophy and the actions taken toward its realization.

Notes

1. It is unfortunate that I found it impossible at this time to make the all-out frontal attack on the whole territory originally contemplated when this paper was titled. It will be done as soon as circumstances permit.

2. "A great book is one that leaves scars on the mind." Mr. Justice Holmes.

Appendix

Bibliographic Essay

It is now certain, unless the Republican party comes into power in 1944, that the definitive edition of the writings of Thomas Jefferson will not only be annotated, but will also contain all the important excerpts from the letters of Jefferson's correspondents. Less than thirteen per cent of these letters of Jefferson's have ever been published anywhere. It is to be hoped that the two hundredth anniversary of Madison's birth in 1951 will inaugurate a similar undertaking in regard to his papers.

In the meantime the student of the intellectual origins of Jeffersonian democracy has in published form approximately sixty per cent of Jefferson's letters and miscellaneous writings, and a somewhat larger proportion of Madison's. These are more than ample to furnish all the hints necessary for analyzing Jefferson's and Madison's mental habits. In fact, the lavish number of leads that the two Virginians scatter through their letters and other writings, indicating their intellectual ancestors, are already oppressively great even without the addition of a single virgin manuscript. At any rate, in preparing this paper, the problem was one of too much material on the intellectual origins of Jeffersonian democracy, rather than too little.

The most important sources for the study of Jefferson's and Madison's ideas are the published editions of their letters and papers. The most voluminous collection of Jefferson's writings is to be found in the *Memorial Edition* (20 vols., 1902-1903), edited by Bergh and Lipscomb. The most scholarly and usable edition of Jefferson's writings, however, is that of P.L. Ford (16 vols., 1892-1899); it also contains a few letters not in the later edition. Both of these sets should be supplemented by the earliest major edition: that of H.A. Washington (9 vols., 1853-1854). Two smaller collections of Jefferson's letters are also important: that published in the *Collections of the Massachusetts Historical Society*, 7th series, vol. 1 (1900); and the *Thomas Jefferson Correspondence, Printed from..the Collection of William K. Bixby* (1916).

There are only two major editions of Madison's writings: the Congress edition (4 vols., 1865), and Gaillard Hunt's edition (9 vols., 1900-1910). Both collections must be used together. Hunt prints many letters of Madison's in the period from 1795-1808 left out of the Congress edition; the latter contains far more of the important letters and memos that Madison wrote after retiring from public life. The Hunt edition also includes Madison's *Debates* in vols. III and IV, but since the other records of the Federal Convention, such as the Yates transcript, are not included, historians normally use Max Farrand's *Records of the Federal Government of 1787* (3 vols., 1911), or Tansill's one-volume *Documents Illustrative of the Formation of the Union of the American States* (1927).

The third volume of Jonathan Elliot's *Debates, Resolutions, and Other Proceedings in Convention on the Adoption of the Federal Constitution* (5 vols., 1827-1845), contains the speeches made by Madison defending the Constitution in the Virginia ratifying convention.

Neither the Congress edition nor the Hunt edition contains the essays written by Madison for the *Federalist*. Furthermore, of the score or more editions of this basic compendium of eighteenth-century American constitutional theory, none is remotely satisfactory for modern critical use. There is no annotated edition of the *Federalist*; there is no edition which arranges the various papers into a topical scheme; there is no edition with an adequate index (several twentieth-century editors have borrowed the index made by Dawson in the 1850s and printed it without changing anything but the page numbers); and there is no edition that has settled in a scholarly fashion the authorship of the dozen papers claimed by both Hamilton and Madison. If war does not prevent, Felix Gilbert and the writer hope to publish shortly a usable and scholarly edition of this unread American classic.

Both Madison and Jefferson are fortunate in their earliest and latest biographers. The best life of Jefferson in still that of H.S. Randall (3 vols., 1858), the last biographer to have access to the immense mass of Jefferson manuscripts before it was scattered. Randall's hero-worship and adulation is kept well within check by high standards of critical integrity. Since he also was able to interview Jefferson's immediate family and surviving friends, his *Life* will always serve as a primary source for anecdotes, conversations, and other personal material. A charming picture of Jefferson in the period after his retirement from public life is to be found in the *Domestic Life of*

Thomas Jefferson (1871), by his granddaughter Sara N. Randolph. In it are published many family letters omitted from the large editions of his writings; and nowhere can one obtain a better picture of Jefferson among his books.

During the last half of the nineteenth century and the first quarter of the twentieth innumerable other biographies of Jefferson were published, read, and mercifully forgotten. In 1929, however, Gilbert Chinard produced his *Thomas Jefferson, Apostle of Americanism*, which is generally acclaimed as the best one-volume life. Gracefully written, based on original research among the Jefferson manuscripts, Chinard's interpretation in the first chapters of his book promised to be the first major contribution, since Randall, toward understanding of Jefferson's intellectual conditioning. Unfortunately, however, Chinard, expecting to find that Jefferson had been influenced by the *philosophes*, and prepared to treat of parallels in French literature and the American's theory, was unprepared to work out parallels in classical literature and English seventeenth- and eighteenth-century writings. Therefore, after showing conclusively what an important place the classics and English writers played in Jefferson's reading taste, Professor Chinard slipped back to a revised form of the Turner frontier thesis: Jefferson's ideas were snatched on the wing from his environment, his reading merely confirmed ideas produced by his frontier environment.

In 1943, the year that marked the two hundredth anniversary of Jefferson's birth, Mrs. Marie Kimball published *Jefferson: the Road to Glory 1743-1776*, which promises to give us a full and rounded biography of the man when the other volumes appear. Mrs. Kimball's careful study of Jefferson's youth, education, and activities up until the writing of the Declaration of Independence should kill once and for all the myth of Jefferson as a "pioneer" or "backwoodsman." Giving much space to Jefferson's intellectual habits, Mrs. Kimball shows with conspicuous success the change that took place in Jefferson's reading as the tension with the mother country mounted. It is indeed unfortunate that the hurry to get the book out in time to mark the bicentennial forced the author to skimp her analysis of the ideas that went into the writing of the Declaration. The intellectual climax for which the author prepares her readers turns into a collection of human interest scraps about the writing of the famous document.

James Madison, like Jefferson, found a mid-nineteenth-century biographer who was a hero-worshiping but scrupulous historian, W.C. Rives, a law student under Jefferson, and a personal friend of Madison, produced in his *History of the Life and Times of James Madison* (3 vols., 1859-1865), a monumental old-fashioned study covering Madison's career to 1796, which is just now being superseded by Irving Brant's large-scale biography. Only the first volume of Brant's work has yet appeared: *James Madison: the Virginia Revolutionist, 1751-1780*—an excellent work. Mr. Brant, like Mrs. Kimball, is not a professional historian; and yet (perhaps for this reason) each study may well prove to be the definitive biography of Jefferson and Madison written in our generation. While Madison unlike Jefferson has not appealed to many one volume biographers, two such efforts are worthy of notice. Gaillard Hunt's pedestrian book, *The Life of James Madison* (1902) was long standard, despite its failure to do more than recite the facts of Madison's life without the least attempt at interpretation. A.E. Smith's *James Madison: Builder; A New Estimate of a Memorable Career* (1937) brilliantly rectifies this shortcoming. Smith's book is a model both in its compressed presentation of detail and its sound general interpretation. It comes as near as possible [to] doing the impossible job of presenting Madison's career in one volume.

Of basic importance in understanding the intellectual development of Jefferson is the catalogue of the library of six thousand volumes that he collected between 1764 and 1800. It is published under the title of *Catalogue of the Library of the United States* (1815), with classifications that Jefferson himself devised. A new annotated edition of this catalogue is now being prepared which will indicate not only what editions of various works Jefferson owned, but which of his books have survived the mid-nineteenth-century fire in the Library of Congress, and which are glossed in his own handwriting. Madison's library which was only slightly less complete than that of his friend was left to the University of Virginia, where it was destroyed almost without trace in a fire some forty years ago. Since Madison had access to Jefferson's collection and since he modeled his own library upon it, however, it is possible to treat it as representative of his reading in a general way. Gilbert Chinard's two pioneering discoveries of Jefferson's early scrap books, *The Common Place Book of Thomas Jefferson* (1927), and *The Literary Bible of Thomas Jefferson* (1928), can not be ignored by any one interested in the Virginian's historical and literary tastes at the period when he had finished college.

The best modern attempt comprehensively to chart Jefferson's intellectual tenets is to be found in C.M. Wiltse's mistitled *The Jeffersonian Tradition and American Democracy* (1935). This book is a very good summing up of Jefferson's beliefs in various fields such as philosophy, government, and religion. It makes little attempt at uncovering their origins or pointing out their relationship to the high tide of Enlightenment. Carl Becker's classic study of the intellectual origins of certain of Jefferson's ideas, *The Declaration of Independence* (1922), still stands alone both in approach and treatment of this thorny type of problem. Edward M. Burns, in *James Madison Philosopher of the Constitution* (1938), a study that focuses on Madison's political theory, sets up for the first time in a satisfactory way his theory of State, views on democracy as they originally were held and as they evolved under the pressure of circumstances. As in the case of Wiltse there is no attempt at comparative analysis, but within the limits set by the author it is an able and welcome job.

By far the most brilliant and suggestive study of American political philosophy in the period 1776-1800 is to be found in Edwin Mims, *The Majority of the People* (1940). Though Mims is as interested in nineteenth- and twentieth-century developments of these early American political concepts, his book cannot be ignored by any one interested in the great political tradition of which the Jeffersonians were a part.

Bibliography

Selected sources cited in the main body of the text.

Adams, Henry. *History of the United States during the Administration of Jefferson and Madison.* New York: C. Scribner's Sons, 1889.

Adams, James Truslow. "Daniel Shays," in *Dictionary of American Biography.* New York: C. Scribner's Sons, 1928.

Adams, John. *The Works of John Adams with a Life by His Grandson, Charles Francis Adams.* Boston: Little, Brown and Company, 1850-56.

Joseph Addison. *Essays of Joseph Addison.* Chosen and edited by John Richard Green. London and New York: Macmillan, 1896.

Beard, Charles. *An Economic Interpretation of the Constitution.* New York: The Free Press, 1913.

———. *The Economic Origins of Jeffersonian Democracy.* New York: The Free Press, 1915.

Beard, Charles, and Mary Beard. *The Rise of American Civilization.* New York: Macmillan, 1927.

Becker, Carl. *The Declaration of Independence.* New York: A.A. Knopf, 1922.

Bergh, Albert Ellery, ed. *The Writings of Thomas Jefferson.* Memorial edition. Washington, D.C.: 1904-05

Bolingbroke, Henry St. John. *Works.* London: A. Millar, 1754.

Bourne, E. G. "The Authorship of the Federalist," in *Essays in Historical Criticism.* New York: C. Scribner's Sons, 1901.

Bowers, Claude. *Jefferson and Hamilton: The Struggle for Democracy in America.* Boston and New York: C. Scribner's Sons, 1925.

Brant, Irving. *James Madison the Virginia Revolutionist.* Indianapolis: Bobbs-Merrill, 1941.

Channing, Edward. *The Jeffersonian System.* New York and London: Harper and Brothers, 1906.

Chinard, Gilbert. *Thomas Jefferson: Apostle of Americanism.* Boston: Little, Brown and Company, 1929.

Cobban, Alfred. *Dictatorship: Its History and Theory.* New York: Scribner, 1939.

Collins, Vanum. *President Witherspoon.* Princeton, N.J.: Princeton University Press, 1925.

Commager, H.S. *Documents of American History.* New York: Appleton-Century-Crofts, 1940.

Crevecoeur, Hector St. John. *Letters from an American Farmer.* London: Printed for T. Daniels, 1782.

Dictionary of American Biography. New York: C. Scribner's Sons, 1928.

Dictionary of National Biography. London: Smith, Elder & Co., 1885-1901.

Dionysius of Halicarnassus. *The Roman Antiquities of Dionysus Halicarnassensis.* Trans. by Edward Spelman. London: Printed and sold by the Booksellers of London and Westminster, 1758.

Dunbar, Louise. *A Study of "Monarchical" Tendencies in the United States, from 1776 to 1801.* Chicago: University of Illinois Press, 1920.

East, Robert A. "The Massachusetts Conservatives in the Critical Period," in *The Era of the American Revolution,* ed. by R.B. Morris. New York: Harper & Row, 1939.

Elliot, Jonathan, ed. *The Debates in the Several State Conventions of the Adoption of the Federal Constitution.* Philadelphia: J.B. Lippincott, 1861.

Farrand, Max, ed. *Records of the Federal Constitution of 1787.* New Haven: Yale University Press, 1911.

The Federalist. A commentary on the Constitution of the United States. A collection of essays by Alexander Hamilton, John Jay and James Madison. Also the Continentalist and other papers, by Hamilton, ed. by John C. Hamilton. Philadelphia: J.B. Lippincott & Co., 1885.

Fite, Warner. *The Platonic Legend.* New York and London: C. Scribner's Sons, 1934.

Ford, Paul Leicester, ed. *The Writings of Thomas Jefferson.* New York: G.P. Putnam's Sons, 1892-99.

Ford, W.C., ed. *Thomas Jefferson Correspondence.* Boston: Little, Brown and Company, 1916.

Gabriel, Ralph. *The Course of American Democratic Thought in the Nineteenth Century.* New York: The Ronald Press Company, 1940.

Gillies, John. *Aristotle's Ethics and Politics, Comprising His Political Philosophy,* trans. from the Greek. London: Printed for A. Strahan, T. Cadell, and W. Davies, 1787.

———. *History of Ancient Greece.* London: Printed for A. Strahan and T. Cadell, 1786.

Glotz, Gustave. *Ancient Greece at Work.* New York: Alfred A. Knopf, 1926.

Goguet, Antoine Yves. *The Origins of Laws, Arts and Science and their Progress among Most Ancient Nations.* Translated from the French of President Goguet. Edinburgh: Printed by A. Donaldson and J. Reid, 1761.

Green, Ashbel. *The History of Princeton.* Philadelphia: E. Littell, 1822.

Halevy, Elie. *History of the English People in 1815.* London: T.F. Unwin, Ltd., 1924-34.

Hamilton, John C. *History of the Republic of the U.S. of America, as traced in the Writings of Alexander Hamilton and His Contemporaries.* New York: D. Appleton & Company, 1859.

Hamilton, Walton and Adair, Douglass. *The Power to Govern.* New York: W.W. Norton & Company, 1937.

Hammond, Barbara. *The Town Labourer, 1760-1832.* London: Longmans, 1918.

Harrington, James. *Oceana.* London: G. Routledge, 1887.

Hume, David. *An Enquiry Concerning Human Understanding.* Oxford: Clarendon Press, 1894.

——. *Essays and Treatises on Several Subjects.* Dublin: Printed for J. Williams, 1779.

Hunt, Gaillard, ed. *The Writings of James Madison.* New York and London: G.P. Putnam, 1906.

Jefferson, Thomas. *Jefferson's Commonplace Book.* Ed. by Gilbert Chinard. Baltimore, Md.: The John Hopkins Press, 1926.

——. *Jefferson's Literary Bible.* Ed. by Gilbert Chinard. Baltimore, Md.: The John Hopkins Press, 1928.

Jefferson, Thomas. *Writings of Thomas Jefferson.* Washington, D.C.: Issued under the Auspices of the Thomas Jefferson Memorial Association of the United States, 1903-1904.

Johnson, Allen. *Jefferson and His Colleagues:A Chronicle of the Virginia Dynasty.* New Haven, Conn.: Yale University Press, 1921.

de Leon, Daniel. *James Madison and Karl Marx.* New York: New York Labor News Co., 1932.

Lerner, Max. *Ideas Are Weapons.* New York: Viking Press, 1939.

Levin, L.M. *The Political Doctrine of Montesquieu's 'Espirit des Lois': Its Classical Background.* New York: Columbia University Press, 1936.

Lippman, Walter. *Public Opinion.* New York: Harcourt, Brace and Company, 1922.

Locke, John. *Of Civil Government; Two Treatises.* Intro. by W.S. Carpenter. London: Dent, 1924.

Lodge, Henry Cabot. *Alexander Hamilton.* Boston and New York: Houghton Mifflin, 1898.

Lodge, Henry Cabot, ed. *The Works of Alexander Hamilton.* New York and London: G.P. Putnam's Sons, 1886.

Machiavelli, Niccolò. *Discourses on the First Decade of Titus Livius.* Trans. by Ninian Hill Thomson. London: K. Paul, Trench & Co., 1883.

MacIver, R.M. *The Modern State.* London: The Clarendon Press, 1926.

Madison, James. *Letters and Other Writings of James Madison.* Philadelphia: J.B. Lippincott & Co., 1865.

Mandeville, Bernard. *Fable of the Bees.* Ed. by F.B. Kaye. Oxford: The Clarendon Press, 1924.

Mathiez, Albert. "The French Revolution," in *Encyclopedia of the Social Sciences.* New York: The Macmillan Co., 1930-35.

McMaster, John Bach. *A History of the People of the United States.* New York: D. Appleton and Company, 1895-1920.

Mims, Edwin. *The Majority of the People.* New York: Modern Age Books, 1941.

Minot, George Richards. *The History of the Insurrections in Massachusetts in the Year MDCCLXXXVI and the Rebellion Consquent thereon.* Boston: James W. Burd & Company, 1812.

Mitford, William. *The History of Greece.* London: T. Cadell and W. Davies, 1808-18.

Montesquieu, Charles de Secondat, Baron de. *The Spirit of the Laws.* Trans. by Thomas Nugent. London: J. Nause and P. Vaillant, 1766.

More, Thomas. *Utopia.* Translated by G.C. Richards. Oxford: B. Blackwell, 1923.

Morris, Gouverneur. *A Diary of the French Revolution.* Edited by Beatrix Cary Davenport. Boston: Houghton Mifflin, 1939.

Neville, Henry. *Plato Redivivus or Dialogues Concerning Government.* London: Printed for S.I., 1681.

Oliver, Frederick Scott. *Alexander Hamilton: An Essay on American Union.* New York and London: Putnam, 1907.

Oppenheimer, Franz. *The State.* London: George Allen & Unwin Ltd, 1923.

Pargellis, Stanley. "The Theory of Balanced Government," in *The Constitution Reconsidered,* ed. by Conyers Read. New York: Columbia University Press, 1938.

Pearson, Hesketh. *Doctor Darwin.* London: J.M. Dent & Sons, 1930.

Plato. *The Republic.* Trans. of H. Spens. Glasgow: Printed by R. and A. Foulis, 1763.

Polybius. *The General History of the Wars of the Romans.* Hampton translation. London: Printed for T. Davies, 1773.

Plutarch. *Lives.* Translation of Dacier and others. London: Printed for J. and R. Tonson, 1758.

Randall, H.S. *The Life of Thomas Jefferson.* New York: Derby & Jackson, 1858.

Randall, James. *The Making of the Modern Mind.* New York: Houghton Mifflin, 1935.

Read, Conyers. *The Constitution Reconsidered.* New York: Columbia University Press, 1938.

Riley, Woodbridge. *American Philosophy: Early Schools.* New York: Dodd, Mead, 1907.

Rives, William Cabell. *History of the Life and Times of James Madison.* Boston: Little, Brown and Company, 1870.

Sabine, George. *A History of Political Theory.* New York: Holt, Rinehart and Winston, 1937.

Shakespeare, William. *The Life of Henry the Fifth.* Ed. by Robert D. French. New Haven, Conn.: Yale University Press, 1918.

Smertenko, Johan J. *Alexander Hamilton.* New York: Greenberg, 1932.

Smith, Abbot E. *James Madison: Builder.* New York: Wilson-Ericson, Inc., 1937.

Sparks, Jared, ed. *The Life of Gouvernour Morris with Selections from His Correspondence.* Boston: Gray & Bowen, 1832.

Spurlin, Paul Merrill. *Montesquieu in America: 1760-1832.* University: Louisiana State University Press, 1940.

Tacitus, Cornelius. *The Works of Tacitus.* Murphy, Arthur, translator. London: J. Stockdale, 1793.

Tansill, Charles C. *Documents Illustrative of the Formation of the Union of American States.* Washington, D.C.: U.S. Government Printing Office, 1927.

Toutain, Jules. *The Economic Life of the Ancient World.* New York: A.A. Knopf, 1930.

Turner, Frederick Jackson. *The Frontier in American History.* New York: H. Holt and Company, 1920.

Voltaire, François Marie Arouet de. *Collection Complette des Oevres de Mr. Voltaire.* Geneva: Cramer, 1757.

Von Holst, Hemann. *Constitutional and Political History of the U.S.* Chicago: Callaghan and Company, 1876-1904.

Walsh, Correa Moylan. *The Political Science of John Adams, A Study in the Theory of Mixed Government and the Bicameral System.*

New York: G.P. Putnam's Sons, 1915.

Warren, Charles. *The Making of the Constitution.* Boston: Little, Brown and Company, 1937.

Washington, H.A., ed. *The Writings of Thomas Jefferson.* Washington, D.C.: Taylor & Maury, 1854.

Wiltse, Charles. *The Jeffersonian Tradition in American Democracy.* Chapel Hill: University of North Carolina Press, 1935.

Witherspoon, John. *The Works of John Witherspoon.* D.D. Edinburgh: Printed for Ogle and Aikman, J. Pillans, J. Ritchie, J. Turnball, 1805.

Woolf, Leonard. *After the Deluge.* London: Hogarth Press, 1937.

Xenophon. *Xenophon with an English Translation.* Loeb Classical Library. London: Heinemann, 1918-1944.

Index

About the Author

Douglass G. Adair was professor of history at the Claremont Graduate School in California at the time of his death in 1968. Prior to coming to Claremont, Adair was on the faculty at William and Mary and had taught at other universities including Yale, Princeton, and the University of Washington. In addition to his publications, Adair achieved notoriety due to his editorship of the *William and Mary Quarterly*. Adair received his Ph.D. in history from Yale University. The Douglass G. Adair Memorial Award is given every four years for the most significant article in the *William and Mary Quarterly*.

Mark E. Yellin received his Ph.D. from Rutgers University in political science. His work concentrates on eighteenth-century British and American political thought. He teaches at North Carolina State University in Raleigh and has contributed to *The Review of Politics* and the *American Political Science Review*.

Joyce Appleby is professor of history at UCLA and past president of both the Organization of American Historians and the American Historical Association. Among her publications are *Ideology and Economic Thought in Seventeenth-Century, Capitalism and a New Social Order: The Jeffersonian Vision of the 1790s* and *Liberalism and Republicanism in the Historical Imagination*. She received her Ph.D. in history from the Claremont Graduate School and, prior to coming to UCLA, taught at San Diego State University.